THE DECLINE OF

AMERICAN PLURALISM

THE DECLINE OF

AMERICAN PLURALISM

Henry S. Kariel

STANFORD UNIVERSITY PRESS

STANFORD, CALIFORNIA

1961

STANFORD UNIVERSITY PRESS
STANFORD, CALIFORNIA
© 1961 BY THE BOARD OF TRUSTEES OF THE
LELAND STANFORD JUNIOR UNIVERSITY
ALL RIGHTS RESERVED
LIBRARY OF CONGRESS CATALOG CARD NUMBER: 61-5505
PRINTED IN THE UNITED STATES OF AMERICA
PUBLISHED WITH THE ASSISTANCE OF THE FORD FOUNDATION

FOR

Sheila

Acknowledgments

As my footnotes will amply testify, this book is a kind of collage of ideas. But if I have had innumerable collaborators, they have been, with the significant exception of a sophomore tutorial group at Harvard and a sophomore class at Bennington College, entirely innocent ones; they cannot in any case be held for the uses I have made of their conclusions.

Although the particular synthesis I offer is original, its components are hardly of my own making. While I was an undergraduate at the University of Washington in Seattle, Professor Thomas I. Cook (now of Johns Hopkins University) first made me aware of the need to distinguish between a realm of means and one of ends in assessing the propriety of governmental action. It was the late Professor Arnaud B. Leavelle who, at Stanford University, called my attention to the self-contradictory character of ideological conservatism in American thought, before it became fashionable to write books about it. And it was Professor Charles Aikin at the University of California at Berkeley who forced me, leaving little quarter, to think within the context of American public law. Because no senior political philosophers were on the permanent staff of the University of California's Political Science Department while I was a graduate student there, I was exposed to the reflections of three eminent visiting professors: George E. G. Catlin, Leo Strauss, and Hannah Arendt. My thinking owes much to each of them. More specifically, however, I am indebted to the late Lloyd H. Fisher, a political economist who came to Berkeley from Harvard with an attitude toward prevailing political ideas which now pervades my own approach. Stressing the play of individualism, tension, and conflict not as prelude to harmony but as a good in itself, he made me question the fraternalism implicit in both the institutions and the academic analyses of American political life. The impact of these individuals on my thinking should not go unacknowledged, for, in various ways, they have all changed my mind.

I remain indebted, furthermore, to Professors V. O. Key, Jr., and H. Mark Roelofs for their constructive criticism of parts of the manuscript version of this book; and I am especially grateful to Professors Thomas I. Cook, J. Roland Pennock, Samuel P. Huntington, Franklin M. Fisher, Sanford A. Lackoff, Rush Welter, and Wallace P. Scott, who struggled through earlier versions of my manuscript and often took issue with my interpretations. In many instances, I have not accepted their advice, but their failure to persuade me may testify more to the limits of my understanding than to the merit of their points.

My special thanks are due to Mr. J. Christopher Herold for helpfully criticizing the organization of my manuscript and to Mr. Gene Tanke of the Stanford University Press for helping make each sentence as sensible and telling as I would permit. I should also like to express my appreciation to Nancy L. Machler and Bryant C. Danner for checking and rechecking numerous references. Bennington College's enlightened administration and flexible curriculum greatly facilitated my efforts, as did the generous support of one of the smaller of the philanthropic foundations whose policies contribute to a healthy pluralism in the academic world. Finally, I am grateful to the editors of *The Western Political Quarterly, Political Studies* (The Clarendon Press, Oxford), *The Journal of Politics,* and *The American Journal of Sociology* for permission to draw on articles of mine that first appeared in their publications.

Henry S. Kariel

Bennington, Vt., June 1960

Contents

Introduction   1

PART ONE: AMERICAN PLURALISM

1. The Constitutional Basis   7
2. The Technological Frame   14
3. The Incorporation of Business   27
4. The Incorporation of Labor   49
5. Private Power and Public Purpose   68
6. The Entanglements of Organized Agriculture   76
7. The Dependencies of the National Government   88
8. The States as Captives   103
9. The Norms of Social Research   113
10. The Case for Devolution   138

PART TWO: THE CONFLICT WITHIN PLURALISM

11. The Challenge of Individualism   179

PART THREE: THE TRANSCENDENCE OF
                   PLURALISM

12. The Articulation of American Statism   191
13. Standards for Public Action   213
14. The Regulation of Groups   252
15. The Reform of Government   273
16. An Orientation for Research   292

     Notes   301

     Index   333

And Abel was a keeper of sheep, but Cain was a tiller of the ground. And in process of time it came to pass that Cain brought of the fruit of the ground an offering unto the Lord. And Abel, he also brought of the firstlings of his flock and of the fat thereof. And the Lord had respect unto Abel and to his offerings; but unto Cain and to his offering he had not respect.

GENESIS 4:2–5

Introduction

During the last two decades, the political activity of business corporations, labor unions, agricultural associations, and other organized groups in the United States has been the subject of a tremendous number of studies. This abundance of investigations has made it possible to learn and generalize about the changed nature of our public order.

Organizational giants such as General Motors, the Teamsters Union, the Farm Bureau, and the American Medical Association have emerged as full-fledged political regimes, each embracing varied interests while speaking with a single voice. They have been free to mature under a system of constitutional government designed for a preindustrial era. As they have come to exercise the power to govern multiple-interest constituencies, we have again and again sought to bring this constitutional system to bear on their behavior. To protect the rights of individuals against them, we have had to interpret and reinterpret the Constitution. And to keep the principles of constitutionalism alive, we have required essays in constitutional interpretation. This work purports to be such an essay. It seeks, always in reference to American constitutionalism, to put contemporary organizational practices and the various rationalizations offered for them under critical pressure—indeed, it proposes to indict them.

What will be indicted here has not, of course, been without its defenders. But those who have framed apologies for the newly emerging public order have generally employed a rhetoric designed for another day. Essentially, their rhetoric has defended a state without a government. Such a state, at best, is believed to be com· posed of a plurality of voluntary associations so guided by an un· seen providence that their interaction constitutes the public good. There is a manifest factual foundation for this belief: voluntary associations are still very much alive in the United States. But for many years now they have not been alone. Above them is a newer set of large-scale organizational power blocs. Today, it is these blocs that comprise most of the public order and occupy much of the public mind. They require new credentials of legitimacy, because whatever they may be, they are not that wonderful and wholly legitimate conglomeration of little groups which visitors from abroad have traditionally identified with Americanism.

In describing and ultimately challenging what I believe to be the new public order, I hope to force aside an outdated but still conventional way of discussing some of the major issues of public policy, to move beyond the debate of the 1930's. Our problem then, or so it appeared, was how to reinvigorate private groups, how to give new life to business, to labor, and to agriculture. If this could be done efficiently, it seemed, the whole body politic would be revitalized.

There are many today who have a vested interest in continuing the debate on precisely this premise—the premise of political pluralism. Public action based on it serves them well. Business still wants "partnership"; labor still wants "security"; agriculture still wants "support." Each desires governmental reinforcement of its conduct and its aims, and all are prepared to assume that the inevitable result is the good of the entire American public.

Yet our problem today, as I see it, is not how to strengthen the hierarchies of organized private power, but rather how to control them by some means short of establishing an illiberal political order.

To lay some foundation for an understanding of this problem, I will attempt to show in my first two chapters that our constitutional system works toward the fragmentation of power while our technological system works toward the consolidation of power. I will then discuss and forecast some instances of how the leading elements within private groups effectively control our work and leisure, often using public agencies to underwrite their decisions. I cannot, of course, consider every organization that significantly raises questions about the legitimacy of its power to govern. To be sure, a full appreciation of the prospects of a genuine and desirable pluralism would demand an examination of the relative freedom from public control enjoyed by the New York Port Authority, the College Entrance Examination Board, the American Legion, the Pentagon, the League of Women Voters, the National Safety Council, the state teachers' colleges, the Passport Division of the Department of State, and innumerable other groupings from the Boy Scouts of America to the Federal Bureau of Investigation. All of these patently raise the question of political responsibility in a free society. None the less, I have found it sufficient for my purpose to consider only the kind of power that groups grown large as a direct result of modern technology now exercise over their constituents.

In the last two chapters of Part I, I shall first discuss the kind of academic studies which, derived from the premise of pluralism, proceed compulsively to vindicate it; I shall then consider some of the more resolute, explicit prescriptions for both group autonomy and governmental dispersal.

Having discussed three variants of American pluralism—the institutional, the analytical, and the prescriptive—I propose to show in Part II how they conflict with the basic moral aspirations embedded in the theory of pluralism itself. This will entail pushing to a conclusion what students of American politics have generally left inconclusive. Where, thanks to a positivist respect for the facts, they have remained normatively ambiguous and "practical," I shall abstract and generalize. It will be seen, not for the first time but hopefully with a new sense of relevance, that the organizations which the early theorists of pluralism relied upon to sustain the individual against a unified government have themselves become oligarchically governed hierarchies, and now place unjustifiable limits on constitutional democracy.

Because the theory of pluralism under conditions of large-scale technology conflicts with the principles of constitutional democracy, we may perceive the need for a new basis for debate, a debate which we as Americans have not, at least so far, been driven to insist upon. Part III seeks to provide this basis. To encourage the debate itself, I will review a generally de-emphasized segment of past American public policy—its affirmative interventionism— and restate what I take to be the traditional theory of constitutional democracy.

My effort, it should be clear, is intended to recall us to a tradition far more contradictory than its apologists have made out, to have us acknowledge that the dialectical nature of our past allows for a shift in emphasis. My bias should be equally clear. I would have us move, if this be possible, from the much-celebrated ideal of Tocqueville toward the still unfashionable one of Rousseau, from a hierarchical public order toward an equalitarian one.

Part One: American Pluralism

We are standing on the threshold of an unpolitical age. Politics has fallen from its high estate. Since the floodgates of political privilege have been opened and participation in political affairs has been vouchsafed to all, we find everywhere a progressively increasing apathy in matters relating to politics. The pre-eminence of the State politically conceived, has been called into question. . . . Its sovereignty has been shorn of many of its mystical characteristics. Other forms of corporate organization are pressing for recognition. We may in turn see arising before our eyes a new great social institution. Like feudalism, it is in its essence unpolitical. As Lord Bryce has pointed out, "feudalism was a social and legal system, only indirectly and by consequence a political one." We may today note that industrialism, which may serve to denominate this new institution, is a social and economic system, only indirectly political. Such would appear to be the trend of history.

—William Kay Wallace, THE TREND OF HISTORY (1922)

Of all perversions of political authority, the most obvious and the most detestable is the subservience of public power to the private interest of the men who hold power.

—Yves R. Simon, PHILOSOPHY OF DEMOCRATIC
GOVERNMENT (1951)

1

The Constitutional Basis

Those concerned with joining justice and power should be willing to inquire into any exercise of the power to govern, into all of its manifestations and justifications. It should not matter where the governors are located, what verbal façades or legal fictions shield them, or in what journals their defenders may publish. The familiar distinctions between the governmental and the nongovernmental may not be wholly the result of convention; possibly they are expressions of some natural law. But considering the number of miracles, mysteries, and authorities men have falsely idolized, it may be wise to ignore the "Keep Out" signs and invade, for the sake of analysis, some of the less well-traveled sectors of contemporary American political life, both public and private.

Certainly it has long been recognized that the American community, like all constitutional regimes, is multi-associational and multi-governmental, that innumerable organizations clutter up our social landscape:

Americans of all ages, all conditions, and all dispositions, constantly form associations. They have not only commercial and manufacturing companies, in which all take part, but associations of a thousand other kinds

—religious, moral, serious, futile, extensive or restricted, enormous or diminutive. The Americans make associations to give entertainments, to found establishments for education, to build inns, to construct churches, to diffuse books, to send missionaries to the antipodes; and in this manner they found hospitals, prisons, and schools. If it be proposed to advance some truth, or to foster some feeling by the encouragement of a great example, they form a society. Wherever, at the head of some new undertaking, you see the government in France, or a man of rank in England, in the United States you will be sure to find an association.

These observations by Tocqueville are scarcely dated. "It is natural for the ordinary American," Gunnar Myrdal was to write a century later, "when he sees something that is wrong to feel not only that there should be a law against it, but also that an organization should be formed to combat it." There is no count of our clubs, lodges, societies, federations, and leagues. Kenneth E. Boulding has in fact spoken of an "organizational revolution":

We now have what seems like a vast jungle. In the United States 15,000,000 workers are organized into labor unions. At least half the farmers are organized into three large farm organizations. Great corporations dominate many fields of industry. Every trade and every industry, almost without exception, has one or more trade associations. Every profession is organized with its professional associations. There are innumerable organizations representing special-interest groups, from Audubon societies to Zoroastrians. . . . Veterans' organizations cover millions of ex-soldiers, and wield immense political power. Lodges and fraternal orders have multiplied. Not only are there many more organizations, and many more kinds of organizations, than a century previous, but the organizations themselves are large, better organized, more closely knit, more efficient in the arts of attracting members and funds and pursuing their multitudinous ends.[1]

Our social virtuosity is even more vividly suggested in Peter Viereck's lyrical appreciation of "the living traditionalism of parochial religious schools, the living traditionalism of our small private colleges . . . ; the geographic diversity of our regionalism, with the shared cultural or historical experiences that enrich many a decentralized, idiosyncratic locality . . . ; [our] local public libraries; town-hall forums; city music-festivals, museums, playgrounds; voluntary fire-brigades, blood donors, the voluntary service of great surgeons in public clinics."[2] It would seem that

America virtually bubbles over with pluralism, fraternity, and cooperation. Reconciling voluntarism and association, this untroubled image of America renders irrelevant all theories of society as atomized masses and all politics based on the unaffiliated individual. Were this description of the community to be completely accepted—as, for example, Max Lerner has so resoundingly done in his *America as a Civilization* (1957)—it would be hard to conceive how any plea for national convergence and centralized public power could possibly evoke a lasting response. America, it would seem, is miraculously both singular and plural, organized and scattered, united and diffused. We may boast of or rail against Washington, D.C., while remaining convinced that our real capitals are in the provinces. We may think of *The New York Times* as representative while believing that our real press is regional. We can affirm that we are governed by no national business, labor, educational, or religious elite. What is more, we tend to be happy in our knowledge that every group generates its countervailing one: an association for the elimination of predatory animals inevitably finds its opposite number in an association for the preservation of wildlife.

Above the private realm, at least in hallowed theory, stands the public realm, in which it is no less difficult to perceive a barely countable number of intelligible governments, each entering into the complex process which somehow results in public policy. However much this reality may be concealed by a high school civics-course approach envisaging a federal system as a national government with defined powers, states protected by the Tenth Amendment, and the sovereign people standing behind both, the fact is that a fresher vocabulary and an antiformalist tradition of research have for some time been cutting through the legal formulas and revealing observable units of government long known to the practical politician, reformer, or businessman. For 1956 the Census Bureau tabulated a total of 102,328 governmental units in the United States. These included 3,047 counties, 17,183 municipalities, 17,198 townships, 14,405 special districts, and 50,446 school districts. The average number of governmental units per state turned out to be 2,131; and there are eight states, not including California or New York, with more than 5,000 governments within their borders.

Yet even this list is radically incomplete. There is no mention here of soil conservation districts (2,300 in 1951), public housing authorities, government corporations, regulatory commissions, interstate bodies such as the Port of New York Authority, or the mosaic of independent jurisdictions within metropolitan areas. Once the handy, well-worn classification schemes are put aside, thousands of decision-making centers reveal themselves between the mass of citizens and those who are publicized as wielding the great power of the national government. More than that, the formerly useful distinction between the public and the private blurs, and it becomes impossible to specify what is foreground and what is background. All the ingredients of sovereignty emerge as intricately meshed, as intersecting, crisscrossing, and smoothly competing, as maneuvering to countervail power, upset balances, and block opposition.

To the extent that this image is a true one—and not merely convenient for those who would keep criticism from taking root—one may correctly speak, in Daniel Boorstin's phrase, of the genius of American politics. A special genius would seem to have been at work, inspiring the development of an intricate, complex pluralistic system, a system developing at a leisurely pace, its growth unforced by rigid public laws or social blueprints, which has saved us, by the very gradualness of its development, from that regimentation and standardization which tends to be the lot of all those who seek to copy the American Plan by imposing "Americanism" on populations determined to break with their past.

The all-too handy explanation for the peculiar quality of the American community has been obvious enough, especially to constitutional engineers: it is the United States Constitution which allegedly provokes the social practice. It explicitly delimits public government, keeping electors geographically apart, staggering elections, separating power into departments, dividing it among regions, and, in the realm of private, human ends, prohibiting its exercise altogether. Public government, in short, is fragmented and distributed by the Constitution. And to the degree that the government is successfully prevented from acting in unison to enforce policies aimed at some singular public end, groups are encouraged to seek in private what the Constitution was contrived to frustrate in public.

Yet precisely because the gap between constitutional norms and social practice has been small, the appeal to the Constitution as an explanation for the American experience begs the question. Why is it that the government was framed as it was, and, more importantly, why do we still esteem its framers? Why do we invite the proliferation of power blocs?

In parceling out sovereignty, in preserving a wildly complicated, interlaced federalism, we have actually accepted the ground for a community structure which in many revealing ways resembles that of previous, seemingly remote societies, notably the Western European society of the *Ancien Régime*. No parallel could better illustrate the vague, ill-defined image of those modern political theorists whose case for pluralism—for a pluralist, corporate, or federalist society—seems less than fully informed by reality. In the power structure of the court of Louis XV we see in its fullness what is merely suggested by some of the current models for the reorganization of society, whether these models are embedded in our social practice or articulated in our social theory.

Another point may be made here. Unlike eighteenth-century continental Europe, we have never had to concentrate power in the hands of one man in order to upset an outworn corporate system. Significantly, our only rebellions against the remnants of feudalism have been rhetorical. In language too often marked by shrillness, betraying a suspicion that no one is really listening, we have talked of individual rights, economic liberty, inevitable progress, free enterprise, laissez-faire, and equal opportunity. But we have never had to destroy the institutions to which these ideals stood opposed. We were never compelled to strengthen the state in order to dissolve the old corporate order. In Tocqueville's classic terms, we did not have to "endure a democratic revolution." Nor did we have to formulate a coherent ideology to challenge the defenders of those decadent feudal institutions which survived in the *Ancien Régime*. In the realms of practice as well as theory, we could leave well enough alone.[3]

Thus we could remain undisturbed by all domestic manifestations of a feudal order, by a vast decentralization of power, states' rights, private corporatism, local autonomy, and home rule. Traditionally unreconciled to bigness, especially in the form of trusts, unions, or parties, we carved out huge zones of anarchic, pluralistic activity—extraconstitutional zones in which private law has been allowed to keep the peace. And we have thought it only natural to give expression to our widely shared inclinations in a written constitution, one which, assuming widespread consensus about what is seemly in private, checks and balances public government, keeping it disunited to prevent power from falling into the hands of a sovereign monarch.

It is no accident, therefore, that we have generated a twofold pluralism: a tremendously complex governmental apparatus —diffuse, unintegrated, centrifugal—and, second, a prodigious cluster of innumerable groups buoyantly, chaotically seeking to achieve privately and voluntarily what we have forbidden ourselves to do publicly. We might plausibly argue that our freedom to associate is merely an extension of a right of free speech, an extension made necessary only because the technological complexity and continental size of our society impose limits on individuals. But this is not an adequate explanation, for our freedom to associate is equally derivable from our separation of means from ends, of state from church, of public enactments from private definitions. Denying public support to the immoderate believer who seeks state aid to achieve his ends, we have traditionally forced our governmental agencies to operate within the realm of means. Our basic demands, as embodied in the Constitution, are characterized by an extraordinary lack of specificity. We ask our government to "establish Justice, insure domestic Tranquility, provide for the common Defense, promote the general Welfare, and secure the Blessings of Liberty"—nothing less ambiguous. Because we assert our constitutional goals in such bland terms, we all but entreat the organization of groups with well-defined goals. Our private associations are consequently always impelled to convert private ends into public ones, to engage in action which, in a constitutional polity such as the American, will always end in partial defeat. Yet prospective defeat, it must be noted, has rarely seemed intolerable even to the most conscientious of dissenters. Only during the Civil War did one appreciable set of interest groups believe its *entire* definition of the good life to be compromised, as indeed it was. It has been far more usual for special interests to respect an underlying consensus, one which steadies the ground for organizational and cultural diversity.

It is this assumed but concealed harmony at which we must look more closely. To grasp the nature of this basic agreement and the immense institutional order based on it is difficult in the extreme, for it is so completely our own. Our very language protects us from truth. No wonder, then, that the visitor from abroad (like the American expatriate, at home or away) has always been more perceptive, recognizing that the areas of compulsion and freedom in America are not necessarily those our clichés lead us to expect. It is precisely because we did not have to revolt against feudalism that we could quietly build up institutions resembling those of the old order. Unaware of its hold on us, we could remain oblivious to its influence. To review the past is thus to expatriate ourselves. It should enable us to understand those parts of our present environment to which we are all too comfortably adjusted. Thus we should force ourselves to recall not only the ever-attractive multiple-group state of the medieval period but also the modern efforts to give life to it under the impetus of a fascist ideology. Recalling how the ideal of a corporate society can work out in practice, especially under conditions of modern technology, should extend our self-awareness and suggest specific American developments that now stand in need of reform.

2

The Technological Frame

In the name of enlightenment, eighteenth-century physiocrats and encyclopedists, thinkers as diverse as Adam Smith, Quesnay, Locke, and Voltaire, uniformly opposed the compulsions and rigidities of a decadent feudalism. But while we in America long ago appropriated the libertarian ideals of the eighteenth century, or at least the rhetoric in which these ideals were couched, we have never found it necessary to engage in a thoroughgoing rebellion against the institutions of feudalism. In normal times, it has been easy for us to accept a profusion of effective and imposing public and private governments—so easy, in fact, that we have seldom taken the trouble to look for any theoretical significance in the daily interaction of these many governments. With the important exception of the *Federalist Papers* and Calhoun's *Disquisition,* both written during critical times, we have formulated no systematic apologetics for either pluralism or federalism; neither has ever seemed much in need of defense. We have ingenuously allowed a pluralistic point of view to express itself in the federal structure of our government and in our innumerable private associations— in short, in the corporate nature of America's industrial society.

In recent years, as we have become increasingly aware of the relentless expansion of the organizations that surround us, we have sought explanations of their nature and their lines of development. In this search we have often looked to Europe, and ultimately to the work of Marx, Weber, Michels, Simmel, Mosca, Pareto, and Mannheim. These writers have helped us recognize that the character of our organizations cannot be explained simply by seeing them as relics of an unpurged feudal past. The present structure of American society has not developed solely from our acceptance of pluralism; it has been shaped just as significantly by the impact of technology on our means of production—and this is precisely what gives pluralism and federalism a novel, awesome dimension. This impact has affected our very way of thinking. The substance of American life, as contained in its various organizational forms, is so radically touched by technology that unless we consider some of technology's social implications, we shall remain ignorant of the way an evolving, nonutopian ideology can slowly eclipse a concern for human purposes. It thus becomes important to inquire into some of the theoretically possible social effects of a productive process in which mechanical energy displaces human energy. Once aware of these effects, we may consider more specifically how the impact of technology on production has influenced American society, and how our pluralism, unfolding under the conditions of modern technology and large-scale industrialism, has tended to fix the texture and substance of our lives.

An industrial regime always entails more than physical facilities. Technology necessarily imposes limits on social organization. In order to produce automobiles, "men—and women—must leave their homes and gather in factories, and there the relationships between them are determined not solely by 'human' factors but by the imperatives of steel, heat, synthetics, typewriters, and so forth. An assembly line is a way to relate *things,* but it is also a relation of *people.*"[1] To supply gasoline, both private and public organizations necessarily cluster about the specialized tasks involved in its processing:

An oil operator brings oil to the surface of the ground; the local government prevents the theft of oil or the destruction of equipment; a railroad corporation transports the oil; State and Federal Governments prevent interference with the transport of oil; a refining company maintains an organization of workers and chemical equipment to convert the oil into more useful forms; a retail distributor parcels out the resulting gasoline in small quantities to individuals requiring it; the Federal Government supplies a dependable medium of exchange which allows the oil operator, the railroad, the refining company, and the retailer to act easily in an organized fashion without being under a single administrative authority, and enforces contracts so that organizing arrangements on specific points can be more safely entered into; finally, government maintains a system of highways and byways which allow an ultimate consumer to combine the gasoline with other resources under his control in satisfying his desire for automobile travel.[2]

The organization of production—compelled by our irreversible determination to "fill the earth and subdue it"—is thus expressed in more than the physical realm. The man-constructed plant, be it business office, oil refinery, airline terminal, communication grid, or fish cannery, will articulate the lives of individuals. It constitutes a system which will respect and reward precisely those skills that serve its purposes. It will prescribe what manner of men are to be its members lest it fail to use its members fully. It will mechanize and regiment men rather than recognize their diversity.

Historically, the mechanization of production engendered the familiar shift from diffused small communities of workers to concentrated large ones, from rural life to urban life, from agricultural pursuits to industrial ones—a shift that produced a new fourth estate of lonely and hence community-seeking people. Their old attachments to farms and villages were replaced by attachments to the new slots provided for them within the industrial order. And to the extent that the industrial order kept changing, so did their attachments. Their homes became little more than places to depart from, easily relocatable places.[3]

Industrialization necessarily implied a systematic rationalization of the work process, a scrupulous effort to keep work from being anything more than a function of the finished product. The rigorous exclusion of irrationality—of whatever may be incalculable and unpunctual, irritating and shocking, subjective and ambiguous—was and is its logical inner imperative. By limiting the range of alternatives, it provides the standard for social health and disease. To be sure, the dynamism and momentum of industrialism could be tempered in practice and resisted in theory. Other definitions of an industrial social order could be proposed, as they were by the romantic conservatives of the Victorian age. But to resist always meant to succumb, as Marx perceived, to either reactionary or utopian sentiments.

It may be fruitful, therefore, to ask again just what, theoretically, is likely to follow a full-scale rationalization of the work process. Toward what is technology likely to lead when unaffected by public policy and left to follow its own inner logic?

A comprehensive theory of the mechanization of work would have to accept the functional incompatibility of machines with unadjusted and unintegrated human activity. Clearly, the use of machines in the systematic mass production of uniform goods requires both a division of the work process and a continuous control over the separate tasks created. An industrial system thus requires a fragmentation of labor under integrated control.

The manner in which the system disrupts the social solidarity of men in order to make them serviceable has of course received the attention of innumerable writers. Seen in the abstract, technology is believed to destroy the timeless community, the organic whole, as well as the autonomous personality. Thus Ernst Jünger could see society becoming an apparatus impressing its style on man, making his life automatic; Marx and Engels could see man transformed into a mere commodity; Le Bon and Tarde could diagnose his readiness to sway with the crowd as an expression of his anonymity; Weber, Simmel, and Mannheim could see him becoming routinized and bureaucratized; Arendt and Lederer could see him as ripe for totalitarian manipulation.

To understand the extent of the consequent impulse to reintegrate and achieve wholeness once again, it may be useful to recall just how a technological system is believed to shatter the traditional order of both work and leisure. While technology ultimately unifies a fragmented industrial society, the individual is attached to only one part of the whole, and only dimly grasps how his part fits. He knows of his dependency but finds the order upon which he depends unintelligible. However rational the total process of production may be, from this rationality he is alienated; barely able to perceive it, he has no personal attachment to it. On his own, he is unlikely to develop a comprehensive view, and even if he does, it will probably take the form of an off-duty philosophy unrelated to his work. Whatever his role—even his role as a consumer of products—it tends to absorb him, to sap his humanity and creativity. He is displaced and pacified by a system which cannot permit him to take the initiative. There is no end—at least no end in clear sight—to his participation in the work process, for there is no objective other than the maintenance of the process itself.

This perspective is not only relevant to the passive assembly-line worker. Managers, too, can be seen as little more than functions of a bureaucracy; owners can be seen as inactive recipients of income from property which is not meaningfully theirs; consumers can be seen as unreflecting purchasers whose market calculations are socially determined.

That this is a strained, systematically exaggerated picture—as it surely is—does not keep it from helping to explain the ever-present ideological push from both the left and right toward some form of social reunion. For if man is believed to be catastrophically self-alienated, it becomes reasonable to support whatever forces might give him a feeling of order and a sense of belonging. Thus the cry of the radical and the reactionary alike is for integrity and convergence. The status quo will not do. Although it is true that industrialism reunites what it breaks apart, its new order is synthetic and hence held to be an unnatural foundation for a community of men. Industrialism's imperative to coordinate is unacceptable, for it is but the counterpart to its imperative to functionalize. Industrial organization may extricate men from one kind of community, but will it not, so the question runs, reattach them all the more smoothly to another?

The organizational archetype almost invariably invoked to support this line of thought is the modern factory, even though the factory pattern is hardly universal. Daniel Bell has noted:

A skilled worker may find his job monotonous and a chambermaid in a bustling metropolitan hotel may not. Nothing may be more deadly, perhaps, than the isolated, hermetic life of the bank teller in his cage or the elevator operator in his sealed jack-in-the-box. Longshoremen swear by their occupation, gaining satisfactions in the free use of muscle and the varieties of excitement on a big city pier, while scorning those who are tied down to the bench or lathe. Musicians, typographers, miners, seamen, loggers, construction workers all have their special cast of work. Yet the factory is archetypal because its rhythms, in subtle fashion, affect the general character of work the way a dye suffuses into a cloth. Coal mining, once spoken of as "underground farming," now—with the mechanisation of cutting and conveying—takes on much of the routinisation of factory work. In offices, the installation of rapid highspeed calculators, tabulators, and billing machines tends to turn the white-collar workers into mechanically paced drones. The spread of mechanisation into "materials handling" (e.g., supermarkets) introduces mechanical rhythms into the distributive sectors of the economy.[4]

It is the system that prescribes, and the constituency—managers, workers, consumers—that conforms. In the name of economical production, the various parts of society are induced to serve. Their progressive adjustment to the imposed rhythms of work is made mandatory, for the system must remain free from all disturbances. To assure the progressive realization of a stable rationality, all manifestations of entrepreneurship must be absorbed and neutralized. Conflicts must be reconciled. Decisions, which involve choices and hence risks of failure, must be emptied of their personal decisiveness: they must seem to emerge as spontaneous expressions of the system as a whole, or, less perfectly, as directives gently issuing from a network of committees. Whatever touches the industrial apparatus, whether from within or without, must be made friendly and manageable.

To order the system, it is imperative to control all its variables. This means creating a society whose members are fully understood, and whose interests are fully accounted for and then guided so as to reduce the risk of discontent. It becomes essential to plan for the future, and, because of the expenses always entailed by change, to stick to the plan. Men must be motivated to find satisfactions within the prescribed contours; they must be stimulated to want only the goods that will actually be available to them. At the extreme, what is demanded in the industrial and economic order is the stabilization of progress itself, the elimination of whims and accidents so that, in Schumpeter's words, innovation becomes the "depersonalized and automatized" concern of "teams of trained specialists who turn out what is required and make it work in predictable ways."[5]

Relating all the complex particulars of an industrial order to its central purpose—self-perpetuation—requires the kind of continuous supervision that is uneconomical to maintain. Industrial operations must be coordinated, and yet supervisors cannot be omnipresent. However, the areas of judgment and discretion beyond the external control of a supervisor may be made subject, as John Stuart Mill wrote in 1848, to "the monitor within."[6] An internalized code of expectations, decked out and kept sharp by a science of mood engineering, thus becomes a significant means of keeping order. The seeming independence of the worker and the remoteness of his supervisors make it all the more essential to secure his psychological dependence. He must be part of the system not because he is physically forced into line but because he himself accepts imposed demands, freely behaving as he must. Without ideology, without a shared sense of obligation, the system remains inefficiently managed. The worker's concern must be deep and abiding, especially when it is not feasible to blame him for a breakdown, or to hold him personally responsible for a team failure. Hence the demands of the system, on the worker as well as on the ultimate consumer, must be legitimized. The demands of the production plan must be perceived as just. It must become the worker's duty to adjust happily to the system, to be no less involved and devoted to it than the managers who formulate his schedules and seek to maximize his output. All must give freely to the great common cause; all must be implicated in it and responsible for it.

To operate harmoniously and continuously, the fully rationalized system of mass production demands not only an internalized code, an organization-wide *esprit de corps,* but also a hierarchical apparatus of control which can encompass the continually proliferating parts of the system. Complexity and fragmentation in an enterprise are tolerable so long as an ideology of common purpose pervades the system and a level of technology has been achieved which actually allows for central control. A scattering of production units no more implies the absence of central control than the mere bunching of men and machines in one locality guarantees the presence of it. After all, technology does not, in theory, make centralization and diversity incompatible. If the diverse parts consent to the policies flowing from the center and if the center remains in touch with the parts, extreme specialization and extreme centralization will be natural complements to one another.

Of course it is true that multiplant operation by a centrally managed single firm will be technologically efficient only up to a certain point.[7] Increasing the size of the firm need not in practice make for increasingly efficient production. What seems likely, indeed, is that after a certain size has been attained, specific non-technological failings begin to make themselves felt—failings that have led worldly economists and reformers to advocate measuring efficiency not by a performance test but by a market-structure test. In principle, however—following only the dynamics and possibilities of technology—nothing should inhibit the continual drive toward the larger firm and toward more centralized direction.[8] Theoretically, firms must be big in order to save on the costs of administration and marketing, to allow for full specialization in machinery and products, to economize in the assembly and transport of raw material, to govern the allocation of expansion funds, to satisfy the need for long-term commitments of venture capital, and to engage in research, assume the risk of its failure, and exploit its unanticipated developments. Objections to bigness rest on non-technological values—a fondness for miniature communities, or possibly an unwillingness to realize how much can be achieved by truly efficient concentrations of power. Such objections are theoretically meaningless: doubts raised about the efficiency of the ever-expanding industrial establishment simply lose their relevance when applied to an economy uncorrupted by history and chance.

Ideally, in the fully mature technocracy, efficient industrialization comes to mean concentration in decision-making. And since it is primarily the extent of industrialization that will determine the degree of concentration in an economy, we should naturally expect the steady emergence of the centralized firm.[9] Provided always that it is large enough to bridge a multitude of diverse components, provided it is a pluralist order, its ascendancy becomes historically likely and objectively imperative. In maturity, the single firm will embrace its complex constituents.

Such industrialization obviously requires the extension of a hierarchical structure of control. To integrate variously skilled work teams at the appropriate moment and place in the productive process requires a management capable of making the plans and the schedules. Those who perform these functions constitute a hierarchy of specialists. Such hierarchies imply inequalities that are virtually inescapable. Moreover, as they speed the development of centralized control, they also promote the growth of an employee constituency in which all but the very top and the very bottom ranks are *both* the managers and the managed. What unites them all is the inherent needs of the autonomous productive order, not any ideal transcending it.

The incentive for maintaining an industrial equilibrium by drawing together men and machines is basically the desire to overcome what appears to be a self-evident disequilibrium. In his great efforts to reorganize the railroads the elder J. P. Morgan is said to have been motivated not by the desire for the immediate realization of profits but rather by the hope of making a manifestly untidy transportation network rational and neat. From this point of view, an appetite for wealth, and for the culture it may provide, is at odds with the demands of technology. The standard controlling those at the corporate top and center who plan to assure uniform productivity, who devise and impose the system of rules, is not a personal one. Those who coordinate work are not irresponsible; they weigh alternatives carefully. The supreme ideal governing their decisions is the successful perpetuation of the productive system itself. They are most concerned with the self-sufficient goods of efficiency and economy. Their "values" are self-referential; their orientation is solely toward means and techniques. Their power, in other words, is validated by their success, every failure calling simply for a more concerted exercise of power, not for any reconsideration of the ends toward which it is exercised. Thus those who formulate the rules for the industrial apparatus are as divorced from ends as those who obey them. For both groups, the ends infinitely recede. Every concern with ends—even personal gratification and the selfish accumulation of wealth—becomes a kind of stalling, an irrational diversion from the need to remain ascetically dedicated to the system.

To be sure, this outline of industrial organization has pushed possibilities to unrealized conclusions. It would surely be absurd to see American industrial enterprise as a homogeneous, monolithic system. Yet there is no slackening in the push toward the rationalization of production, toward centrally controlled, functionalized, and stabilized work. All those concerned with the maximum utilization of productive processes, and especially with planning for automation, endorse the current tendency toward eliminating subjective impulses within the industrial order. The overriding aim is conservative—the reduction of variables, whether by coercive trimming or subtle tranquilizing. Management, if the words of one commentator are representative, understands the problem:

Now men by definition are difficult and tricky things to play around with. You have employee-relations men, time-study men; you have training and educational directors; you have personnel men, washroom men, cafeteria men. That all costs money. My point is this: that if we could take some of the money that we are spending in trying to ease the pain of our assembly-line personnel, and apply that money for some research to get the men out of there entirely, we would be better off in the long run.[10]

The automated plant, with its interlocking parts and its requirement of uninterrupted output at the same rate over an appreciable period of time, must make specific social demands. Because the production process itself must not be interrupted, the worker (now actually the semiskilled or skilled engineer) must be infinitely conscientious, for any lapse on his part may affect the entire mechanism. He must be all the more loyal because he seems to work alone; his interest must be genuine, for there can be little check on his inclination toward indifference or carelessness.

Given a highly integrated technology, men and machines share what we think of as responsibility. It is often virtually impossible to fix the blame for breakdowns. By the same token, the possibility of assessing the value of the employee by his output is slim, since there is no way of gauging his personal responsibility for the rate of production. Because the extent of his contribution is not readily measurable by results, it is necessary to engage as caretakers of the process only those who will not have to be blamed, those who will spontaneously act as they are expected to act. Hence the value to the system of applicants for employment must be predetermined. While screening is certainly not new in business and industry, careful scrutiny of the worker's set of predispositions—as revealed in his total record—is being radically intensified. Just as his history is used as a precise index to his prospective value, his past will standardize his future.

To take the risks out of production also requires control over consumers. It becomes necessary to "understand" society, to deal with it by motivating the newly leisured so that they will find satisfactions within the prescribed boundaries of consumption, to diminish elasticity of demand by stimulating the market and channeling goods toward it in an even stream. It becomes necessary, in short, to tie the market to the system. This requires not only an economy free from the vacillations of depression and prosperity, but also the most sensitive of public relations so that all can clearly grasp the needs of the system.

The imposition of a rational pattern on major economic events, employee behavior, and consumer preference demands the installation of the kind of control centers that are rapidly becoming technologically feasible. There is no reason to expect the dispersal of the centers of policy-making in a society that accepts a mature technology. In the past, the centralization of policy formation was made possible, as C. Wright Mills has noted, by

the now primitive office instruments of typewriters, calculators, telephones, and rapid printing, and, of course, the transportation grid. Now the technique of electronic communication and control of information is becoming such that further centralization is entirely possible. Closed-circuit television and the electronic calculator put control of an enormous array of production units—no matter how decentralized such technical units may be—under the control of the man in the front office. The intricately specialized apparatus of the corporation will inevitably be more easily held together and controlled.[11]

Perhaps the giant corporation is not alone in its ability to take advantage of a mature technology. Perhaps the costs of automation are not so formidable as to keep the small enterprise from meeting them. And perhaps heavy capital outlays invested over long periods of time will not really be required. Still, it is hard to believe that the market and capital position of entrenched firms will not be crucial. Even more significantly, there is a technological imperative favoring the large-scale enterprise. To make full use of special-task machines such as computers demands nothing less than a *de facto* organization large enough to absorb their entire output. No matter how geographically dispersed or legally separated such organizations may be, they must increasingly emerge as economic, social, and technological concentrates. As this trend continues, political control from the outside can only become more annoying. The conclusion seems inescapable: modern technology, as Peter F. Drucker has put it, "is a concept of the structure and order of economic life, the design of its basic patterns integrated into a harmonious, balanced, and organic whole."[12]

Technology, then, tends to integrate not only business enterprises but also the patterns of social life which today must seek primary expression in the matrix of industrialization. Whether this integration should be described in such rhapsodic terms as "harmonious, balanced, and organic" or whether it might better be regarded as dehumanizing, its momentum is bringing out a heretofore concealed paradox in American society. Whereas the thrust of technology is toward integration, the thrust of American constitutionalism is toward disorganization, and hence ultimately toward stalemate. On the face of it, nothing would seem more likely than that these two seemingly opposed forces should meet in mortal combat. And indeed, we have had collisions between the technological order and the political order in the days of the serious antitrust crusades. But we are beginning to understand why these have always turned out to be sham battles. Although we are only vaguely aware of it, the centripetal forces inherent in technology and the centrifugal forces of our political order are steadily fusing on a new, as yet unnamed, level. Until recently, this has been difficult to see. After all, it has been quite within our political tradition to keep these two opposite tendencies in different tracts of life, one labeled public and the other private.

Traditionally and easily distinguishing between them, we have been pleased to apply the argument for power dispersal to governmental operations and that for power concentration to private enterprise—always in the name of individual freedom. Whether this argument remains valid today depends on the character of our corporate economy.

3

The Incorporation of Business

The paramount organizational form in which the processes and imperatives of industrialism define themselves in the United States is unquestionably the large-scale business corporation. What sort of an institution is it? How, within the immense physical, social, and psychological area it spans today, does it affect the rights of individuals to direct their lives? How does it stabilize and centralize the power to pursue diverse ends?

The answers to these questions are difficult not only because the modern business corporation fails to conform to some singular type—General Motors and H. J. Heinz, Sears, Roebuck and Safeway Stores all have different personalities—but also because its various types are always changing. Yet even though it is constantly transforming both itself and its public image, it is now being cast in a mold sufficiently well defined to enable students of society to consider it anew, to contemplate it as Madison contemplated the unratified system of states within a union under a constitution. It would seem, if present research is to be trusted, that we are witnessing a fundamental shift in both our aspirations and the organizational forms which contain them. The existence of such a major historical transformation—perceived by writers as diverse as Overton H. Taylor, Roderick Seidenberg, C. Wright Mills, David Riesman, Hannah Arendt, Daniel Bell, and William H. Whyte, Jr.—can hardly be verified empirically. To speak somewhat casually of shifts from inner-directed to other-directed persons, from a Protestant ethic to a social ethic, from an old liberalism to a new conservatism, without rigorously attaching these labels to recognizable social groups is to permit the proffered concepts to become all too slippery. Still, the hypotheses most difficult to verify may be the most useful ones. Moreover, an awareness of the distinguishing features of a past economy of values may help accentuate a peculiarly modern development and sharpen our view of the nature of America's emerging industrial order.

For our present purpose, there is no need to analyze in detail either the tenets or the actual structures of the early American corporations, or to retrace the gradual transformation of property, the seemingly destined growth of multiple ownership of single enterprises, and the steady centralization of control.[1] Whatever the past, within the present economic system, as Berle and Means wrote in 1932, "there exists a centripetal attraction which draws wealth together into aggregations of constantly increasing size, at the same time throwing control into the hands of fewer and fewer men."[2] While this statement has not gone unchallenged, the facts are clear in one respect: by whatever standard it is measured, the degree of industrial concentration in the United States is appreciable. It is irrelevant here whether we consider such concentration un-American (i.e., deviating from the American past or from American ideals) or inefficient (i.e., incapable of maximizing output). Hence there is no point in characterizing the statistics as "staggering" or "striking," or in noting with studied surprise that oligopolies behave oligopolistically and that executives lead the executive life. Nor need we make much of economic trends. The shift from agricultural to industrial pursuits has of course meant a shift from small production units to larger ones; inescapably, the result must be ever-increasing concentration until the shift is completed.

We must remember, of course, that the industrial sector itself is highly varied and filled with complexities that discredit any analysis of American capitalism as monolithic and centrally controlled. The mixture of the forms of economic power is so incredibly complex that it is no wonder that economists are unable to furnish unambiguous formulations of likely trends.[3] To the question whether monopolistic market control is increasing, Edward S. Mason has candidly—and, it would seem, correctly—responded that "the answer in a nutshell is—we do not know."[4] It may be true that firms have grown in size, that the open market is being replaced by a planned one, that research is governed by corporate giants, and that competition from imports is diminishing. But it is no less true that markets too are growing in size, that improved transportation and communication are making local markets national, and that there is no necessary relation between size and monopoly. In short, there is no clear evidence of a trend. Nevertheless, the existing picture, regardless of whether it reveals a trend, is enough at odds with our economic mythology to justify attention.

Of the more than 4½ million business units in the United States, a relatively small number hold a predominant position. Their share of resources, of assets, of production, of the market, of employed manpower, and of spending is of a magnitude vastly disproportionate to their number. They are responsible for a disproportionately large share of output in manufacturing, mining, power, transportation, communication, and finance—though not, it should be noted, in distribution, service, construction, and agriculture.[5] One hundred and thirty-five corporations own 45 per cent of the assets of America's nonfarm economy. Industries in which the four largest producing firms turn out half of the total value account for 57 per cent of the value of all manufactured products. In 22 industries the four largest do 80 per cent of their industry's business.[6]

Embracing various interests, raw materials, and goods, these industries frequently contain elements which compete with one another. The Radio Corporation of America produces both radio and television sets; Anaconda processes both copper and aluminum; the Koppers Company sells both natural gas and bituminous coal; the New Haven railroad, through the New England Transportation Company, operates passenger buses and trucks.[7] Thus the fact that large-scale corporations are internally decentralized is not relevant when the corporation can dictate performance criteria to its decentralized units. As Corwin D. Edwards has said, "In a concern that has chosen to raise prices, restrict output, avoid improvements in the product, or limit new investment, internal competition does nothing to overthrow these decisions."[8]

Not only are the corporate giants the predominant producers; they also cover the major portion of the market. It is not surprising, therefore, that their share of national assets and resources is massive. About 150 corporations hold the assets of roughly 50 per cent of American manufacturing. The most recent compilation shows the 200 largest firms to hold about 40 per cent of all corporate assets and between a fifth and a fourth of all income-producing wealth.[9] Decisions to invest capital saved by individuals are no less concentrated: while there are 609 life insurance companies, in 1950 70 per cent of their assets ($63 billion) were in the hands of the largest ten companies. Moreover, the finance power of banks and of the investors of pension trusts is far from diffused. In fact, both pension trusts and mutual funds give further impetus to centralization because their managers, for the best of reasons, favor investments in the giant firm.[10] Nor is the power to affect employment a scattered one. In terms of asset values, the 200 largest employers (though not necessarily the same 200) account for about 20 per cent of all employees in nonagricultural establishments. Put differently, less than two-tenths of one per cent of all manufacturing and mining companies employ half of all the people in these industries. Their share of the nation's spending power is no less considerable, with a small number of firms investing disproportionately large amounts. Baratz has calculated that "in 1953, for instance, net private domestic investment amounted to about $24 billions. Of this the three largest firms in the steel, automobile, chemical, and oil industries together accounted for more than $2.7 billions, or approximately 12 per cent."[11] And to call attention to the actual concentration of so-called small business—gas stations, restaurants, car dealers—is merely to underline what should be evident enough: an immensely important sector of the American economy is succesfully affected by a plurality of giant corporations that provide the conditions not only for sheer survival but also for the good life of the community as a whole.

However, to obey the soundest of dramatic instincts and say more than this—to insist on the existence of a unified and interlocking power elite of business—is to place an accent where none belongs. The top corporations are not, as C. Wright Mills has rightly insisted, a set of splendidly isolated giants. Yet is it true, as has also been maintained, that they have been knit together by trade associations which unify the managerial elite?[12] There is ample evidence that trade and employer associations, often controlled by an unresponsive leadership, have seriously attempted to "organize a unity," seeking to provide a united front for conflicting interests.[13] But today they actually seem far less significant than organizations such as Du Pont, General Motors, United States Steel, Standard Oil of New Jersey, Radio Corporation of America, Metropolitan Life, American Telephone and Telegraph, General Electric, and their surrounding satellites. To understand the range of corporate power, it is not necessary to look beyond these at associations such as the Iron and Steel Institute, the American Bankers Association, or the Petroleum Institute.

We are concerned with these corporations, then, not because they are statistically typical, but because they are paramount instruments of production and distribution, predominant sources of wealth and employment, and primary agents of material progress— because they influence the pace and style of living pursued by an accessible and obliging twentieth-century public.

We should no longer be surprised by the discovery that corporate decisions are made by the few. The tendency toward oligarchical management is an altogether natural result of the historical development of industrial and business enterprises. An industrial bureaucracy is relentlessly replacing the independent entrepreneur. While in 1870 two-fifths of the working population in the United States were self-employed, by 1955 only one-fifth was. And within industry itself, there has been a parallel over-all increase in the ratio of administrative to production personnel.[14] Focusing on Swift and Company as representative, Reinhard Bendix has noted that in 1923 this meat-packing firm employed 50,000 workers who were managed by 500 executives.[15] In 1950, it employed 75,000 workers managed by 2,150 executives. The ratio changed from one executive for every 100 workers to one executive for every 35 workers.

There can be no doubt, in any case, about a gradual change from independence to dependence, or, more accurately, from one kind of dependence to another. This transformation implies new ways of managing people. It has resulted in new power relations, and consequently in new political and social obligations. It has brought about an elaboration and a refinement of managerial functions to cope both with the increased number of the managed and with the ever larger, ever more intricate technological plant. As company officials have been vested with the power to perform special tasks in standardized ways, the expert has been brought to the fore. Industrial statesmen may preach the need for getting young men of liberal education into the ranks of management, but when the chips are down and company personnel representatives make the rounds every spring to interview the nation's prospective college graduates, it is the specialists—engineers, market analysts, statisticians, or lawyers—who turn out to be the better employment risks.

It is only natural that this appreciation for managerial expertise should ultimately have come to be shared by the industrial worker. Given our prevailing economic goals as well as the nature of industry's existing physical plants, nothing is likely to induce production employees to discuss and decide matters of policy. What is more, they probably would not care to. To assure the constant study of relevant facts and the prompt reaching of decisions, one can hardly count on mass participation. Only specialists skilled in planning and budgeting, in allocating resources and coordinating work, can be continuously prepared to act speedily and objectively.

There is nothing new in the recognition of this. Robert Michels's classic, *Political Parties* (1915), long ago prepared social scientists for the discovery of seemingly irresistable bureaucratic tendencies in the modern organization. Thus there can be no excuse for any sting of surprise in finding that when we look carefully, we behold oligarchy. Leadership, secure as long as it does not make blatantly wrong guesses about what the law forbids, will naturally stand aloof from groups affected by its policies.

It now appears that the foremost managerial aim of corporate leaders is not so much to maximize immediate personal profits as to negotiate equitably with whatever interests compose the large firm—including those which, from a purely legalistic point of view, are not incorporated at all. Today, its function is to conceive of the corporation's constituencies in the broadest terms and to deal with them in statesmanlike fashion. This swelling of the corporate role was anticipated by Keynes, who wrote in 1926:

One of the most interesting and unnoticed developments of recent decades has been the tendency of big enterprise to socialize itself. A point arrives in the growth of a big institution—particularly a big railway or public utility enterprise, but also a big bank or big insurance company —at which the owners of the capital, *i.e.* the shareholders, are almost entirely dissociated from the management, with the result that the direct personal interest of the latter in the making of great profit becomes quite secondary. When this stage is reached, the general stability and reputation of the institution are more considered by the management than the maximum of profit for the shareholders.[16]

This expansion of managerial goals is necessarily reinforced when the intensity of the quest for profits is diminished because it is widely felt to be in poor taste to gain social prominence by conspicuous spending. When a high margin of profit is recognized as only one of several ways to social power and prestige, it becomes inviting to explore others, to sponsor whatever may help one's reputation for altruism, service, and patronage. Thus the entrepreneur, less bent on enriching himself and the corporate shareholders, may be inclined to offer his administrative talents to the government, the charitable organization, or the public welfare group. He may be inclined to make the facilities he controls available to educational, recreational, or cultural institutions. This does not mean, of course, that he disdains profits (profits remaining a decisive index to the success of his enterprise), but rather that he is likely to direct them to public uses. By such redirection he may protect his status—at least in the affluent society where conspicuous consumption as Veblen had described it loses relevance—while at the same time extending the range of his influence.

There is certainly ample evidence that a narrow definition of the corporate role has become less and less palatable. "Industrial management," Alfred P. Sloan has insisted, "must expand its horizon of responsibility. It must recognize that it can no longer confine its activities merely to the production of goods and services. It must consider the impact of its operations on the economy as a whole in relation to the social and economic welfare of the entire community."[17] Ralph J. Cordiner, president of General Electric Company, has declared:

There was a time when the manager felt that if his shareowners were happy and if his customers were not going over to his competitors, he was satisfying his managerial responsibilities. Today, the manager knows that continuing usefulness and profitability depend on a much wider spectrum of relationships. . . . All this is to say that a new dimension has been added to business leadership: the social dimension. . . . Increasingly, the people expect business not only to satisfy their material wants and desires, but also to satisfy a whole range of psychological and ethical expectations. . . . We in business will have to become far more sensitive to the social and political currents and undercurrents in this country. . . . We must anticipate the major social, political, and economic trends, both nationally and internationally, and help to shape them for the common good. . . . We must construct a more appealing vision of the future. . . . [We must make our] opinions heard, understood, and believed. . . . And, finally, we in business need to learn how to be politically effective.[18]

The belief that "ownership carries social obligations, and that a manager is a trustee not only for the owners but for society as a whole," as the editors of *Fortune* put it in 1951, is widely, if somewhat compulsively, repeated.[19] A vice-president in charge of the industrial relations of the Ford Motor Company has characteristically affirmed the conviction that management "has learned to take, and has the motivation to take, a balanced approach to its problems. In the nature of its function, it must take into account a number of varied interests in arriving at its decisions. This is so because the health of the enterprise depends vitally and directly on management's ability to achieve a proper balance among all of these sometimes conflicting interests."[20] Honorable men managing key firms, not the market, are expected to play the mediating role. According to Frank W. Abrams, speaking as chairman of Standard Oil of New Jersey, top management must conduct corporate affairs so as "to maintain an equitable and workable balance among the claims . . . of the various interested groups: the stockholders, employees, customers, and public at large." But this is not all:

Management's responsibility, in the broadest sense, extends beyond the search for a balance among respective claims. Management, as a good citizen, and because it cannot properly function in an acrimonious and contentious atmosphere, has the positive duty to work for peaceful relations and understanding among men—for a restoration of faith of men in each other in all walks of life.[21]

Dean Donald K. David of the Harvard Business School has seen the businessman's new opportunity in his capacity to "help society determine—in a continuing and purposeful program—the most effective ways of furnishing the maximum of human satisfactions and security."[22] Appropriately enough, the prescient social philosophy of Owen D. Young, late chairman of the board of General Electric, has been resurrected. "To whom," Young had decided to ask, "do I owe my obligations?"

My conception of it is this: that there are three groups of people who have an interest in that institution [General Electric]. One is the group of fifty-odd thousand people who have put their capital in the company, namely, its stockholders. Another is the group of well towards one hundred thousand people who are putting their labor and their lives into the business of the company. The third group is of customers and the general public. . . .

One no longer feels the obligation to take from labor for the benefit of capital, nor to take from the public for the benefit of both, but rather to administer wisely and fairly in the interest of all.[23]

An all-embracing community perspective comes readily to a managerial elite whose task it is to compose and calm corporate constituencies in the name of that natural homogeneity of interests which is assumed whenever spokesmen for the large firm identify the interest of their institution with the public good. To serve one's self is, ineluctably, to serve the public.[24] It is at once easy and essential to take an expansive, over-all account of the public good, to celebrate the kind of business, as one United States Chamber of Commerce president is said to have observed, that "views its own work through the eyes of the community and looks to the total welfare in terms of the long pull."[25] To conform to *Time* magazine's new creed for modern capitalism, businessmen "must shoulder a host of new responsibilities, must judge their actions, not only from the standpoint of profit and loss on the balance sheet, but of profit and loss to the community."[26]

With these benign sentiments echoing in their ears, it is no wonder that corporation leaders consider themselves proper interpreters of public expectations. "The majority of Americans," a president of Crown Zellerbach has been quoted as saying, "regard business management as a stewardship, and they expect it to operate the economy as a public trust for the benefit of all the people."[27] It is a sense of responsibility, a chairman of the board of United States Steel has proclaimed, that makes business move ever upward from individual entrepreneur to partnership, from partnership to corporation. "And now," he concluded, "we see these great corporations themselves necessarily forming partnerships—for one reason and one reason alone: to do the job that is expected of them in an enterprise system where size and responsibility are companion words."[28]

To do the job expected is to handle the various corporate interests with that zest for negotiation which is the recognized mark of the politician. In an economy in which management has become professionalized, the business leader cannot help but resemble the successful political figure. He becomes, above all else, the specialist in business administration, in scientific management, in human relations. In considering this trend, C. Wright Mills (quoting from Ida Tarbell's biography) has rightly singled out the archetypal figure of Owen D. Young:

In the early twentieth century . . . the typical industrial leader was a domineering individual, offensive in his belief that business was essentially a private endeavor. But not Owen Young. During World War I and the 'twenties, he changed all that. To him, the corporation was a public institution, and its leaders, although not of course elected by the public, were responsible trustees. . . .

So he worked with people outside his own company, worked on an industry-wide basis. . . . He came to feel trade associations, in the corporate age, performed one role that once "the church" . . . performed: the role of moral restrainer, the keeper of "proper business practices." During the war, he became a kind of "general liaison officer between the company and various [government] boards . . . ," a kind of prototype of the many executives whose co-operation with one another during the wars set the shape of peacetime co-operation as well. . . .

His face was always "friendly and approachable" and his smile, one colleague said, "his smile alone is worth a million dollars."[29]

Today, Young's successors may be recognized, in Reinhard Bendix's apt language, by "the calm eyes which never stray from the other's gaze, the easy control in which laughter is natural but never forced, the attentive and receptive manner, the well-rounded good-fellowship, the ability to elicit participation and to accomplish change without upsetting relationships."[30] Their professional concern is with the integration of decisions, and toward this end they see the firm as a whole, seeking to keep it functioning in its entirety as an always viable and peaceful organization. Sensitive to disturbances, anticipating them where possible, they act as diagnosticians and therapists, relying on planning, staff work, and group decision-making. They envisage their primary task as the creation of group attitudes that will dispose their constituents favorably toward the system, that will give them the feeling of being needed members of a wholesome fraternity. They see the governed as a big happy family, its members not commanded to obey but rather encouraged to participate. They unobtrusively engineer obedience to authority, inspiring *esprit de corps* and job enthusiasm. To the extent that they are successful, they tend, in C. Wright

Mills's words, to relax their autocratic hold and to widen their "manipulative grip over the employees by understanding them better," doing so by "countering their informal solidarities against management and exploiting these solidarities for smoother and less troublesome managerial efficiency."[31]

Of course, it may be true that top management, unlike some academicians, gives little verbal credit to techniques of manipulation. Explicit authoritarian control may not, in actual practice, have been replaced by amorphous, paternalistic forms of employee persuasion. Yet why should we expect industrialists to concede frankly that, merely because they are beginning to assume new public responsibilities, they are suddenly prepared to become solicitous in the governing of men? After all, their creed, however contradicted by their action, has traditionally demanded an unsentimental indifference to employee welfare. And the creed is likely to be abandoned far more slowly than the practice.

By its techniques of government, whether harsh or gentle, the corporation defines not merely its own goals but those of outsiders as well. In so doing, it is gradually and persistently trying to bring under control the environment in which it lives. As its millions of day-to-day decisions take cumulative effect, it manages to reshape the physical foundations, the emotional dispositions, and, ultimately, the political ideology of the American community. The makers of corporate policy, by their *ad hoc* decisions, suggest what is painful and what is pleasurable, attach prestige to some forms of behavior and detach it from others, and legislate the relative soundness of popular indulgences and deprivations. Above all, they are in the position to use their power to establish and maintain an attitude of approval in those segments of the public whose interests are assumed to be the same as the corporation's. From one point of view, first articulated in 1949 in Harold J. Laski's *The American Democracy,* the various publics surrounding the great industrial corporations are quite unconscious of their interests; they are therefore apathetic, easily diverted and readily directed by a power elite which they cannot or will not influence. This view, however, is incomplete. American corporations have obligingly responded to many of the special interests with which they deal, at times not imposing what the customer might accept; they have remained sensitive even to latent public opinion, at times not charging what the market might bear; and they have accommodatingly bent to the will of the national government, at times adjusting their foreign policies to the dictates of American foreign policy.

To understand this kind of behavior—whether virtuous or merely prudent, responsible or merely expedient—requires thinking of the corporation in nonlegal terms. It is misleading to think only of the managers on top and the host of the managed at the bottom, to picture managerial decisions as flowing but one way—down. More importantly and realistically, the corporation must be seen as at least one group of economists has seen it right along—a far-flung, working institution. Approached in this light, its boundaries are not set by public laws or individual contracts; they range as far as the network of ties which all involved interests habitually respect. From this expanded point of view, it is possible to see how public policies privately enacted by the managers of a few firms can effectively govern a set of major groups in society—owners, employees, and consumers. Each of these groups might be considered in turn.

The classic exposition of the extent to which corporate management has become immune to owner interest is still the study by Berle and Means.[32] In detail, it shows how the evolution of the corporate system—which the authors in 1932 expected to become "as all-embracing as was the feudal system in its time"—involved the progressive separation of property ownership and managerial power. Because individual wealth (in the form of stocks and bonds) tends to be dispersed, minorities can and do exercise corporate power. The devices by which they retain control with relatively small investments are familiar enough: pyramiding through holding companies, using nonvoting stock and voting trusts, exploiting the proxy machinery, or simply exercising control in those common situations in which no group of owners happens to have a share large enough to outweigh that of the management.[33] Under such conditions, the influence of owners on management decisions is negligible, especially when shareholders are appeased by the steady returns (dividends of about half of average earnings) they have learned to expect. Their legal rights, formally guaranteed,

become practically meaningless. As Robert Aaron Gordon under-
stated the facts in 1945,

By the nature of the case, the rank and file of stockholders cannot continuously initiate or approve leadership decisions, nor can they exercise
any continuous co-ordinating function. Their participation . . . is limited to voting at stockholders' meetings. The range of decisions open to
them at these meetings is very narrow.[34]

Management necessarily initiates decisions, the stockholder
"saying yes or no to proposals submitted to him." The obstacles
in his way to opposing management, while they can sometimes be
overcome, are formidable. The organization of factions, requiring
the means to communicate with potentially dissident stockholders,
is expensive and difficult. "Viewed in this fashion," Gordon has
concluded, "the proxy machinery is not so much a means of depriving the stockholder of his vote as an alternative to his doing
nothing with his vote at all. The proxy machinery becomes a
partial—and by no means completely satisfactory—substitute for
complete disfranchisement." This is confirmed by later observations. As Berle was to attest in 1954, "when an individual invests
capital in the large corporation, he grants to the corporate management all power to use that capital to create, produce, and develop,
and he abandons all control over the product."[35] Management,
favored by every legal presumption, is all the more unencumbered
by the wishes of owners because, with the notable exception of
utility companies, it generates its own capital to plow back into
the enterprise.[36] And when it is able, like Sears, Roebuck and Company, to depend on the trustees of its own pension trust fund to
invest voting stock back into the very corporation whose employees
make compulsory contributions, there is no need for management
to feel intimidated by the latent threat of individuals who might
invest or withhold their savings. "A corporation like General
Electric or General Motors which steadily builds its own capital,"
Berle has written, "does not need to submit itself and its operations
to the judgment of the financial market. Power assumed to be
brought under the review of banking and investment opinion a
generation ago is now reviewed and checked chiefly by the conscience of its directors and managers."[37]

While equity owners tend to be passive and hence marginal to the self-replenishing enterprise, employees in production, maintenance, and management—including those working for suppliers and distributors—are its integral human material. They are properly the members of what is publicized as the corporate team.[38] They do not merely agree to work for the organization; they model themselves on provided criteria so as to belong to it. They become attached to the corporation by a fealty transcending the rational demands of legal documents or economic necessity. As members of industrial families serving the nation, they voluntarily live within the corporate realm, cooperating for their mutual advantage and united by a common interest. Their attachment as individuals is as free and unforced as that of the 26,000 firms (all with less than 500 employees) that General Motors boasts of supplying with goods and services. There may be occasional resistance, such as an attempt by an automobile dealer to appeal over the heads of his corporation to a committee of the United States Congress. Or there may be an occasional revolt by a supplier or a distributor. But to the extent that they are all linked to the corporate order, moving carefully and willingly within it, they come to identify themselves with it, realizing, as one president of Du Pont has calmly noted, that "they have something to conserve."[39] Thus the automobile dealers themselves have seen the wisdom of maintaining intimate relations with the manufacturers. At least the well-established, conservative dealers have sought to strengthen their ties with Detroit. Asking for "equality of competitive opportunity," they urged Congress in 1958 to bypass the antitrust laws and stabilize their sales territories. Fighting a distribution system one of them likened to an oriental bazaar, they petitioned Congress to permit the manufacturers to penalize the non-professional upstart who makes deals and sells outside his own territory.[40] While such distributors may appear to be detached outsiders, they in fact constitute a voluntary fraternity of individuals jointly nourishing what they know to be their enterprise, faithfully and often proudly serving through generations.

At best, the corporation develops its own work force entirely. When it can, it schools its own executives by its own training programs. What is actually "its own" must be understood, however, in the broadest of terms. It employs the output of universities which, by responding not so much to direct business pressure as to diffuse but cumulatively significant student preferences, cannot help but tailor their faculties and curricula to satisfy vaguely anticipated corporate needs. Moreover, the potential members of corporate teams are not caught unaware when confronted by their new jobs. As one survey has made clear, they quite naturally groom themselves to become what the corporation desires, always on the lookout for helpful cues.[41]

When their alertness, dislayed perhaps by acceptance of a "career-oriented summer job," has been rewarded by employment, they remain aware of the unspoken demands of the hierarchy of their institution. The institution, it is true, will provide them with genuine opportunities for advancement—indeed, with a surfeit of undefined ones. But an organization's internal looseness does not necessarily enlarge the freedom of the individual determined to move up. The task of orienting himself is merely added to his managerial duties. The very generosity of the organization is likely to make him sensitive to his peers and superiors, slowly turning conditional into compulsive loyalty.

Once adjusted, the executive finds it difficult to detach himself from his firm to join another. Of course, to gauge his value or respond to an itch to move, he may quietly offer himself to competing firms and thereby, in the fashion of automobile industry executives, manage to circulate, entering a seemingly new environment. There is, however, a specific penalty even for specious mobility: promotions tend to be made from within the firm. And long tenure has its rewards. The corporation has come a long way since, in the effort to control labor turnover, it first distributed free tulip bulbs and planting advice to the wives of production workers. Today, organizations captivate their members not only with decent salaries and agreeable working conditions; they also offer that host of schemes which, however hard for the individual to size up, specifically weds him to the corporation—plans for health and welfare, for sharing profits and purchasing stocks, for obtaining pensions and insurance, for supplementing unemployment benefits, for reducing the cost of moving, housing, travel, entertainment, and recreation. And at the higher levels, loyalty may be additionally secured by such emoluments as stock options and elastic accounts for private expenses. Thus as benefits accrue by virtue of membership, privileges are collectivized.

Nor is the rank and file left unadjusted. The reward for labor is fixed by well-synchronized decisions determining wage patterns which workers, for understandable reasons, cannot take part in formulating. It is the fully unionized giant firm which sets the pace in deciding the level and structure of wage rates. Negotiating on an industry-wide basis, its agreements tend to be made "at the expense of the real incomes enjoyed by workers in less favored industries, in less protected mercantile and white-collar employment, and in the low-income industry of agriculture."[42] Favorably situated power blocs, rather than begetting countervailing ones, are thus reinforced. They find themselves in a position to govern the economic standard of living of their memberships.

As an advancing technology makes jobs more demanding, as it requires the upgrading of production employees, and as economic and social distinctions between worker and bureaucrat consequently tend to fade, the opportunity to find fulfillment within the corporation opens up to the career worker no less than to the career bureaucrat. Encouraged to become involved in an expanding community, both are driven to use the corporation as a status-bestowing institution, as a point of reference for their values. Yet at the same time, they exercise no meaningful control over the forces which drive them, especially when they have uncritically permitted those forces to work within themselves. Management employees no less than workers are affected by decisions establishing dovetailed patterns which remain unchallenged and unassessed—patterns of leisure and work, of capital investment and personnel allocation, of education and character. These are legislated by corporate management, which feels impelled to define the expectations of the very individuals who own the enterprise and labor within it.

If owners and workers are engulfed by the corporation, what of the market where it meets the consumer? The free, competitive market in which the sovereign consumer rationally chooses between alternative goods and services is an ideal so remote from reality that deference to it remains only verbal. While the extent of corporate power over the market is certainly debatable, its presence is undeniable.

With their unchallenged power to capitalize on major innovations, to pool patents to exploit unexpected research results, to consign resources, to influence advertising media, and to control retail outlets, corporations are certainly not without power to regulate competition. Furthermore, they can employ the manifold forms of legitimate private or quasi-private price administration which mark especially the steel, textile, oil, and cement industries.

In its more subtle variants, corporate power affects the consumer not by rigging the market but by reaching him directly. The freedom of the large corporation to decide what kind and quality of product or service it will promote gives it a unique power first to confuse and then to straighten out its customers. By the process Schumpeter called "creative destruction," it may supply new products of greater comfort, convenience, or serviceability; but it also manages, as Bernard De Voto once observed, to build worse mousetraps and then to force the world to beat pathways to its retail outlets. For large sectors of the economy, it imposes positive values on new goods and makes old ones not merely undesirable (which they may or may not be) but undesired. By dramatically portraying esteemed social groups as appalled by the old and gratified by the new, it provides the standards of seemly consumption. With the help of brand names, it plans well-marked routes of escape from the very anxieties it has created. In fact, it forces the adaptation of tastes even when one of its particular sales campaigns fails, even when the consumer moves on to a competitive product. For while he moves, the consumer nevertheless remains within that realm of values upheld by advertisement and consumer education.

What sellers and their advertisers establish is not a specific value standard to be rejected or shared by the purchaser but a set of speciously alternative standards within a pervasive climate of consumer taste. It is a standard of taste to which, in practice, it is uncomfortable to take exception. More is involved, however, than offering the consumer goods whose values are rationally debatable; he is at the same time encouraged to believe, as he scurries about to register his preference at the retail outlet, that he exercises significant options.

The point here is emphatically not that some corporate elite rules autocratically, but rather that our basic commitment to unceasing productivity induces corporations to spend some twelve billion dollars annually on advertising (not to mention an incalculable amount for consumer education) in order to initiate the productive process. Thus corporations and consumers become thoroughly integrated through their joint commitment to productivity. All talk of the manipulators versus the manipulated to the contrary, both parts become but complementary functions of a larger whole in which all find peace.

It is the corporation's widely accepted power to create preferences, coupled with its growing skill to appraise what the partially frozen market is likely to yield, which enables it to engage in those diffuse activities the gains and losses of which simply cannot be reflected on annual reports and balance sheets. No wonder, then, that corporate trustees are irresistibly driven to attempt to form a more perfect union, endeavoring to establish justice, to insure domestic tranquillity, to provide for the common defense, to promote the general welfare, and, ultimately, to secure the blessings of liberty to ourselves and our posterity—endeavoring, in short, to invade, occupy, and govern the realm of human ends. Of course, the effort to secure community benefits and underwrite public virtue (rather than to increase dividends, raise salaries, or expand facilities) may also represent an attempt to maximize longrun profits. But the possibility of taking such an elastic view of profits suggests the need to shift the vocabulary away from economic to broadly political terms, to talk not of "profitable" public relations but of "beneficial" ventures pursued in an "altruistic" spirit so as to achieve what is morally "good" in obedience to right reason and sound ethical dictates.

There are innumerable manifestations of an attempt—still undesigned, fumbling, and reticent—to deal with a social system immeasurably larger than the one acknowledged by the rhetoric of early capitalism. Clarence B. Randall, in one of the less timid of the available pronouncements, has urged that businessmen participate in community affairs, that they lend-lease themselves to the national government (there saving "us more money in two years . . . than they possibly could by staying at their desks in our plants and offices"), that they become active in party politics, and that they vigorously support the higher learning in America.[43] As one report has it:

Jersey Standard has kept up with the times, and recognized the structure and the obligations of the modern corporation. It is in part a money-making machine, but in greater part it is an economic agent of the community, responsible to the community. . . . A recent editorial in *The Lamp* states the company's philosophy: "If today's managers of private enterprise are to justify their positions, they must conceive their duties in broader terms than simply the production of goods. They must have a sense of public responsibility, and must assume active roles."[44]

In 1956 *Time* magazine claimed that "the average top executive spends up to one third of his time on community projects, expects his subordinates to follow his example,"[45] A widespread interest in symphonies, art, architecture, community parks, and nontechnological research centers is but another manifestation of the enlarged vision of business.

More weighty, perhaps, is business activity in the field which most intimately and elusively shapes the character of a society—that of education. Rarely taking the crude form exposed by Veblen's *The Higher Learning in America,* rarely appearing as Charles E. Wilson's proposal to have the businessman define "goals of attitude, outlook, and knowledge" and "provide high policy guidance for the action-taking body of the college," it is more commonly concealed by corporation-supported charitable foundations. These, at least according to one student, have become increasingly important "in the determination of educational policy, the goals of research in all spheres, and the direction of thinking in international affairs." And as foundations are "increasingly becoming a by-product of the large business corporation, the latter can, to a significant extent, influence educational and cultural policy."* To

* Wolfgang F. Friedman, "Corporate Power, Government by Private Groups, and the Law," *Columbia Law Review* 57 (February 1957), 155–

the extent that industrial research is carried on within the private realm, which is well protected against infringements on its arsenal of patents, the speed and the direction of scientific and technological progress is quietly fixed by those who exercise corporate power.*

Cooperating with the major organs of the national government and more or less peaceably disposed toward the leadership of the great labor unions, the corporate giants occupy a strategic economic position. Well-disciplined organizations with control of their material and financial resources, they have the means to promote not only their social but also their economic policies. Generously permitting smaller corporations and public governments at all levels to share a portion of their surplus, they constitute a formidable reservoir of public power. However sensitive to the aspirations of the groups that they govern, however inefficient their rule in practice, and however responsive to a government-endorsed national interest when it is virtually unanimous, they wield power in a stupendously large sector of our economic order. They determine the level and the distribution of national income. They direct the allocation of scarce resources, and they decide the extent and the rate of technological and economic development.[46] They fix the level and the conditions of employment,[47] the structure of wage rates, and the terms, tempo, and season of production not

---

86, 162–63, 177. "When a foundation," Friedman writes, "bears the name of an operative enterprise, any adverse publicity may affect the competitive position of the 'parent' corporation. Some months ago there was some concern whether the action of the Fund for the Republic . . . might affect the sale of Ford automobiles. Even when such direct implications are absent, most foundations will prefer to finance uncontroversial rather than politically controversial fields of education and research. . . . The result may, in due course, be a very gradual, though indirect, restriction of the freedom of research . . . [and] likely to operate less through direct censure than through the narrowing down of the scope of research."

* This is not to suggest that matters are markedly different under nominally public auspices, as the development of atomic energy during the Second World War indicates. Nor, to point to a field in which the pressures of narrow interests play an even greater role, has the research engaged in by the Department of Agriculture been consistently disinterested.

only for themselves but also for those who use their bargaining agreements as models. They decide which labor markets to exploit and which to reject.[48] And they control the quality of goods and services as well as the standards and quantities of consumption.

Insofar as corporate oligarchies effectively control industrial systems, and insofar as the systems manage to bring under their influence vast areas of the public, it is corporate oligarchies that control public life. As their environment remains at peace, they become secure; as the world outside becomes dependent, they become independent. Their law becomes *de facto* constitutional law; their economic behavior becomes statesmanship; their social conduct becomes public morality. The organizations they control emerge as self-maintaining political communities prospering in a social setting made ever more hospitable. Their professional duty becomes to govern well, to operate as self-appointed stewards, responsible but unaccountable, integrating a multitude of interests, not selfishly but for the sake of the enterprises they rule. Their systems are self-centered: once properly primed, they generate, replenish, and purify themselves. Above all, they provide their own validation, their own excuse for being. Ironically, they come to resemble the sovereign, conscience-burdened individuals in whose behalf John Locke vindicated the Glorious Revolution.

4

The Incorporation of Labor

The contemporary labor union, whether active within the business corporation or facing it from the outside, places the classical problems of governing men in a modern frame. As one of the most important organizational variants within American political pluralism, unions provide a fertile field in which to examine individual rights and obligations. Extending from the relatively autocratic Federation of Musicians to the relatively democratic Upholsterers Union, they raise problems of governmental centralization and decentralization, of membership participation and apathy, of citizenship and subversion. They necessarily do so in a fresh idiom, one which begs for newly formulated answers. They invite the attention not only of a political science interested in rules of prudence or in manipulative knowledge but also, in so far as unions find themselves operating publicly in the realm of human ends, of political philosophy.

The interest of American labor unions in the good life—an interest which properly makes them a target for political philosophy—has been far from constant. In view of the conditions shaping their development,[1] it is understandable that the first men who successfully led American workers could not be preoccupied with programs outlining forms of leisure, retirement, education, and recreation, or with theories prescribing a level of culture and a style of life away from the job. Because they could gain their victories most easily by concentrating on economic benefits, theirs was predominantly a bread-and-butter unionism. Whenever a broader moral and social orientation was nurtured, as it was between 1860 and 1880, it either fell by the way, as every effort to create a national labor party has collapsed, or was simply an orientation which could be shared with management, namely, the belief that the given system must be made to work. This belief always meant accepting the "realities" of American life, in particular the workings of the great American market. Accepting this, the concern of organized labor has been with bargaining on wages and working conditions, and, more rarely, on standards of production and ways of introducing new technological processes. True, there have been expressions of interest in the efficiency of particular managements, the wisdom of certain product designs, and the desirability of alternatives for industrial development. But on the whole these have been no more than interesting but improvised scouting expeditions into well-defended territory. The significant fact, to which recent explorations are no exception, is that American labor unions, accommodating themselves to the prevailing way of legislating reforms, have sought to improve the welfare of their members not by subverting the law but by hiring lawyers to put the law in their service as best they could. Moreover, in seeking to come to grips with the market itself, they have worked within the existing industrial structure and thereby reinforced it.

In order to deal effectively with the market, unions have steadily expanded. Today about 17 million members belong to some 200 national unions. Excepting the Roman Catholic Church and Baptist bodies, the AFL-CIO encompasses more individuals than any other organization in the United States. In 1957 membership in the Teamsters Union alone—not to mention the more recent coalition of workers in the transportation industry—was reported at 1,700,000. Twenty per cent of the labor unions have more than 100,000 members, and about seventy per cent of all members are enrolled in these large unions. About one third of all members are in the seven largest ones, each with a membership of more than 600,000.

In reaching their present dimensions, unions were inevitably forced to develop tactics and organizational arrangements that would assure their survival. Somehow they had to respond to the potent antagonistic forces in their environment: to ideology, public law, and the sheer violence of business. Nor was the worker himself always the friend of organized labor. He could often afford, literally, to be indifferent; he could *feel* that he was free to move from plant to plant and from one social group to another. As unions sought to come to terms with these environmental forces, they naturally discarded practices that proved wasteful, and they became increasingly similar. They began to rationalize their affairs under a leadership which slowly had to become centralized. Labor leaders, unable to accept anything approaching pure democracy, yet encouraged by successes to abandon militancy, gradually lost their roles as heroic fighters. Initially tough and uncompromising, they were impelled to emerge as efficient coordinators. As such, it became their major task to keep their vast social machines together, forcing rival interests to work in unison; in attempting to maintain what was typically a conglomeration of power blocs, they were led to create relatively autonomous national offices which, in turn, were eventually to be linked with the AFL-CIO. Although the AFL-CIO can hardly be said to *govern* 180-odd nationals, it could insist, as George Meany did for the first time in 1957, on the expulsion of unsavory ones.

The obstacles to such internal consolidation have been considerable. The unions have had to absorb a stream of new members whose political education had been European and who, when they did not permit themselves to be infatuated by Horatio Alger, contentiously urged their organizations to fight on a broad front for social justice. Nevertheless, the organizational drift almost invariably obeyed Michels's iron law: what began as a movement to protect individual members from outsiders generally ended as one to protect the leadership from insiders. Not unexpectedly, the power to make decisions has come to reside in well-protected, self-perpetuating incumbents whose prestige and skill—backed by an extensive staff of professional attorneys, economists, statisticians, writers, and administrators—is such that the rank and file, perhaps gratefully unconcerned, only rarely challenges their word.*

It was never likely that union leaders would find it expedient to keep their organizations small and voluntary, and thereby homogeneous. The advantages of large size and compulsory membership have always been evident, with heterogeneity and the consequent need to impose discipline a small price to pay. The involuntary nature of membership is no secret. "I don't know," James C. Petrillo has mused about the musician expelled from the union, "where he would get a job today. An expulsion is a very serious matter for a man who is making his living with his instrument."[2] What is more, voluntary departure is certainly inhibited when seniority may be lost and when the accumulated benefits of unemployment, retirement, medical, and pension plans may be forfeited. The incentive to stick it out is consequently strong. Finally, unions have also become increasingly unwilling (or unable) to discriminate against applicants with unorthodox viewpoints, differing racial backgrounds, or great variations in education, skill, and age. Therefore the kind of homogeneous membership which had characterized the early craft union—and which had made it possible to identify the policy of the leaders with the wishes of the members—has clearly become a thing of the past.

While the large-scale, heterogeneous, and involuntary union has thus emerged, procedures for taking account of the various newly incorporated interests have not been welcomed. Oligarchies

---

* This massively documented tendency toward oligarchy is not, of course, confined to unions. But the union leader finds himself in a peculiar situation. His stake in his office is doubly great since, unlike his counterpart in the business corporation, the loss of his office is likely to be a serious matter for him. There is nowhere else to go, at least in the present stage of the labor movement when his managerial skills are likely to be appreciated only in the more competitive industries. Ironically, the less he is corrupted by business interests beckoning from outside his union, the more unscrupulously he will secure himself within it. Unless he has cultivated nonunion business, he must remain attached. Hence his effort to prevent his displacement may be formidable.

remain entrenched; the rank and file is kept in line; and a semblance of policy consensus is achieved either by straightforward coercion or by a more oblique engineering of consent, with slight concessions to voluntarism, parliamentarianism, and politics. These propositions are not hard to document.[3]

Hostility to intra-union politics is widespread, and certainly understandable. Factional fights are bitter. And since they make for disunity, members are not likely to take issue with what was forcefully expressed in Philip Murray's address to the 1942 convention of the United Steelworkers:

I do not want—as a matter of fact, I shall fight any attempt that is made to have little back room caucuses while this convention is going on. There is going to be one convention in the city of Cleveland and it is going to be held in this hall. We are not going to permit sharp practices and petty politics to be played in the Steelworkers. So if any of the boys are thinking right now of midnight sessions in strange places in the city of Cleveland, just begin to forget about it right now. There is going to be one convention. . . . That is the democratic way to do business.[4]

"If we started to divide up and run a Republican set of officers, a Democratic set, a communist set and something else," Harry Bridges frankly told his Longshoremen in 1947, "we would have one hell of a time."[5] What occurred in 1958 at the biennial convention of the Steelworkers is distinguished by its dramatic management, not its uniqueness. Without naming his major opponent to presidential office, incumbent David J. McDonald asked 3,522 delegates to "rip this cancer out of your bowels through your own doing and don't leave it up to me." He did not have to point out that he was referring to one of the delegates, Donald Rarick, a local union president who had had enough support the previous year to cut into McDonald's majority. Actually, McDonald need not have worried, for Rarick had no base whatever for effective opposition. Not only did McDonald have an "administration" on his side—some 750 union employees prepared to lobby for him— but more important, as the incumbent he himself had the power to determine how his challenger might get a hearing. What President McDonald did, giving no advance warning, was to summon Delegate Rarick to his side on the speaker's platform. Ostentatiously tolerant, he then stopped the booing from the floor and asked that Rarick be given a chance. Although caught off balance, Rarick made an attempt to state his position. But McDonald had little trouble presenting his rebuttal and obtaining a solid majority to vote for trials to purge the rebel and his lieutenants.[6]

Legally, of course, a national convention ratifying such decisions is the supreme legislative organ. But a president who controls a convention's committees—especially a credentials committee able to screen out delegates unenthusiastic about the machine in power—effectively influences its behavior. He is in a position, not surprisingly, to secure the approval of his policies, to assure his own re-election, and to designate his associates and successors. He is the great allocator of the union's resources—its legal skill, its fighting power, its ability to reward and punish. Funds flow to him from locals which collect per capita taxes, initiation fees, reinstatement dues, and special assessments. Of course not all locals are equally dependent. Yet wherever the president is empowered to grant or revoke local charters, to funnel the resources of his office to his adherents alone, local autonomy is necessarily a fiction —as it was well illustrated by the case of the Teamsters in the 1950's. At best, locals become administrative agencies of the nationals. Paul Jacobs's comments on the relation between the president of the Teamsters and his organization are to the point:

The president has "authority to interpret the Constitution and laws of the International Union and to decide all questions of law thereunder. . . ." He alone determines whether strike or lockout benefits will be paid. The bylaws of local unions are subject to his approval. He appoints and may remove all the international organizers. And the president appoints the four chairmen of the conferences, the most important informal power bases within the International. . . .

Except to say that vice-presidents are members of the general executive board, the union's constitution is silent on their duties and responsibilities. In practice, an informal, reciprocal relationship of mutual protection and dependence exists between them and [President] Beck.[7]

His extensive appointive power gives the president the opportunity to absorb potential dissidents within his administration; and once absorbed they are without a base on which to build their own reputations. Thus, even though a union president and his top officers, like those who govern the Amalgamated Meat Cutters and Butcher Workmen, might be legally responsible to both the national convention and an executive board, this means little if the members of the executive board serve without compensation and draw salaries because they fill positions to which the president has power to appoint them. In the United Mine Workers, this control has been even more forthright: the president simply appoints and removes board members. Such arrangements for leadership continuity are merely amplified when a union constitution—for example, that of the Hod Carriers, Building and Common Laborers—permits the membership, by referendum, to postpone holding a convention for as long as 30 years. Add to this the leadership's power to act as accuser as well as judge in disciplinary proceedings, and the union membership remains as little more than a massive organ of assent and affirmation.[8]

Union oligarchies, presuming to take full account of men whose purposes cross, transform these purposes into unified policies. They enforce harmony despite many real conflicts: between old workers and young workers, employed and unemployed members, those in competitive concerns and those in stable ones, those who want pensions and those who want pay increases, those who exercise union power and those who desire to. When the leadership deals with business concerns or addresses the community outside, it has no alternative. Although the interests spoken for are plural, the voice with which the union speaks must be singular. Thus every union policy effectively discriminates against some internal union interest. Every agreement circumscribes the lives of members: it creates and distributes their rights and their duties; it defines the nature and pace of work as well as the duration and locale of strikes.

On another level, union policies have more subtle consequences. Cumulatively, the agreements reached through negotiation create a body of law regulating not merely the lives of union members but the place and the role of the organization as a whole. They establish its position in the larger social and economic environment. What assumes importance here is not any specific set of contracts but rather the general framework within which all of them are drawn up, the framework settling the status of the parties engaged in bargaining and determining their respective jurisdictions.

As union leaders find fewer reasons to protest against specifiable employer injustices, they become less concerned with promoting the expressed interests of workers and more concerned with making organizational demands. It becomes less essential to raise wages (the sound contract will automatically take care of this) than to guarantee the efficient operation of the organization and the effective governing of its constituents. To maintain the organization as a viable entity—to secure its funds, its own economic enterprises, its network of contacts in the world of business and politics—those devices which make control possible (such as the closed shop or the dues checkoff) must become stock-in-trade. The attainment of union autonomy under rational top-echelon control gains priority as a goal.

This does not mean that the union will lose interest in extracting from the labor market as much as the market can be made to yield; it does mean that union bargaining is likely to be keyed to organizational imperatives. More specifically, the union will seek to eliminate the islands of independence preserved by localized, firm-by-firm, short-term bargaining. Negotiations with an entire industry over long terms can thus be seen as necessary for getting power over the market, for stabilizing the rank and file, and for dealing authoritatively with management. The union leadership does not actually strive for the resulting sense of worker detachment, the pervasive apathy fostered by the long-term contract negotiated on a regional or an industry-wide basis. It simply acts on the realization that wages will be depressed when specific industries are "too competitive," when the market is fickle because firms fail to perceive the wisdom of cooperation.

The tendency therefore must be to bargain with an industry as a whole, or, when this proves impossible, to cope with the market head-on. In areas where competition remains vigorous, the union is unavoidably thrust into a managerial role when it attempts a more direct policing of the market, whether by limiting production (as in the case of coal), by fixing price lines (as in the garment industry), or by stabilizing wages (as in the construction trades). In a competitive market, the union thus tends to play the role of an independent entrepreneur.

The economy of impulses underlying the behavior of labor unions may be illustrated by considering the case of the International Brotherhood of Teamsters, Chauffeurs, Warehousemen, and Helpers of America. A rapidly growing organization quick to change tactics and to make the most of opportune moments, the Teamsters revealed during the late 1950's some of the essential organizational traits of an ascending unionism.

The difficulty of welding together a labor force of dispersed, independent workers who are attached to a great variety of industries had always been formidable. To achieve stability and hence strength of bargaining power, the organization of the Teamsters had to be integrated as it was enlarged. And where no arrangements to tie men together existed, they either had to be imposed (as, for example, in the form of region-spanning "conferences") or had to be allowed to develop freely so as to fill organizational gaps as specific needs arose.

The 1957 Senate investigation of some of the practices of the Teamsters has made it easy to see the picture in greater detail.[9] The hearings did not reveal so much as is popularly supposed about abuses of granted power. About this, the record, at least in part, remains ambiguous. We shall never really know what share of the Teamsters' membership may have gladly taxed itself to get that sense of well-being which comes from the vague awareness that one's elected officials and their relatives lead richer and more comfortable lives than reported salaries suggest. What the hearings did succeed in demonstrating is just what it takes to make a union such as the Teamsters fully functional in its own terms.

What provoked the Senate investigating committee, and what seemed to call for Congressional action, may certainly have been the union's blatant nepotism, its reliance on illegal deception, its fondness for shakedowns and kickbacks, and its use of violence. But at bottom, the most disturbing element was the joining of conflicting interests, primarily those of management and labor. Because this joining of interests was so timid, unsystematic, and informal, providing for a partnership which generally rested not on hard-won contracts but on personal friendships, it proved to be a scarcely discernible pattern. Indeed, the actual fuzziness of the relations may yet cause us to look back on them wistfully. For if mature unions led by men of integrity should manage to integrate conflicting interests and make the resulting integration respectable, we may someday feel about the present state of labor unions as we now do about political bossism; we may nostalgically recall those swampy regions of waste and planlessness which permitted the acquisitive, self-reliant improviser to act with bold ingenuity (albeit without scruples), somehow doing what had to be done.

Some clues to organizational imperatives are to be found in the career of Nathan W. Shefferman. An agile, energetic purchasing agent for various union leaders, including Walter Reuther, he was a peripatetic entrepreneur who operated in a corporate twilight zone in which only the well-attuned can expect to survive.[10] The impersonal, organizational needs that Shefferman served so well were none the less real for being hardly recognized. He sensed what was demanded and built a flourishing business on answering the calls of others. It would seem that in serving as a procuring agent for labor chieftains, especially his good friend Dave Beck, he acted not by design, for the profits were never noteworthy, but instinctively, following the course of least resistance, sensitively and loyally responding to the requirements of friendship and power.

His business, it seemed, was a vague sort of labor-management consulting, exclusively for employers. Thus he dispatched an "industrial psychologist" to Whirlpool Corporation, one of the 300 clients of his Labor Relations Associates, so that concealed pro-union sympathies of employees could be exposed through "Human Equation Tests." At the same time, and while his staff was engaged in more forthright anti-union activities within various plants, Shefferman himself exuded good will at scores of union conventions. What is more, he did what he could to settle President Beck comfortably on his union-financed estate, to furnish and decorate the Teamsters' international headquarters, and to provide the friends and relatives of top union officials with salaried jobs or the comforts of life. "From the Desk of Dave Beck" went memos asking "Nate" to pay for some $85,000 worth of goods and services—from golf balls to diapers, from landscape gardening to interior decorating. With these memos Shefferman complied, for there were always union funds to reimburse him. "I never questioned it for a moment when he sent me the bill," he was to tell the Senate Committee. "When he said 'Pay it,' I paid it. I didn't question it for a moment."[11]

Insofar as the cues to which Shefferman unthinkingly responded were given insistently and repeatedly, does it not become justifiable to speak of his middleman operations as a necessary by-product of organizational behavior, as a natural function of the type of large-scale regime he served? His testimony was wholly candid; he saw nothing truly incriminating in his conduct. In fact, it must shock the ignorant more than those labor and business groups that "understand the system," for given the system to which Shefferman so skillfully catered, his solicitude was not so much wrong as it was haphazard, fumbling, and unsystematic. What did seem wrong, in the final analysis, was merely the personal element, his failure to make his transactions more impersonally and more efficiently. And if it is only this that made a Senate committee as well as the conscience of the rest of American labor indignant, it is reasonable to expect that Shefferman's transactions—and the transactions of the innumerable lesser fixers and brokers whose model he is—will eventually become legitimate, that they will become fully institutionalized and bureaucratized. Before long, we may see them as routine components of the labor movement, which, far from being morally repugnant, are functional parts of an ascending political order.

What is true of the half-hidden roles so suggestively played by Shefferman has been no less true of the roles played by other actors on the same stage. The part of the labor racketeer might also be seen as only a symptom of immature labor-business cooperation; it has often been pointed out that racketeering is a practice designed to cut off access to the market and eliminate competition.

Should labor decide to rectify itself, should it actually furnish the basis for a commendable public image, we should not expect major changes in its orientation, its organizational structure, or its network of relations with the community outside. It will seek to preserve the nature of these foundations while finding reputable substitutes for them. And in this search for legitimate equivalents, unions will necessarily purge themselves, much as the United Steelworkers did in the 1930's when they kept the leaders of wildcat strikes in line after contracts had been signed. Thus we might look forward to the replacement of a Shefferman, but not to the replacement of the structure within which he functioned. This structure may be expected to emerge as one which successfully balances its component parts, economically keeping them in line to move the organization more efficiently toward its goal.

On the surface, that goal has been both to preserve the organization and to extract the maximum from an economic surplus for the membership. Although the fight to fatten the pay envelope has never guaranteed the elimination of conflicts within labor organizations, it has almost always contributed to a union's cohesiveness. Conflict is likely to arise only as goals become more specific, doctrinal, and ideological while a union remains heterogeneous and broad-based in its membership. Ever since Adolph Strasser and Samuel Gompers first spelled out the interest of their organizations in getting more money for their workers rather than in fighting for some specified social order, we have noted with C. Wright Mills that "labor leaders do not connect specific demands with general images of the kind of society they want, nor do they integrate immediate demands and general principles into programs."[12] In 1957, Jimmy Hoffa spoke up almost as if intending to reinforce this view:

Senator Mundt. . . . Basically, do you believe in socialism?
Mr. Hoffa. I positively do not.
Senator Mundt. Do you believe in our private-enterprise system?
Mr. Hoffa. I certainly do. . . .
Senator McNamara. I think we are talking in vague terms when you endorse or reject socialism. I do not know what it means in the context that it was used here. Are you talking about a political philosophy or something else?

Mr. Hoffa. I assumed it was political philosophy.

Senator Mundt. His assumption was correct.

Senator McNamara. What was that again?

Senator Mundt. I say his assumption was correct. I was talking about the same thing.

Mr. Hoffa. I understood, sir.

Senator McNamara. I did not think they were an important political party and I do not know why it enters into the affairs of this committee. I thought socialism was pretty well dead.

The Chairman. Gentlemen, let us get back on the track.[13]

But in an area where practicality and especially praise for practicality are highly esteemed, it may be more appropriate to explore what is being done than what is being affirmed. Today, the power to run the union—the power to consider a union's administrative staff, in the words of Hoffa, as "*my* men" paid out of "*my* payroll" to run "*my* business"[14]—has been given an extra dimension first by the far-flung operations of organized labor and, second, by its intent to assume responsibility for the "whole person" in a balanced community. These two factors might well be considered in turn.

In a society whose workers had overwhelmingly accepted the proposition that the business of America is business, a class-conscious labor point of view could become neither emphatic nor clear. However much resistance there has actually been to the creed of the businessman, it has been so sporadic and isolated as to be unable to overcome a gradual blurring of the distinction between labor and business. Labor's own involvement in business became inevitable, in fact, as soon as vast union pension and welfare funds began to accumulate and beg for sound investments. Formed to fight for economic benefits and political rights, to use their financial resources to organize the unorganized, and to gain the favor of legislatures, unions had no significant investment problems in the past. Nor, as long as industries remained incompletely unionized, was there any problem of finding fields in which union functionaries might find outlets for their skills. There was little surplus of either capital or talent, and hence little excess of power. But as unions developed the capacity to generate their own capital and found themselves unable to plow it back into their own organizations, the issues of market power and political power were bound to arise.

To the extent that the straight political road had been blocked by the non-ideological orientation of American labor, it was only natural for unions to seek outlets in the market and to create or use business outlets—illegitimate ones in vice and crime when labor leaders were so addicted, legitimate ones when the rewards of community respectability seemed in the offing. Not infrequently, their ventures into business were tied, if not to the personal interests of the leadership, then to the job interests of their members. Thus in 1956 the United Mine Workers agreed with mine operators to establish a joint shipping company to promote the export of American coal. Similarly, the Teamsters have come to the aid of Fruehauf Trailer Company, and the Hatters' Union has become a major stockholder in a hat factory. Since the aim was for more than a sound investment of pension funds, these enterprises were not necessarily the best available business risks. Still, they did have the effect of confounding traditional trade union and business motivations.

Again, the Teamsters present the extreme case. In the trucking field especially, labor and management often overlap and become indistinguishable. After all, drivers who accumulate capital or credit have no trouble becoming operators. Operators who go broke in what is a highly competitive industry may easily return to driving. Moreover, there are thousands of owners who, because they drive their own rigs, are union members. When management and labor are hardly distinguishable, the union becomes an integral part of the trucking business. It is hardly startling, therefore, to find Hoffa, while still a ninth vice-president, speaking simply of "the labor business" and his "friends in the labor business," as Paul Jacobs has reported. In 1956, despite a long and bitter strike by the Retail Clerks against a Minneapolis department store, Hoffa loaned the store $200,000 out of a union welfare fund. Asked about the loan's propriety, he called it a "business deal," "strictly a sound investment."[15]

Jacobs concluded his study of the Teamsters by observing that the more labor is inclined to be business-like in its dealings, the more it will share business practices and incentives. The relationship between business and labor "becomes that of two giants vying for economic power or collaborating in its joint exercise."[16] Such a pattern of harmonious, reciprocal relations between labor and business implies a change in the role and direction of American labor. It suggests, at a minimum, a new degree of labor's "understanding" of the "problems" of management. "We must raise our sights," Walter Reuther wrote early in 1959. "We must shape policies in the knowledge that free labor and free management are less antagonists than partners, that they have more in common than in conflict. We need to broaden areas of understanding and minimize areas of conflict."[17]

Perhaps the epitome of fraternal worker-management relations is the set of arrangements between the United Mine Workers and the Bituminous Coal Operators' Association. One BCOA executive, Edward G. Fox, believed it necessary in 1956 to point out ("emphatically," as he put it) the error of those who felt that "the present method of arriving at new contract terms could not be properly defined as negotiations." That simply is not how it is: as union and management learn to operate harmoniously in the coal industry, they will merely keep out other interests, jointly combating "the influence of competitive fuels, government interference, and unreasonable safety regulations."[18] Such spontaneous collaboration requires that union and business negotiators use joint machinery to discover "the logic of the situation," agree upon a solution, and then act less as agents than as principals in persuading their respective constituencies of the objective soundness of their bargains. Why not, as the counsel to the AFL-CIO Ethical Practices Policy Committee seriously urged in 1958, resolve impending conflicts in a formally established labor-management assembly?[19] Who could resist an assembly expressing the consensus of big business and big labor?

Labor-management agreements, negotiated in an atmosphere of a calm preserved by two professional teams and concluded in the privacy of the bargaining chamber by principals capable of anticipating the reactions to all proposals and counterproposals, are not alone in extending the range of oligarchically formulated policy. There is some evidence that American labor leaders themselves are beginning to be exhilarated by the prospects of securing not only readily calculable economic benefits but of guaranteeing the worker self-realization in all phases of his life. In 1955, Walter Reuther asked publicly for the first time just what "positive human values" the labor movement might satisfy. While he offered no conclusions, affirming only the need for bringing "economic and material values" into greater harmony with "basic human and moral values," he significantly raised a question which the pragmatism of American labor leaders had until then consistently deflected.[20]

To raise this question seriously, and to propose answers intended to furnish a basis for action, is to consider organized labor as something more than a limited and special interest in American society. Thus Arthur J. Goldberg has rightly observed in his quasi-official history of the AFL-CIO merger that "with labor's growth and maturity, American unions have rapidly emerged from the status of a narrow pressure group into an area of broader interest in the general problems of the nation and the specific community."[21] This concern with general interests, the chairman of the AFL-CIO Community Services Committee has acknowledged, constitutes a "departure from the traditional pattern of unionism."

This departure, in turn, has required a redefinition of the standards governing the union member's relations with his community. Most narrowly, it has meant that full-time labor representatives could join the staffs of community organizations under an AFL-CIO sponsored program.[22] In 1956, the AFL-CIO executive council could affirm:

Unions have a responsibility for the health and welfare of their members and their families which extends beyond the place of employment. This responsibility includes not only the emergencies caused by strike, unemployment, and disaster, but extends to helping the employed member meet his personal and family problem.[23]

In contemporary American practice, such pronouncements, like the similar ones previously cited from business leaders, may have very little actual significance. There is a considerable amount of vacuous rhetoric in the announcement that "in the states and cities, men and women from the unions are active in community services work of every description—not just as individuals with a hobby, but as representative spokesmen for their fellow union members."[24] What is more, such concern with the worker as a member not only of his union but also of the community is not altogether new. Before the 1920's, the Amalgamated Clothing Workers, under Sidney Hillman and Jacob S. Potofsky, instituted workers' banks, insurance companies, housing projects, health centers, and educational facilities. Addressing the delegates of the Ladies' Garment Workers' Union in 1959, David Dubinsky did not jar anyone by asserting that his union aspires to more than additional money in the pay envelope: "Dignity, not just dollars; freedom, not just less working time; self-fulfillment, not just labor for hire, these are the real goals toward which we in the ILGWU and our fellow workers in sister unions . . . have been moving."[25] Although he did not specify what dignity, freedom, and self-fulfillment substantively consist of, his union's educational and recreational activities do suggest definitions.

This broadening of union interests may still appear to be exceptional. Yet it is likely to become less so as it gains support from the employer's realization that he can hardly avoid contributing to it. It was during the great General Motors strike of 1945–46 that one management negotiator, recognizing a turning point in labor history, indignantly denounced Walter Reuther for pushing beyond bread-and-butter benefits.[26] But reflection might have shown him the futility of his indignation. Once company insurance schemes and pension plans provided the condition for it, a union interest in education, recreation, housing, hospitals, medical schools, consumers' cooperatives, community projects, and civic enterprises entered the employer-employee relation. However disguised, it was bound to become the very subject of negotiation.

Not only does this interest extend leadership control over the rank and file—incidentally relieving the leadership from having to remain in touch during times of tranquillity—but it also justifies the assumption that unions can be stewards of the public interest.[27] David J. McDonald, addressing the American Management Association in 1956 as head of the United Steel Workers, has put the case clearly:

After all, union leaders and company executives are trustees. We have it within our power to build our great enterprises, not only in size and volume but in service—service to the economy, service to the worker, service to the housewife and the family. We can do much to make life easier, better, more enjoyable, safer, healthier—for the people, giving them peace of mind and confidence. . . .

The recognition that we each have a role to play and that together we can progress is the key to future prosperity. This mutual acceptance and knowledge of our trust is what I mean by "mutual trusteeship." It is a logical expression of our American way and our progressive traditions.[28]

McDonald's reflections were buttressed by the thoughtful statement drafted in 1959 for the Fund for the Republic by Gus Tyler, director of the Training Institute of the ILGWU. Maintaining that present-day American labor aspires to a balanced fusion of ideological and bread-and-butter unionism and that a sound "philosophy" for labor must reflect this, Tyler nevertheless came down on the side of ideology:

Labor needs a broad view, conceived outside its parochial shop experiences, so that it may help formulate a program for the world within which it functions, so that it may relate intelligently to other groups in the community, so that it may be effective in its broad political appeals and electoral coalitions. But labor has other needs for a philosophy. Sheer business unionism is not enough, for the cash nexus has hardly ever been the basis for inspired, ethical conduct in any walk of life, anywhere in the world, at any time.[29]

The ethical level of union behavior must be raised, Tyler urged, by "a dedication to enduring ideals, a sense of duty to the community, an economic program, a concern for democracy. . . ." What is needed, he said, is "a greater goal than the contract, a broader religion than the dollar sign." Labor needs a "sensitive social interest and conscience." The keeper of labor's conscience should be the professional—the union officer distinguished by his rectitude. And for this, Americans were informed, the best guarantee would be his sense of dedication.[30]

If we are left uneasy by these formulations, it is because organized labor (or, for that matter, organized business) is decidedly not some sort of private, close-knit group of individuals who are in general agreement on life's ultimate objectives. We find ourselves vaguely troubled by its immense scale, its oligarchical government, and its concern with prescribing human ends. We may be reassured, of course, by our vision of a vigilant, unified state behind our economic and industrial organizations. Above the increasingly integrated economy, we can tell ourselves, the state exercises sovereign governmental power. But this soothing vision is still to be set against the facts.

5

Private Power and Public Purpose

American constitutionalism and an advanced technology, intimately linked, have encouraged a trend toward policy formation within a plurality of entrenched oligarchies. Constitutionalism has done so by fostering the growth of associations to attain private ends and technology has done so by favoring the concentration of control within associations. At bottom, this development is not affected by the occupational orientation of associations. It would not seem to matter whether an organization is composed of businessmen, industrial workers, farmers, attorneys, or morticians, provided only it is large in scale, complex in its interests, and heterogeneous in its membership. The rights of members to dissent, and to make their dissent effective, are not being habitually exercised in the giant-size group, even where such rights are nominally granted. And this is the case despite the wide range of interests which organizations contain and discipline, despite the repressed conflicts between all those who today are compelled to cooperate—producers and dealers, exporters and importers, jobless union members and employed ones, wheat farmers and cotton farmers, hog raisers and wool growers, surgeons and general practitioners. Associations, more specifically those who run them, effectively coordinate the diverse interests of these groups.

To stabilize the social organism, an incumbent leadership relies either on loyalty freely pledged or on the coercive tactics which monopolistic positions make possible. It avails itself of plebiscites, mood engineering, need manipulation, or more forthright economic sanctions. This is not to say that it despotically captures and victimizes the powerless. It may in fact realize that the membership really can be pleased, or at least can get the feel of pleasure, and that reliance on the light touch and the soft sell is ultimately the least wasteful technique. In adjusting barely articulate intimations of public wants to policies it identifies with the public good, it can become paternalistic and benevolent, fondling innumerable latent interests and emerging as a caretaker of public aspirations.

Regarding the individual exclusively as part of the social organism, managerial cadres may at first seek to energize him directly. They may approach him as a pliable creature and try to make him fit compartments in which he can be efficiently supervised. Once he is under control they may carefully guide him toward an open, public life, one which is secure, satisfying, and politically neutral. This guidance requires quieting his prejudices, channeling his extracurricular interests, and making him alert to the likelihood of harm if he should do the unexpectedly frivolous, have his impractical fling, or sit the next one out altogether. If these supervisory efforts enjoy a measure of success, it may become obvious that he need not really be coerced at all. It may then become sufficient to relieve him from pressures, to take genuine pains that he will not be made anxious by meaningful choices. And this should require little more than arranging his environment so as to make him truly comfortable, giving him the opportunity to become the communal, self-renouncing creature he naturally seems to be.

Those who are assuming such managerial responsibilities may now purposefully intervene in the individual's life by administering what affects his drives. As they scrupulously observe whether his motions and emotions tend to conform to the ideal of social harmony, as they test whether the myths calculated to galvanize him will in practice induce him to behave appropriately, they make man's industry correspond with what has been identified as his true interest.

Once this ideal is realized, the leadership will no longer need to tamper with human aberrations, with those unbecoming urges which make men think first of all of themselves. All taxes on idleness and nonconformity can finally be repealed, for as men are stimulated to join voluntarily in the great common purpose, they are led into genuine freedom.

The new tutelary leadership, then, is penetrating, but also soothing. It is extensive, but gentle. It slowly breeds a contented, homogeneous mass of men, a mass untroubled by the derangements which spring from the reverberations of the playful imagination, a mass free from that irreducible mystery of spirit upon which man had traditionally sought to base his dignity. As Tocqueville had speculated in his second volume on democracy in America:

Above this race of men stands an immense and tutelary power, which takes upon itself alone to secure their gratifications, and to watch over their fate. That power is absolute, minute, regular, provident, and mild. It would be like the authority of a parent, if, like that authority, its object was to prepare men for manhood; but it seeks, on the contrary, to keep them in perpetual childhood: it is well content that the people should rejoice, provided they think of nothing but rejoicing. For their happiness such a government willingly labors, but it chooses to be the sole agent and the only arbiter of that happiness; it provides for their security, foresees and supplies their necessities, facilitates their pleasures, manages their principal concerns, directs their industry, regulates the descent of property, and subdivides their inheritances—what remains, but to spare them all the care of thinking and all the trouble of living?

This extreme view of the mass society may seem utterly irrelevant today. After all, it takes no account of the good will and generous motives of Americans in positions of power. Have their intentions no weight? And isn't the picture overdrawn because of what it omits—most significantly, the role of the federal government?

Indeed, voices made shrill by repeated defeat might well ask if it can really be denied that the instrumentalities of government —regulatory commissions, boards, and bureaus, investigating committees of Congress, and, not least, the courts—have fined, licensed, certified, chartered, reorganized, taxed, harassed, and even busted America's great organizations and their high statesmen. Is it not true, the question runs, that above the race of adjusted men and the array of integrated interests stands not merely the immense and tutelary power of private government but also the far greater power of an effective, undivided, and purposeful, public government? Is not private power transcended by public unity?

In far softer terms, it is often asked whether a healthy balance of powers does not actually characterize the American political scene. Thus in 1957, in his effort to survey the whole of America as a civilization, Max Lerner furnished a view of the character of public power which, while corresponding closely to our wishes, seems also to correspond with the facts:

A new constitutional structure of industry and government is emerging, with a new separation of powers that is more relevant for contemporary America than the classical separation of governmental powers. The corporation and the union have tacitly agreed roughly on the boundary lines beyond which neither interferes with the other, while there is a common area between these boundaries where they bargain collectively; and the government has agreed roughly on the limits beyond which it will not interfere with either the corporation or union, nor will they seek to overthrow it.[1]

If this neat delimitation of powers were to remain uncontradicted by a pattern of collaboration—by an overlapping of corporation, union, and government—there would be no reason for concern. There would be every justification to join Lerner and attach the pleasing label "welfare democracy" to the amalgam of the welfare corporation, the welfare union, and the welfare state. Indeed, every sentiment favors such attractive labeling. A picture of a society composed of a multitude of self-regulated interest groups all acting in unison will always look engaging. Such a society would seem to be wonderfully suffused by a wholehearted consensus, whether depression-inspired or war-borne, on what ends are good. In their joint endeavor, these groups—so the picture must appear—preserve their diversity and yet contribute to the cause of all. Provincial interests felicitously coincide with the national interest. They do not usurp the sovereign power of government, nor does the government impose on them; their action is spontaneously parallel. Sovereignty is equitably distributed among them. Government need not coerce them, for they know the true path and march along it willingly. Relations between them are amiable: friction is controlled; boundaries are clear; competition is workable. Despite their superficial diversity, they are mutually deferential, respectful, and forbearing. And from their friendly interaction, a common denominator of sound public policy inevitably emerges.

The accuracy of this image of pluralism is put to an ultimate test during times of national emergency, when interests would seem to harmonize most completely. Under conditions of war or depression, when we might expect to see a widespread consensus on public policy, the effects of acting on pluralistic premises, of giving pluralism an institutional embodiment, should rise in bold relief. An examination of such times is likely to suggest more clearly what occurs in periods of normalcy, when the same forces are more unobtrusive, less efficient, and more easily diverted. At least two home-grown combinations of pluralism and idealism, of private power wedded to a public purpose, should therefore bear another look: (1) the depression-nurtured experiment of the National Industrial Recovery Administration and (2) the attempts during World War II to enlist the cooperation of diverse groups in shaping public policies.

The short-lived program of the NRA was based on the tacit assumption that the prevailing system of investment and employment might best be protected against the destructive effects of the depression by providing an institutional frame within which a plurality of existing economic groups might govern themselves and freely negotiate agreements. These agreements, it was felt, would necessarily reflect the variety of affected interests, for all would share in their drafting and execution. In fact, the NRA concretely expressed a hope which was the motive power behind many New Deal policies.

Reviewing the first eight years of the New Deal, the Brookings Institution rightly called attention to "the currency in official circles of the view that through the expression of . . . partisan interests and through bargaining among them, the formation of sound public policy is to be achieved."[2] This view explains the procedures and tasks Congress was asked to lay down for the new agency in 1933. A host of industries were to send their delegates to Washington, there to form a board with two members representing industry, two labor, two the general public, and one—the chairman with final authority—the President. These delegates were to fix the terms of business—prices, wages, and working conditions. Codes were to be drawn up jointly by business and labor. Section 7A of the Act invited labor to organize, and section 7B sought to secure industrial solidarity by asking labor to cooperate with business. The codes were to have the effect of public law, enforceable in the courts.

Brief as it was, this experiment in industrial self-government had at least one clear and unambiguous result. Wherever one company or a small number of companies dominated in industry, as Walton Hamilton has pointed out, the small independents were at the mercy of their large competitors.[3] In effect, the NRA stabilized a pre-existing situation. Thus Hamilton concluded:

The tightly organized industries did not demand the assistance of the NRA in imposing their discipline upon their members, although governmental sanction for their restrictive practices was recognized as an asset. In the conglomerate industries, such as poultry, cleaning and dyeing, the manufacture of clothing, the mandates of the NRA were not adequate to the task of subduing into orderly entity a medley of firms long accustomed to intense rivalry. It was to the intermediate group that the sanctions held out by the NRA were most appealing.

While the NRA affected industries in which the concentration of power varied greatly, those that were most concentrated, most tightly organized, and most oligopolistic quite naturally used their newly granted freedom from competition to reinforce their positions. And in doing so, far from encountering governmental resistance, they received official encouragement. This was not because government officials were biased, but because they had been furnished no definite economic objectives to guide them in administering the Act. As a result, interests that were weak, inarticulate, or amorphous simply found themselves eclipsed. The consumer was left unprotected against a management-labor coalition.

At the same time, given the relatively weak position of labor, management emerged triumphant vis-à-vis labor, ultimately always finding the Administration solicitously on its side. This is a point made by at least one detailed case study: "The history of the [automobile] code . . . revealed clearly that despite the talk of partnership of government, industry, and labor in the operations of the NIRA, organized labor, where it did not have the power to challenge organized industry, was, at best, a limited partner."[4] Thus the public policy behind the NRA, while not responsive to all interests, proved to be responsive to the most potent. Undirected from above, it was free to assume its own shape, or rather the shape which the prevailing group imposed. The arbiter between the competing claimants was the force, including the forceful language, brought to bear upon the government.

A review of the operations of one World War II program might suffice to show that even when national survival or victory in war is the pre-eminent goal of virtually all groups in society, there is no assurance that permitting diverse interests to compete freely will in itself secure the perpetuation of free competition. According to one exemplary study, which is no less telling for being narrowly focused, a deliberate pluralistic diffusion of power, even when consensus on ultimate ends is virtually unanimous, will enforce the concentration of power in private hands. Shortly after World War II, Lloyd H. Fisher examined the effects of the decentralization of the power to fix wages under the wartime Wage Stabilization Program; he studied the experience with the program in California, where he felt it was probably more significant than in any other state.

Grounded in the Jeffersonian faith that the public government which governs best will also govern least, Congress had left the program under the control of the very interests who were, so it seemed, affected by it—those competing at the grass roots. According to Fisher, the initial question whether to adopt a wage stabilization law or to live without one

was left where prudent agricultural administrators thought it ought to be—in the hands of the farmers at the grass roots. By what must have been a unique or nearly unique view of the proper exercise of a public function, the War Food Administration provided the administrative machinery for a program of wage regulation with the decision as to whether it would be employed or not left to the employers of those whose wages were to be regulated.[5]

The result of this decentralization of a governmental function was obvious: in effect, it gave to one of the parties, the organized growers and those who financed them, the power "to dictate the terms upon which they would accept a wage stabilization program." Congress, institutionalizing pluralism by granting democratic rights to functional interest groups, "merely recognized and formalized authority which pre-existed any congressional action."[6] Precisely as in the case of the NRA, an existing balance of power was officially cemented.

When times of national emergency make it possible to assume the existence of a common public purpose, the acceptance of pluralist premises in the design of public policy only serves to strengthen entrenched corporate enterprise. To act in the faith that private groups within a federal system will spontaneously pursue the public good has the effect of liberating private hierarchies of power and enabling them to make their own settlements. If the strongest among them triumph merely by default or fail to exploit their victories, their ascendancy is no less real.

The very crisis which makes a nonpartisan convergence of all economic interests seem so imperative will also compel a collaboration between citizenry and government which allows predominant private interests to emerge as the public interest, a result which a community under pressure will acclaim uncritically. As the cause of private lobbies becomes the cause of the nation, we are prepared to ignore the small voice—it was Senator Truman's in the midst of the Second World War—which might remind us that those who work for public benefits without compensation do not thereby neglect their selfish interests, that "in a very real sense the dollar-a-year and WOC men can be termed 'lobbyists.' "[7]

6

The Entanglements of
Organized Agriculture

The administration of agricultural policy illustrates profusely
what happens when pluralist premises inform the making of public
policy: interests which have already gained a commanding position
through the power technology has given them to act in concert will
be further fortified. Still, a pluralist approach to governmental
action has always seemed especially appropriate in the field of agriculture. So closely have farming and democracy been identified
with one another in America that an overlapping of private and
public pursuits can hardly be seen as objectionable; indeed, this
identification can be given a convincing historical explanation and
an appealing moral defense.[1] But whatever its basis, the longstand-
ing identification of farming with democracy helps account for our
general willingness today to entertain claims for the autonomy of
organized agriculture.

It was no physiocrat but Alexander Hamilton who had written
in his *Report on Manufactures* that "the cultivation of the earth,
as the primary and most certain source of national supply . . . has

intrinsically a strong claim to pre-eminence over every other kind of industry." As late as 1830, when the rural population was calculated at over 90 per cent, the national interest could justly be identified with the needs of those who did have some tie to the soil. Pressure for governmental policies affecting farmers was simply general public pressure. After all, despite the energetic growth of industrial, commercial, and shipping groups, farming was the major source of income.

Initially, farmers gave voice to their wants and transformed them into legislation at the state level. They did so in a loose, *ad hoc* manner, well described in 1807 by Isaac Weld:

The Americans . . . are for ever cavilling at some of the public measures; something or other is always wrong, and they never appear perfectly satisfied. If any great measure is before congress for discussion, seemingly distrustful of the abilities or the integrity of the men they have elected, they meet together in their towns or districts, canvass the matter themselves, and then send forward instructions to their representatives how to act. . . . Party spirit is for ever creating dissensions amongst them, and one man is continually endeavouring to obtrude his political creed upon another.[2]

Gradually, a loose network of regional interests, and hence pressures, began to emerge. These pressures were further differentiated along occupational and economic lines, the former reflecting differences such as are entailed by dairy farming and corn raising and the latter reflecting various levels of income. As formal and informal farm organizations began to absorb the existing localized and specialized pressures, a plurality of interests found representation in various agricultural groups. During the latter part of the nineteenth century, some of the objectives of these groups became public policies, fostering a corresponding growth of governmental agencies to implement them. To the extent that pressure groups became continuously concerned with the administration of legislation, aware of the range of administrative discretion and the need for sympathetic interpretation of the law, they naturally enough cultivated friendly relations with the agencies established to minister to their interests. This complex pattern of overlapping private groups and administrative agencies was not especially striking until the Great Depression, when the voices of farmers (aided by the pro-farm bias built into the American electoral system) produced radically amplified programs in agricultural marketing, housing, labor, credit, research, and education.

What became apparent then was that a prevailing complexity of interests did not make for a multiplicity of competing organizations. If the existence of a complex system of competing pressures and organizations is the necessary condition of a pluralist democracy, it could become proper to speak, with L. Grant McConnell, of the decline of agrarian democracy.[3] Not unexpectedly, agriculture seemed to have partaken in a natural history of group life which Earl Latham—writing of business, not agriculture—has taken note of:

Simple groups tend to become more complex. And the more complex they become, the greater is the tendency to centralize their control. The structure of the business community of 1950 is different from that of 1860 precisely in that relatively simple forms of business organization have become complex—have gone through federations, reorganizations, mergers, amalgamations, and consolidations in a growing tendency to rationalize the complexity and to integrate the elements in comprehensive structures. Monopolies, combinations, cartels, giant integrated enterprises are characteristic of a mature phase of the evolution of group forms. Furthermore, the history of federal administration amply shows that the tendency of simple forms of organization to become complex by combination and to develop centralized bureaucracies to cope with this complexity is to be observed among official groups as well as among the groups, like the CIO and the American Legion, which dwell outside the domain of public government.[4]

However diffuse and sporadic the pressures determining the policies affecting the farmer had been originally, by the turn of the century they began to become increasingly concentrated. When the national government responded to these pressures, its response was not to the self-reliant, independent yeoman of the Jeffersonian dream, nor even to the petition-dispatching factions Isaac Weld had observed, but rather to the most unified of the existing organizations. Although governmental policy appeared to be coherent enough, this was seldom due to the foresight of legislators, and surely not due to any constitutional scheme for fragmenting public power. It must instead be attributed to those nominally private organizations commanding enough unified power to nurture or starve the myriad of public agencies acting within their sphere of interest: managing soil, water, forest, and other natural resources; regulating farm labor and housing; fixing interest, credit, tariff, and freight rates; studying the weather and the nutritive value of foods; governing the production, marketing, and exchange of commodities. All these activities have been carried on by agencies markedly free from central public surveillance and control; in adjudicating confllicting claims, they have enjoyed great freedom to interpret Presidential pronouncements, executive orders, and acts of Congress. Independent of public power, they could easily become dependents of private power.

The record of this ascendancy of private power vested with public authority is not without lessons.[5] The first clear, though trivial, response to pressure for special benefits for agricultural interests came in 1862 with the establishment of the Department of Agriculture, which was allocated no more than $100,000, to be used primarily in giving farmers useful information. In the same year, the Morrill Act set up land-grant colleges to provide education in agriculture and engineering. The Hatch Act of 1887 gave federal support to state agricultural experiment stations. The Department itself, while expanding into such fields as weather reporting and product inspecting, remained a service agency.

By 1914, Congressional action began to shape an Extension Service to disseminate agricultural information. The Extension Service grew out of and in turn contributed to various types of extension work already under way. It was generally supported by a local county "bureau" which maintained an "agent" from private funds or a mixture of private and public funds. The agents were thought of as representatives of both the Department of Agriculture and the state colleges; in fact, however, they never hesitated to represent the other assorted interests of their home county. They did this with the acquiescence of the colleges—more specifically, the Association of Land-Grant Colleges and Universities, a potent pressure group in its own right since 1887.

The nationally federated county-agent system, as John M. Gaus

has pointed out, has rested on three major assumptions, com-
pounded equally of facts and ideals: (1) The farmer is an independent owner-operator, and he enters the market as such; (2) the
farmer himself, freely participating in the formation of policies,
specifies the problems with which agricultural education must
cope; and (3) because the diverse interests of American agriculture,
springing especially from geographical peculiarities, cannot be
served by a standardized policy, policy must become progressively
more variegated as it is channeled toward the counties.[6] These assumptions, and the county-agent system which gives them the
weight of an institution, still guide American agricultural policy
despite the fact that the farmer is simply no longer an independent
producer, free to enter or leave the market as he sees fit and free to
accept or ignore the services of government. The farmer is now
governed if not by his government then by his organization. His
organization treats him as it must, and perhaps as he expects: as
both producer and consumer in a national market to which he is
inextricably tied. At the same time, however, the notion that he
is not, as a farmer, merely a functional part of a large-scale commercial system continues to sustain agricultural policy, particularly by underwriting the county-agent system.

In order to administer the first Agricultural Adjustment Act of
1933, which was designed to restore the farmer's share in the economy, the Secretary of Agriculture felt it necessary to rely on the
only existing agency equal to the task: the Extension Service, with
agents in more than two-thirds of the counties in the United States.
And once its services had been enlisted, the Extension Service remained the nucleus of the field service in most states until the
Second World War. Given the belief in an agricultural community
of autonomous farmers, there seemed no alternative. It is true that
the land-grant colleges argued as if an opposition existed. They
fought national integration and advocated the "democratization
of administration," hoping to have local elective committees of
farmers, served by extension personnel, carry out national policy.
But, significantly, no one espoused what they opposed. Even
Roosevelt, making his way through Kansas in the fall of 1932,
promised decentralization. Only this, he said, would check the

threat of centralized bureaucracy, give responsibility for programs to those affected by them, and infuse "vitality," as he put it, into governmental schemes.[7]

The AAA of 1938, counting on the kind of sympathetic Supreme Court which was to decide *Wickard v. Filburn* in 1942, gave the county-agent system statutory basis. The Act aimed at reducing the supply of basic farm commodities (primarily by a curtailment of acreage) and providing an equitable distribution of subsidies. By these means, an always normal, nationwide granary was to be approximated. To achieve these purposes, production and marketing quotas were to be fixed and then translated into individual acreage allotments and production quotas by county committees elected by participating farmers.[8]

To stifle the charge originating with land-grant college officials that agricultural policy was actually being forced on the unwilling farmer, undermining his initiative and making him more dependent on official Washington than on his own organizations, the so-called Mt. Weather Agreement of 1938 was negotiated between representatives of the Department of Agriculture and the land-grant colleges. According to this agreement, new agricultural policies were to be germinated by millions of farmers themselves.[9] The compact specified that "land use plans, programs, and policies [were to be] developed by community and neighborhood planning committees." These were to be "established as the cornerstone of the whole planning organization." What these committees brought forth was then to be coordinated by county committees consisting of farmers, the county agent, and representatives of governmental agencies concerned with land use. While a farmer was to head the county committees, the county agent, presumably to preserve continuity, was expected to be an executive officer. At the state level, in turn, an agricultural program committee, headed by the State Director of Extension, was to function. Thus administration was imbued with democracy.

Even after setting up this organizational pattern to prevent the national government from capturing the committee system, organized agriculture still thought it necessary to remain on guard against other possible forms of central control and coordinated

government. One of the efforts which threatened to achieve integration and to effectuate a truly national agricultural policy was
the Administration's attempt to strengthen the Bureau of Agricultural Economics in the late 1930's. This Bureau had been elevated to lead in the shaping of policy recommendations, and to
enable it to implement its recommendations, it had been put in
charge of the state and county land-use planning program. By
1940, just before it was permitted to wither, the BAE had actually
carried on its activities in almost 2,000 counties. It has been argued
that its rapid growth deprived it of vitality; it allegedly became the
victim of geography. But geography was not without allies. The
farm organizations, it turned out, lost interest in keeping the bargain they had struck at Mt. Weather, Virginia. Because the committee system was becoming increasingly independent, they decided to attack the BAE and ultimately the committee system itself.

Nor was this the only area in which centralized power independent of American Farm Bureau Federation control was attacked. The Farm Security Administration was forced to with-
draw from the field as well. It was opposed in part because the
Farm Bureau's Southern wing feared that the FSA program of
tenant rehabilitation would diminish the supply of cheap labor.
But the more decisive reason, which McConnell was to note, was
that whatever the Farm Bureau could not control, and it had
trouble with both the BAE and the FSA, it simply sought to destroy.[10]

Whether in obedience to the implicit demands of American
federalism or to the explicit pressures of organized agriculture, the
Department of Agriculture in practice had no recourse but to
route its policies through seemingly independent, democratically
elected committees. Theoretically, of course, there was always governmental authority to direct the committees from above. In 1942,
to give this authority some point, an effort was in fact made by the
Department to extricate the county agents from the system: county
committee and county agent were presumably divorced.

But how real was the divorce? Were the committees the pliable
instruments of the Department? Or was the Department too powerless to use them for promoting its policies? Reed L. Frischknecht

has maintained that the state committeemen served completely at the pleasure of the Secretary of Agriculture under one-year appointments, that they were screened for loyalty, and that they supported the Secretary "nearly 100 per cent."[11] On the other hand, Charles M. Hardin concluded earlier that actual control had slipped away from the Secretary, becoming vested in state chairmen who, operating from an independent base, were able to modify Department directives.[12] We are likely to emerge, Hardin speculated, "with an agricultural field organization built upon a network of state and local farmer-elected committees which effectively interlock with influential persons in state and local farm organizations. Such organizations would be responsible neither to the Secretary of Agriculture nor to any effective general electorate."

The offered evidence does not permit firm conclusions. But ending on the note struck by Hardin may be justified by two other investigations bearing on the pluralism of American agriculture: McConnell's study of the Farm Bureau and Philip Selznick's study of the Tennessee Valley Authority. Focusing on the private rather than the public sector and seeing the latter absorbed by the former, their conclusions are relevant.

Clearly, the Farm Bureau influences both Congress and the Department of Agriculture, exerting pressure directly as well as through the Extension Service. When seen in detail this is interesting, but in an open and representative society it is hardly alarming. The two-million-odd commercial farmers who farm not for themselves but for the market do not, today, constitute a monolithic bloc. And although the Farm Bureau remains powerful, the Farmers Union began to counterbalance it in the late 1950's.

Yet it remains true that the farm organizations are quite naturally led so as to exert pressures favoring their membership in unequal ways. It is significant, as McConnell has painstakingly shown, that the Farm Bureau acts for only one part of its membership. Thus when the government happens to respond to demands from the Farm Bureau, it serves not the variety of agricultural interests but merely some, and grass-roots democracy is willy-nilly transformed into a system which misrepresents those affected by administrative decisions. Recognition of this situation is far from new. It was in 1937 that the representative of the Southern Tenant Farmers' Union on the President's Committee on Farm Tenancy declared in his minority report that his experience kept him from believing that "the Department of Agriculture will be able in any near future to remove itself from domination by the rich and large landowning class of farmers and their political-pressure lobbies." And he saw the county agricultural agent as the symbol of such domination.[13]

In 1949, at the Annual Conference of the Production and Marketing Administration, Secretary of Agriculture Brannan affirmed:

The leaders of some organizations apparently take the view that they and they alone speak for the farmers. They seem to feel that farmers and the Secretary of Agriculture should be gagged and muzzled unless their voices are filtered through the purifying plants of a particular organization.[14]

The systematic filtering and purification of contradictory and confusing voices is made possible by modern technology, which enables us to maintain organizations of enormous scale. In a pre-industrial environment there had been good reasons for thinking that nature itself limited organizational power, and that if it did not, federalism would shatter the power to govern. In a nation whose interests are diffuse, geographically decentralized, and pluralistic, no majorities, so Madison had written in *The Federalist*, were likely to "concert and execute their plans of oppression." The sources of political power would necessarily be narrow.

But what happens, McConnell has asked, when the large organization, unhampered by a constitutional division of power and supported by modern technology, steps in?[15] Initially, it organizes where it can—on the local level, at the grass roots. But to maintain its organizational integrity, to integrate the geographical units which compose it, it must proceed to control them. In practice this requires the control of no more than a bare majority of each of the units—less than a bare majority when apathetic members acquiesce. Moreover, if power is pyramided—as it is in the Farm Bureau, which stacks its units so that the larger becomes a holding company for the smaller—the organization can be governed oligarchically. McConnell found himself concluding that under contemporary conditions, when technology allows us to ignore the former "limits of nature" in our effort to integrate human organizations, governmental decentralization leads to a pattern of domination based upon narrow constituencies.[16] It provides a specific class with the opportunity to shut off competing interests and then to rule in its own behalf. It makes the private power to exert influence on public officials the property of the self-chosen, self-regarding, self-sufficient few. And when private and public power blend, it is the few who turn out to exercise the very power to govern.

These conclusions find support in Selznick's examination of the Tennessee Valley Authority. Selznick's interest, unlike McConnell's, was in showing just how organizations, especially those exemplifying "democracy on the march," manage to retain their integrity in the face of the group pressures that surround them. He characterized the TVA's grass-roots approach to policy-making as inherently ambivalent. Relying on Extension Service machinery, the TVA permits its program to be influenced by local demands. This has of course brought its policies into conflict with national agricultural policy. One might expect the TVA to have made compromises. It has, and then some: "In delegating its agricultural program to a group which carries the banner of local constituency," Selznick wrote, "the Authority comes to reject in principle—not simply as a matter of temporary expediency—those elements of the national program which are opposed to the constituency." And at the local level, the constituency is defined in such limited terms that an existing pattern of discrimination is reinforced:

In strengthening the land-grant colleges in its area, the TVA has bolstered the position of the existing farm leadership. There is some evidence that in the process of establishing its pattern of cooperation, TVA refrained from strengthening independent colleges in the area not associated with the land-grant college system. Again, the relatively dominant role of the American Federation of Labor unions in TVA labor relations . . . is objectively a hindrance to the development of labor groups having other affiliations. In general, to the extent that the agency selects one set of institutions within a given field as the group through which it will work, the possibility of freezing existing social relationships is enhanced. At least in its agricultural program, TVA has chosen to limit its cooperative relationships to a special group [namely, the well-situated farmer and the AFBF].[17]

Thus as long as the TVA is concerned with preserving the integrity of existing institutions, its use of the most democratic means of executing policy will only bind it more firmly to a non-governmental, privately established status quo.

These considerations of the implementation of governmental policy along geographically decentralized, federalistic, and pluralistic lines should give us more than a sharpened awareness of the capacity of the well-organized to influence the government—a capacity which is infinitely enhanced, of course, when public governments and private groups coalesce legally as well as socially. Of greater, if unrecognized, significance is the fact that a government fragmented so as to make it responsive to local needs will produce a balance of public power unanticipated by the eighteenth-century proponents of decentralization, federalism, and pluralism. What happens is that the decentralized governmental agency, merely to survive and to prosper, tends to become responsive not to all interests in the locality but to the best organized, the most articulate, and the most potent. Weaving an existing pattern of private groups into the fabric of the state, enabling *all* who design the pattern to operate under color of public authority, has the necessary consequence of strengthening pre-existing power relations, whatever they happen to be.

Public government thereby becomes the great conservative force. It promotes those organizational patterns, initially pluralistic but ultimately monolithic ones, which have flourished independent of public control. Since the self-controlled, large-scale, technologically amalgamated organization is not constructed like a constitutional republic but rather, as has become evident, like a closed, oligarchically governed regime, what we publicly conserve is oligarchy. Indeed, public government will sponsor not only the most powerful member of a group of organizations; it will also sponsor the most powerful element of the leading organization.

Therefore, far from being dependent on a system which guarantees that in every final reckoning all interests will be duly accounted for, the government is actually adjusted to and adjusted by the few who lead the few. William Fellner, an economist writing of group competition in an entirely different field, has rightly concluded that to stabilize our equilibrium of groups is in fact to favor "the well-organized—and, within their ranks, the most powerful subgroups—as against the comparatively unorganized."[18] And when such subgroups are oligarchies, the government becomes *their* outpost and dependency; being democratically sensitive to them, it becomes insensitive to their rank and file. Screened off from scattered, unorganized, and unrepresented interests and thus free to ignore them, it discriminates against them. Established to protect the private rights of the individual, the government ends by contributing to their erosion.

7

The Dependencies of the
National Government

When a splintered government responds to an economic order which modern technology is depriving of its pluralist character, it tends simply to sanction the bargains struck by unrepresentative private interests. Both the regulatory commissions and the executive departments of the national government provide illustrations of this.

Although in recent years the importance of the major commissions has declined, at least when measured against the other parts of the Executive branch, they are still extensively involved in public affairs. They are concerned with the regulation of interstate rail, motor, and water transport (the Interstate Commerce Commission), of air operations (the Civil Aeronautics Board and the Federal Aviation Agency), of holding companies and stock and bond transactions (the Securities and Exchange Commission), of monopolistic, unfair, and misleading trade practices (the Federal Trade Commission), of the labor practices of employers and unions (the National Labor Relations Board), of hydroelectric development (the Federal Power Commission), and of radio and television (the Federal Communications Commission). They are in politics. From within the government and from without, pressure is put on them to favor one interest and to withhold favor from another. And they in turn apply pressure—deciding cases, making rules, shaping policies. Much has been written about this interplay of political forces within the administrative branch, and it is no longer difficult to find support for a good number of generalizations about the relation between regulating agency and regulated interest.[1]

It is now beyond doubt that the independent commission tends to be far from independent; indeed, it could not be sovereign even if it ingenuously made the effort. Whatever missionary spirit it initially possessed, at present it is not inclined to experiment creatively, to explore and test alternative policies. Moreover, it is ill-equipped to consider the objectives of groups outside the calm preserve which it administers jointly with its clientele. Even when such objectives are supported by the President or other governmental instrumentalities, the agency remains unmoved. Thus, when the Antitrust Division of the Justice Department challenged the patent practices of the Radio Corporation of America, the Federal Communications Commission was not only helpfully silent on the matter of patents but actually encouraged RCA in the television field.* Similarly, in 1957 the FCC did not delay authorizing a television station transfer to the National Broadcasting Company even though it had just received a communication from the Justice Department noting "a serious question as to whether or not the proposed transfer is unreasonably restrictive, and thus violative of the Sherman Act."[2] The natural result of

---

* "In 1950, the commission did adopt color television standards for a system proposed by a competitor of the Radio Corporation of America, which did not require licensing by the Radio Corporation of America. It should be noted, however, that the commission's intent in this respect was utterly frustrated by the refusal of television manufacturing companies (all of whom were operating under Radio Corporation of America licenses) to manufacture television receivers capable of receiving the color system authorized by the commission." (Staff Report, Special House Subcommittee on Legislative Oversight, quoted in *The New York Times,* January 23, 1958, p. 14.)

such conflicts is that governmental departments instructed to implement national policies, policies concerned with more than the administration of a single industry, tend to be hostile toward commissions.[3]

Severed from the Presidency and the departments of the national government, the seemingly independent agency slowly learns to depend on the very interests it was established to control. Whatever the nature of a clientele's initial opposition to the regulatory agency, a *modus operandi* is easily reached. Clientele and agency quite naturally come to enjoy mutually good working relations with each side intent on the survival of the other. These relations go far beyond a mere *ex parte* link between a member of the agency and a litigant before it. Nor are they confined to the kind of easy exchange of governmental with nongovernmental personnel which Cyrus Eaton detailed in 1949 before a committee of Congress:

> The almost endless procession of lawyers from positions of importance in the SEC to lucrative posts in private practice also helps to account for the Commission's cooperative attitude toward the charmed Wall Street circle. The case of Judge John J. Burns, the SEC's first general counsel, is illustrative. After 3 years in that capacity, he left the Commission to become general counsel of Morgan's United Corporation. . . . The SEC's chief supporters are naturally the Wall Street lawyers who have made a fortune out of their practice before the Commission.[4]

The quality of reciprocal solicitude has been well described in Samuel P. Huntington's discussion of the ICC and the railroads. While there have certainly been disagreements between them, the record of collaboration, of mutual praise and deference, remains impressive. In fact, the ICC, as Huntington has pointed out, is able to boast that a counsel for a railroad has written a book about it in order to demonstrate how well the Commission has performed its duty. The railroads themselves have been the most fervent defenders of the Commission's "independence." Thus they have opposed attempts to reorganize the Commission, to create rival agencies, or to interfere with the Commission's business—whether the source of interference was the Department of Agriculture, the Office of Price Administration, or the Antitrust Division. Indeed, the railroads have supported expansion of ICC power, especially over unregulated groups competing with the railroads. "Insofar as the scope of its authority is concerned," Huntington has concluded, "no stronger support could be asked by the ICC than that which the Association of American Railroads has given to the Commission."[5] The Commission, in turn, has not been ungrateful, even where responsiveness to railroads has meant unresponsiveness to the interests of rate-paying shippers, price-paying consumers, or late-coming entrepreneurs seeking to enter the transportation business. At the same time, when pressure from the late-comers became irresistible, the ICC was not unwilling to make its peace with them too. Thus it may now remind even the motor carriers of its helpfulness since, as one economist has noted, it has "created a government-approved freight cartel—with entry restricted, mergers encouraged, rate fixing tolerated, and outside competition harassed."[6]

In his critical appraisal of the commissions, Marver H. Bernstein has suggested that a governmental agency has a natural history. After it has passed its prime, decay presumably sets in: "Politically isolated, lacking a firm basis of public support, lethargic in attitude and approach, bowed down by precedent and backlogs, unsupported in its demands for more staff and money, the commission finally becomes a captive of the regulated groups."[7] Yet considered from another point of view, agency and clientele are not so much hostile organisms in a war for survival as a functional unit in a self-perpetuating industrial system. Each complementary part of the unit learns to respond to the system's needs. Seen in this light, an agency is not so much captured and enslaved as it is integrated; it adjusts to a system whose status quo it helps protect. Thus it is at once above specific struggles, impartially keeping peace between the interests within its field of jurisdiction, and intensely partisan, preserving the prevailing mode of competition and the prevailing definition of public issues. Interlocked with its clientele, it performs its functional role by being an aggressive foe of forces outside the system and a passive mediator for the system's constituents. To cite but one example, although the ICC is empowered when regulating rates to choose between taking the initiative or responding to a complaint, it seldom exercises either power; its usual practice is to remain silent on proposed rate changes, which become automatically effective if not challenged within 30 days. In this way authoritative ratification of private law—formulated by members of an industry acting in concert—is effectively secured.[8]

When only the clientele has substantive interests, and the agency's chief concern is to preserve its existing position, the clientele necessarily provides the frame within which decisions are made—and the agency accepts this frame. This is not to say that the agency rubber-stamps specific decisions previously reached by private associations; after all, hard contests are fought before it. The point is rather that the agency operates within a publicly unexamined set of values, that in resolving specific conflicts it simply accepts the values of its clientele.*

The inclination of agencies to preserve clientele-determined policy patterns may be illustrated in the federal government's regulation of labor. The way the National Mediation Board has maintained a system of discrimination established by the four major railroad transportation unions—the Locomotive Engineers, the Conductors, the Firemen and Enginemen, and the Trainmen—provides a relevant variation on the familiar theme.[9] The Railway Labor Act (1934) made it the function of the Board to certify the bargaining representative chosen for the majority of any "craft or class." Since a duly certified union becomes the exclusive bargaining agent for *all* workers in the appropriate "craft or class," minority groups within the union as well as nonunion groups within the same class of workers may negotiate only through the union's certified representative. The Board, not without a touch of righteousness, has publicized its adherence to the rule that bargaining

---

* Of course, it may embrace the industry's definition of what constitutes economic health and yet remain extraordinarily active. Its business of making affirmative rulings is not curtailed, and the scope of its activities may remain enormous. But the task of introducing new standards for judgment remains circumscribed. This fundamental limitation is likely to be obscured when a commission insists, as the FCC has, that it constructively formulates criteria intended to account for interests other than those subject to administrative regulation. In such cases, however, it can still be asked whether these new criteria are actually relied upon or whether the old ones remain implicit in specific rulings.

units "may not be divided into two or more on the basis of race or color for the purpose of choosing representatives. All those employed in the craft or class, regardless of race, creed, or color, must be given the opportunity to vote for the representatives of the whole craft or class."[10] What this statement camouflages, as Benjamin Aaron and Michael I. Komaroff have revealed, is that "the privilege of voting for representatives of the whole craft or class has not proved to be an adequate protection for these groups; and that their rights are today consistently violated by the respective union's majority."[11] Board action has simply left privately established discriminatory admission policies untouched. Moreover, efforts by Negro workers to form their own organizations so as to secure protection of their jobs have been thwarted by the Board on the ground that it was desirable to avoid "unnecessary multiplication of subcrafts and subclasses" and to preserve "the customary grouping of employees into crafts and classes as it has been established by accepted practice. . . ."[12] The practical result of this policy has been explained by Herbert R. Northrup:

Since . . . crafts and classes have been "established" principally as a result of the activities of the so-called "standard" railway labor organizations, what the Mediation Board usually does . . . is to place in one craft or class all the workers within the jurisdiction of a standard railway union. In view of the fact that nearly all these unions exclude Negroes, or afford them only inferior status, it is not surprising that the units deemed appropriate by the Board should not be the ones best suited to advance the welfare of the colored railwaymen.[13]

The NMB might have found a sanction for its indifference to internal union affairs in the silence of the statute under which it operates. This escape was closed, however, to the National Labor Relations Board, which, though it operated under a similarly silent statute (the Wagner Act, which makes no reference to revoking certifications), has in fact exercised the power to revoke. "While it is true," the NLRB ruled in 1943, "that the [Wagner] Act contains no express provisions granting the Board the power to revoke certifications, it does not necessarily follow that the Board lacks such power. . . . A certification must be viewed as a means of effectuating the policies of the Act. . . ."[14]

Although it claims the authority to do so, the NLRB has failed to challenge the certification of trade unions made unrepresentative by their discriminatory admission policies. Like the NMB, it has adhered to the seemingly sound principle that "the color or race of employees is an irrelevant and extraneous consideration in determining, in any case, the unit appropriate for . . . collective bargaining."[15] In practice, it has therefore been unwilling to probe fictitious claims like the one made by officials of the Carpenters' Union that their union "does not now, never has, and never will discriminate against any race or creed," and that it "will provide equal representation to colored as well as white locals."[16] Aaron and Komaroff have shown in detail that if the NLRB has safeguarded employee interests and protected minorities, as it has, the protection was not against unions presuming to represent them, but only against employers. It seems reasonable to conclude that the record of the NLRB under the Wagner Act was "one of dubious administrative deference to the principle of the autonomy of the private association."[17]

Such deference to a prevailing private pluralism is deference to an existing pattern of compromises and victories. It has the effect of fortifying an established balance of interests, and thereby of reinforcing precisely those interests which are the most entrenched, the best organized, and frequently the oldest. Hence what appears to be plural turns out in practice to be singular.

This is best illustrated, again, by the history of that most studied of all agencies, the ICC. In its efforts to regulate commerce, the Commission, especially after the First World War, began to focus more and more of its attention on the railroad industry, and particularly on its management group. As Huntington has shown, the railroads, only one of the many groups affected by and involved in interstate commerce, provided the support the Commission required "to expand its authority over other carrier groups and to defend itself against attempts to subject it to executive control."[18] Seemingly self-directed, the Commission showed itself to be remarkably immune to newly emerging transport interests. It responded with measured indolence to technological changes, the appearance of motor and air transport, the development of new methods of warfare, and the growth of industry in the South and the West.[19]

The interest favored by the regulating agency is thus not an industry or business as an undifferentiated whole but as a well-articulated structure whose elements have been integrated under nongovernmental auspices. The regulation which achieves such integration is private. While it is true, as I. L. Sharfman has concluded, that "in the railroad field any clear-cut differentiation between the sphere of private management and that of public control is largely obliterated,"[20] significant areas of distinctively private management actually remain. Within these areas policy is made without consideration for all those who are managed. Furthermore, it is generally executed under the warrant of public law. Thus the Securities Exchange Act, which makes membership in the National Association of Securities Underwriters compulsory, permits the Association to supervise those engaged in the business of marketing securities; it permits the levying of taxes, the maintenance of an internal court system, and the imposition of sanctions. What evidence there is suggests that this quasi-public government is not, however, championed by all of the membership.[21] It has been headed, to quote Cyrus Eaton's testimony again, by "the hand-picked hireling of the 17 indicted Wall Street [investment] houses." And these houses, he said, have their direct representatives on the Association's board of governors and on its national and district committees. In relations with the SEC, it is predominantly the secure, well-poised, blue-chip corporations which are able to

employ the high-priced legal, accounting, and engineering talent needed to assemble the mountains of information required by the SEC. They are also the ones who have the big public relations staffs, with the inexhaustible expense accounts, that are so helpful in currying favor with governmental agencies. The medium-sized and small companies, on the other hand, have neither the financial resources nor the personnel to cope with the SEC.

Similarly, in 1958 the staff of the House Subcommittee on Legislative Oversight noted in the Federal Communications Commission a tendency . . . in recent years to modify the weight given to the different criteria developed by it. Such modification has been in the direction of diminishing the importance of criteria such as local ownership, integration of ownership and management, and diversification of control of the media of mass communications (all of which tend to favor the small newcomer, without established broadcasting interests) and magnifying the weight given to the criterion of broadcast experience (which tends to favor the large established company, with extensive existing broadcast interests).

In a number of recent cases, indeed, the experience factor has tended to be all but conclusive. The result has been a growing number of decisions which increase the already pronounced tendency toward concentration of ownership in the broadcast field.[22]

Whatever a commission's specific rulings under necessarily vague congressional mandates, they are handed down "in the public interest." And what generally emerges as being in the public interest is protection of the dominant interest within the agency's own clientele, a clientele giving focus to diffuse voices, pressing its case on many fronts simultaneously, dealing in unison with myriad governmental commissions, boards, and bureaus which are kept separated by pressure deriving its justification from the hallowed principle of governmental dispersion.[23]

Administrative agencies which, unlike the independent commissions, have been made formally dependent on the Executive branch do not thereby escape their clientele. The fact that a table of organization places them closer to the President does not in itself determine the real source of effective regulatory power. Other, and less formal, conventions seem to be crucial. Two studies of presumably well-integrated governmental units merit special interest, for they are concerned precisely with the results of an agency's dependence on its clientele. They deal with (1) the relation between the Bureau of Land Management's Grazing Division and the National Advisory Board Council and (2) the relation between the Department of Commerce and the Business Advisory Council. Both the Grazing Division and the Commerce Department—not to enumerate the large number of other agencies which are aided by over 35,000 advisory committees operating at the national level—seek to give expression to democracy in administration. They provide for "home rule on the range" in one case and for "business participation in government" in the other.

In 1955, Charles McKinley took note of "the private guild units which have become so enmeshed in the administration of some of the national and state public lands as to constitute vital parts of the administrative, policy-making, and operating systems." If it became possible to delineate "the roles of the livestock advisory boards of the grazing districts, the National Forests, and the state land departments, of the Timber Protective Associations, and of the grazing associations," perhaps, so he wrote, one could learn something about "the real system of federalism."[24]

Whatever may remain obscure about what McKinley called a "web of interlocking practices, buttressed by the consensus of the forestry profession and the timber industry,"[25] it has not prevented others from reaching some conclusions. Thus in 1957, Phillip O. Foss reported what home rule on the federal range really amounted to.[26] Under the Taylor Grazing Act (1934), 483 district boards were established to advise the Department of the Interior on the distribution of range privileges in the respective districts. Board members, elected by persons holding grazing permits, were drawn together into a National Advisory Board Council in 1940, and shortly thereafter state advisory boards were formed in each of the Federal Range States. By 1949 the entire establishment had received full statutory recognition. The result, as Foss has shown, was that the stockmen's associations (the National Woolgrowers' Association and the American Livestock Association), in practice inseparable from the boards, were in the position to administer policy. As might be expected, this regime of organized stockmen was internally stable, untroubled by contested elections, officer turnover, or significant voter participation. At the same time, the boards were far from powerless. According to Foss,

no area of the administration is closed to the boards. Matters which receive most attention at the district level are range carrying capacity, awards and cancellation of grazing permits, range improvements and control of trespass. District boards are also consulted, however, on managerial questions and on such matters as bureau-wide personnel policy. State Advisory Boards and the NABC concentrate most of the attention on congressional bills, grazing fees, appropriations, organizations of the grazing service, and revisions to the Federal Range Code.[27]

In short, the boards made federal grazing policy. Their power may have been only the power to recommend, but they had been right in expecting their recommendations to carry. As one NABC president testified before the Senate in 1941, a revised range code "was written in its entirety by stockmen at the first meeting in Denver. The Grazing Service even asked if we would rather they weren't there." Senator O'Mahoney asked him whether he recalled ever having been overruled. "Not to my knowledge," he said; "there have been—the advisory board has never been overruled." One director of the Grazing Service testified that the recommendations of the Advisory Boards with respect to the issuance of permits were quite simply controlling.[28] The federalism typified by this advisory system could hardly represent all involved interests; nor could it foster habits of democratic participation in politics. In fact, Foss concluded that

through the advisory board system, a small interest group has been able to establish a kind of private government. . . . What was intended to be a device for creating and nourishing "grass roots" democracy seems to have reinforced the position of already powerful elite groups and cast over their activities a cloak of legality. Decentralization, in this instance, does not imply democratization but rather the creation of splinter governments dominated by interest groups and local elites.[29]

The result was that two potent private associations comprised the public in whose interest the public lands were governed.

A review of the NABC's participation in the process by which the Taylor Grazing Act was administered leads to conclusions which follow less obviously but just as surely from an examination of the Business Advisory Council of the Commerce Department. The Council, operating without benefit of statute since 1933, has seen its task as being

to submit to the Secretary of Commerce a constructive point of view on matters of public policy affecting the business interests of the country; to respond to requests by the Secretary for advice and assistance in carrying out his administrative responsibilities; and to provide a medium for better understanding of Government problems by Council membership.[30]

Despite some earnest efforts to learn about the Council, its role and power have been hard to trace.[31] Even though one Secretary of Commerce has conceded that the Council "is not in any sense an official body,"[32] it has, with one brief exception, been shielded from Congressional attempts to investigate its activities. Assumed to be part of the Executive branch, it has been protected by the principle of the separation of powers. However, Norman F. Keiser has shown that "in spite of able representation from smaller businesses the BAC has been dominated and composed primarily of individuals representing our larger industrial corporations." In a formal sense, the Council is not a public organization. Although an office staff is furnished by the Commerce Department, its executive director is not a federal employee; it is financially endowed by its own membership and freely uses its funds for such patently nonpublic purposes as prizes for golf and tennis tournaments at BAC meetings.[33]

Although nominally a private organization, the BAC is publicly influential in a way in which pressure groups without the same ease of access to the federal government can never be. It is apparent, for instance, that it serves as a recruiting and placement agency for personnel in many of the federal agencies. More significantly, it prepares elaborate "studies" and "reports." Although the specific import of such advisory reports is often hard to gauge, the Justice Department has found it necessary to inform the Secretary of the Interior that "fundamental questions of basic policy" are being initially settled by industry advisory committees, with the result that government action amounts to "no more than giving effect to decisions already made by such committees."[34] Decisions which thus emerge as public law have their source in a private organization, an organization whose oligarchical leadership can distort or ignore the wishes of its individual members.

Since private advisory committees were consciously built into public bodies to participate in policy-making, they remain identifiable groups whose influence, while hard to specify, can be expected to be present. But there are other private-public arrangements whose role is more difficult to trace. Less deliberately planned, these, too, are meant to provide equal representation of interests, and these, too, end by producing unrepresentative policies. Thanks to our uncritical acceptance of their role, they make it possible for the well-situated firm to improve its situation by using the government as its outpost. This can be seen, for example, in the formation of monetary policy by the Federal Reserve Board.

Conforming to general economic policy, the Federal Reserve Board controls available credit, and thereby either restrains or encourages investment. Leaving prices and wages untouched, and ostensibly seeking to avoid discrimination between various possible borrowers of funds, it attempts only to control the amount available to all comers. What have been the results? In the 1950's, the Board's efforts to curb inflation have necessarily favored the strong, and its action has in effect discriminated against small business, agriculture, and construction.[35] It may seem that the naturally weak are thus fairly restrained by a Board composed of both private and public officers, were it not that the prevailing policy itself contributes to their weakness. A government-imposed high interest rate will hurt precisely the kind of enterprise which is compelled to abide by the demands of the market, which cannot administer prices and thus pass the given interest rate on to the consumer, which cannot generate its own capital or rely on its established credit rating. In restraining inflationary growth in the entire national economy, the Board's policies have a disproportionately small impact on giant corporations and on such non-banking financial institutions as life insurance companies and pension funds.

One reason for this and other similar economic policies lies in the feeling that no administration can permit the corporate giants to be struck by financial crisis. Indeed, public agencies must be prepared to respond even to potential crises. As Morton S. Baratz has pointed out, there is no choice but to arrange both monetary and fiscal policies so that

at any time the federal government is in a position to bail out the private managers of large enterprises situated in key positions in the economy. Moreover, the dominant position of the giant firms demands that public policy-makers avoid at all costs decisions which could conceivably jeopardize the financial integrity of the mammoths. As a practical matter this means that most doubts . . . on the vigor with which certain regulatory statutes will be applied . . . will be resolved in favor of the corporation in question.[36]

This helps explain why in the Great Depression 1.2 per cent of all industrial borrowers from the Reconstruction Finance Corporation obtained 39.4 per cent of the sums authorized. But even in less critical times, the government is not likely to pursue policies which will fragmentize and equalize economic units. For one thing, working with large-scale producers is simply more convenient and more economical: for each dollar of contract, fewer hours are spent on the phone and fewer forms are routed through the bureaucracy. The pattern of government procurement programs is typically one of cooperation between governmental agency and giant-size firm. To quote Baratz again, there is a

tendency for the largest private corporations to serve as prime contractors for government procurement. In that role the giant firms are in fact serving as arms of government, empowered to distribute largess almost as they see fit. Subcontracts may or may not be granted to the lowest responsible bidder; they may be awarded with the view of building a ring of satellites, smaller firms which are to be made wholly dependent for their future survival on the giant company. Or, alternatively, the general contractor may use the lucrative subcontract as a means of promoting one of the aspects of its operations, e.g., tying a contract award to a promise to buy certain products.[37]

The ramifications of vesting the power to act as general contractor in the private corporation become especially apparent when the government responds to pressures imposed by the nature of our international relations. When military objectives become paramount in foreign policy, an appreciable slice of the national budget is committed to programs facilitating the concentration of economic power. As the Defense Department scrutinizes bids for projects, it is understandably more hospitable to the firm that can handle an entire project. The dominant corporation becomes quite naturally the primary contractor. And as a result, a few giant corporations hold the favored positions vis-à-vis the government.[38] As the aircraft industry, for example, becomes almost entirely dependent on the Air Force, so the Air Force becomes dependent on the aircraft industry. Sound working relations develop, and each party grows more convinced of the rightness of the prevailing balance of power.[39]

It is tempting simply to conclude with C. Wright Mills that, while the bureaucracies of business and government apparently confront one another across the bargaining tables of power, beneath the tables "their myriad feet are interlocked in wonderfully complex ways."[40] But this impression does scant justice to the variations in the pattern of collaboration. In point of fact, the incorporation of an organ of government by its most powerful clientele will occur in highly varying degrees. Clientele penetration into the Bureau of Internal Revenue is far greater, for instance, than in the Federal Bureau of Investigation.[41] Where the groups with which the government is linked are monopolistic, the agencies find it hard to resist capture; that is, where apathy or policy encourages private monopoly, agency-made law gives public sanction to a private domain in which groups have merged under laissez-faire conditions. On the other hand, where competition between strong groups is genuine, or where an unshakeable general consensus on policy objectives gives backbone to an agency, an agency is not likely to be relieved of its power to govern and become an instrument of the dominant element among the regulated groups.

8

The States as Captives

The tendencies characteristic of the relation between the national government and large-scale nongovernmental organizations are even more pronounced at the state level. Far fewer counterbalancing pressures are at work there, and state administrators have far less to gain by holding out against private interests. For these reasons, state governments are more responsive to organized pressure, and their response creates a stronger fusion of the public and the private. At the state level, it is not only that organized private interests make public law, which does not go unrecognized today, but also that law is often conceived by the dominant groups *within* certain industries and professions.

It is not hard to support such propositions. The price of survival of a state regulatory agency—even one as powerful as the Texas Railroad Commission—is accommodation to the dominant interest within its field of regulation, whether the field is insurance, milk, or oil. In his study of the control of petroleum production in Texas, York Y. Willbern had to conclude that the procedures of the Texas Railroad Commission were most informal, in part because the "regulatory pattern was not, generally speaking, imposed on an unwilling protesting industry, jealous of its rights in a procedural as well as substantive sense. Rather, it was done at the request and with the cooperation of the *dominant* portions of the industry, a fact which made it easier to proceed informally." This particular Commission survived not simply because the regulated interests themselves desired regulation, but because the results of regulation were "extremely beneficial to the regulated interests, and have also, very happily and somewhat accidentally, been generally beneficial to the national interests and the interests of consumers in general." Admittedly, Willbern says, "legal purists" might criticize the Commission's procedures, and others might wonder about its "opportunities for favoritism and discrimination," but, by virtue of a happy accident, it has proved to be possible at once to favor public interests and to meet industry needs "without stirring up too much opposition."[1]

The problem of regulating potentially recalcitrant special interests is eliminated entirely when a state law removes the distinction between the private and the public. Thus in providing, for example, that "the Medical Association of the State of Alabama . . . is the state board of health,"[2] the Alabama legislature has radically simplified the political process. It has made politics the prerogative of expert insiders who need hardly worry about opposition from untrained outsiders. Whatever the potential conflicts about medical policy, Alabama law provides for their mediation within the Medical Association itself. The Association meets annually, but, as Robert T. Daland has reported, it does so only to endorse the decisions of its executive body. Every year it hears the State Health Department's summary of activities—and just as routinely approves it. What the Association's membership ratifies is formulated by a group immune to the influence of individual members. This is no accident, for "the internal organization of the Association was deliberately designed to insure stability, and to insure control from the apex of the system." By Alabama law, the Association's executive body is the Committee of Public Health. At the same time, it is the Board of Medical Examiners for the licensing of physicians.

As a result of these laws as well as the corresponding provisions in the constitution of the Alabama Medical Association, the same body of men serves in three different capacities. First, the group acts as the governing body of the Medical Association in its nongovernmental capacity, establishing association policy, considering questions of medical ethics, and managing the affairs of the association in the interim between meetings. Secondly, and under another title, it acts as the board of health in all but name. Thirdly, it constitutes the official state agency charged with examining applicants for licenses to practice medicine in the state.

This governmental arrangement makes it possible, according to one of its defenders, "to divorce public health from politics and the spoils system, and to keep it free of eleemosynary sentimentalism and specious quackery of social reforms." It makes it possible for a dominant group of medical practitioners, as Daland has pointed out, "to influence decisively how much of the ever broader demand [for medical services] to recognize"—and how much to ignore with impunity.[3] It ensures that public law will be made by those who govern private groups.*

There is nothing unique about the Alabama experience. It is easy, at the state level, to exemplify the making of public law by occupational, would-be professional, and professional associations —associations whose leadership is self-serving and whose policies are unrepresentative of their memberships. The fact is that far-reaching decisions—in the fields of medicine, law, public health, sanitation, zoning, recreation, education, religious observances, and sexual practices—have assumed public character when vested with public authority. When these groups have not actually emasculated public government and left the state an empty form, theirs has been the influence of the enlightened expert who has con-

* "The basis of good relationships with a state government," one AMA president has written, "is to have the state medical societies in a position to be consulted about appointments to these boards and agencies. Once this honorable extension of medical society influence has been established, it becomes difficult to put into effect measures which are not compatible with our ideals. Physicians on the boards of such agencies have an unusual opportunity to analyze the effects of proposed measures and oppose them if they are not acceptable to medicine, thus adding the weight of government to the side of medicine and not leave the profession to stand alone as a defensive minority." (Barker, "The State Medical Society and the State Government," *Journal of the American Medical Association,* 133 [1947], 549; quoted in David R. Hyde and Payson Wolff, "The American Medical Association: Power, Purpose and Politics in Organized Medicine," *Yale Law Journal,* 63 [May 1954], 938–1022, 999.)

cluded what constitutes misconduct or malpractice and who therefore knows which groups of individuals should be denied licenses
to practice, permits to build, or certificates to enter.

The decisions of private groups may be as innocuous as the
simple blessing given the job-hunting teacher by the California
Teachers Association.[4] They may be as far-reaching as the American Medical Association's recommendation for legislation setting
the standards of medical education. They may be seemingly nonpolitical choices made by a virtually autonomous educational hierarchy at the county level.[5] Questions of their desirability aside,
all of these decisions are public policies specifically intended to
impose forms of discrimination.[6]

When members of licensing boards practice the trade they are
empowered to license, they will necessarily be tempted to protect
their own stake in that trade. In looking out for themselves, they
will represent their professional groups, or at least the dominant
elements within them. As long as their decisions can be reasonably
related to ends not in conflict with a dormant general consensus,
the action of private groups will appear to have the stamp of legitimacy. Precisely because they tend to be vested with public power
(in Connecticut, to take an extreme case, the medical society's
Board of Censors is the State Board of Medical Examiners),[7] it is
difficult to overcome the presumption that their discriminatory
practices are legitimate, even when it can be shown that their private law aims merely at promoting the integrity of their organization and the security of their leaders.

To recognize that an insulated leadership defines organizational needs and establishes discriminatory patterns affecting both
the membership and those who require its services is not to say
that either the public outside or the members within are dis-
pleased. Indeed, the public might be well disposed toward a
realtors' code of ethics or an AMA-supported program of medical
care. And the members of occupational groups, like those of business corporations and trade unions, might have the warmest feelings toward their organizational hierarchies. Physicians and lawyers, after all, are not alone in valuing professional status. Cer-

tainly there are benefits transcending the honorific for the interested teacher, realtor, beautician, mortician, watchmaker, photographer, public relations counselor, interior decorator, television commentator, and industrial consultant—to offer but a partial list of those seeking the security of the professional.* Under the impetus of technological changes, the professionalization of trade and work is likely to extend, and with it will come increasing insistence on the expert's right to self-regulation. Many more of those who are impelled or called to practice specific trades will have to be duly prepared and accredited to enter the ranks of the incorporated. As Frank Tannenbaum has written,

This compulsory membership is now to be found in a vast number of industries, occupations, and professions, from barbers to steelworkers, from musicians to airplane pilots, from chorus girls to sailors. Skilled and unskilled, professional and learned occupations, small and large plants, highly mechanized and semi-mechanized industries, are being incorporated into and made part of this pattern, and there is no prospect of an immediate end to the movement.[8]

If what Tannenbaum has called a system of estates is finding acceptance, it is worth inquiring into its nature. To what extent does it eclipse various public interests, including those outside its formal boundaries? This question is pertinent even though it may appear to the professionals themselves that they have justly earned state support. Are they not free from partisanship of the grosser variety, moving above politics, in touch only with the general interest? After all, there has been no cry to unseat them. Their self-image, and perhaps increasingly their public image, is one of

---

* "One may not be surprised to learn," Walter Gellhorn has noted, "that pharmacists, accountants, and dentists have been reached by state laws, as have sanitarians and psychologists, assayers and architects, veterinarians and librarians. But with what joy of discovery does one learn about the licensing of threshing machine operators and dealers in scrap tobacco? What of egg graders and guide-dog trainers, pest controllers and yacht salesmen, tree surgeons and well diggers, tile layers and potato growers?" (*Individual Freedom and Governmental Restraints* [Baton Rouge: Louisiana State University Press, 1958], p. 106.)

individuals who have been, on the whole, far from irresponsible in the exercise of their great power.

We must ignore the image, however, and ask some questions: Are the bases for their necessarily discriminatory policies always reasonable? To what extent are the potential or actual memberships of various professional associations governed by oligarchies untroubled by dissident opinions or disapproving ballots? And finally, have we sought to enforce responsibility during times when the public is only marginally affected and hence only mildly indignant? To neglect raising questions about the responsible exercise of power is to invite the erosion of liberty; it is to foster the use of power by private groups which can successfully advance their interests in the name of public authority, carefully exploiting whatever public agency happens to be momentarily disengaged, distracted, and ready to deliver.

We can fairly seek representative answers by examining the one association which we might expect to maintain the highest standards of self-enforced propriety, both because of tradition and because of a near-consensus on its ultimate goals: the American Medical Association.[9] How does it manage its constituents? For what segments of the public does it achieve a policy consensus?

For the doctor not associated with a medical school, a research foundation, or a governmental health service, the price of following his calling outside of the ranks of organized medicine is so high that it is unrealistic to speak of his association as a voluntary one. Advances in medical technology and the resultant division of labor alone are enough to tie the doctor to a bureaucratic apparatus for managing an increasingly cooperative enterprise. Only by availing himself of the facilities for testing, diagnosis, research, and experimentation offered by the clinic, the hospital, and the specialized library is it possible for the doctor to make the most of his potential. As the center of his work shifts from his office, or the patient's home, to the clinic and the hospital, he must rely on organizations, special staffs, and integrated schedules. The image of the autonomous physician related to no one but his patient—portrayed in Sir Luke Fildes's ubiquitous painting, "The Doctor," which has recently been displayed with the subtitle KEEP POLITICS OUT OF THIS

PICTURE—is no longer creditable. To achieve his own ends, the physician finds organization indispensable.

Under these conditions, AMA membership has become virtually compulsory. "Non-membership," David R. Hyde and Payson Wolff showed in 1954, "amounts to a partial revocation of licensure to practice medicine. . . . Defiance of AMA authority means professional suicide for the majority."[10] The reasons are apparent. Membership has generally been interpreted as a criterion of professional competence, even by such outside groups as the U.S. Navy[11] and insurance companies writing malpractice insurance. But discrimination against the nonmember is primarily felt within the profession itself:

In general a physician's ability to continue his professional development is restricted by the loss of participation in scientific programs and professional relationships. And a rejected doctor is denied the use of the medical societies as a forum for bringing his own discoveries before the profession. The non-society member is "quite generally regarded as an outcast." As a non-member he is ineligible for specialty board examinations and ratings. Referrals and consultations, so essential to the growth of a new practice, are denied him. Expulsion or denial carries the stigma of unethical practice so that members who have professional relations with a rejected practitioner may themselves be considered unethical. Thus, as part of its enforcement program one medical society circulated a "white list" of approved doctors to its members. The disapproved physician will also be handicapped in caring for his patients. Unless he relinquishes control over the patient he may be unable to secure assistance in time of emergency. Perhaps most important, he will be denied the use of most hospital facilities.[12]

The preponderant majority of those affected by the policies of organized medicine unquestionably appreciates what is done in its behalf. This is true not merely of a wide public which respects the word of the doctor; it is surely also true of the actual AMA membership. The membership generally is quite indifferent about both alternative medical organizations and internal organizational politics. A former AMA president has remarked that "if 10 per cent of the membership [in many areas] attend a meeting it is about average and it is usually the same 10 per cent at each meeting."[13]

Those who choose to be active can consequently make the most of their opportunities. Incumbent officers tend to determine who will succeed them. Campaigning by the soliciting of votes is considered unseemly. Few elections are contested. The same names reappear on ballots. As Hyde and Wolff have reported, "The nominating process, in combination with the apathy of the average doctor, assures domination by a single faction within the AMA."[14] This self-perpetuating faction cannot be challenged effectively, for there is no ground on which to take an opposing stand. In part, this may be due to the failure to provide a forum for dissent and opposition: minorities rarely get space in the *Journal of the American Medical Association,* nor can they find representation in the national body.[15] But actually more is involved. Opposition is by no means deliberately fought off and then disarmed. It is initially without opportunity to find itself and to conceive of alternative policies. Thus an incumbent leadership determines—not casually, but by concerted effort—the range of possible controversy. It poses and limits the issues.*

Those who fail to accept the provided frame of reference, whether in the area of professional ethics or public policy, may be brought into line either by professional ostracism or by the verdicts of county medical society boards from which the ultimate appeal is to the AMA's own Judicial Council.[16] Thus consensus is preserved by the nature of the law-making process, by the power of the leadership to formulate the terms of debatable policies, and by the ultimate threat of using sanctions against the recalcitrant—especially the competitive, new practitioner. The consequent agreement on policy objectives, engineered by the controlling group within the AMA, makes it possible for this very group to speak with a single voice for American medicine.†

* "The [medical] profession's leaders over a period of years did a thorough job of educating the rank and file; such dissent as remained was drowned out by the sheer volume of official AMA propaganda." (V. O. Key, Jr., *Politics, Parties, and Pressure Groups* [New York: Thomas Y. Crowell, 1958], p. 139.)

† There are groups which appear to challenge the monopoly position of the AMA. But like the National Medical Association, composed of Negro physicians, they generally seek AMA affiliation. None are serious competitors.

What "American medicine" appears united on may, however, touch various groups in society in unequal and conflicting ways. All groups are not equally benefited by the decisions about the cost of medical services, the number of available practitioners, and the geographical distribution of doctors. Nevertheless, a small faction within the AMA decisively influences policy in these areas. This faction has decided just how the costs of medical services should be met. It has answered the questions of whether society or the individual should pay, of whether he may make prepayments while healthy, and of whether he should freely choose to assume the risk of financial disaster or be compelled to insure himself. It has secured the "integrity of the profession" and has sought to secure the income of one group of its members by discriminating against the physician who participates in plans tabooed because they provide for prepaid, non-price-discriminatory medical service.[17] It has opposed, with a measure of success, the utilization of doctors as salaried employees. It has fixed the number of physicians available by "reporting" on the quality of medical education, both in this country and abroad. Anticipating the number of doctors "required," it has defined the "desirable" level of medical care. Relying on its campaign to glorify the general practitioner, it has frustrated nation-wide planning for the distribution of doctors.

In all of these policy matters, organized medicine has not only had its say by acting as a legitimate and persistent lobby, participating in the making of public policies by pressuring the state from the outside in order to influence decisions. More importantly, to enforce its verdicts and maintain its position, its dominant faction has effectively blended with the state. The standards it has set have been embraced by the state for the simple reason that they are believed to be exclusively professional standards, not fit to be debated by laymen. They have been made to appear as objective assessments impartially formulated by an elite capable of speaking at once for American medicine and the public interest.

It would be wrong to conclude from this necessarily selective survey of quasi-private, quasi-public governments at the national as well as at the state level that "politics has fallen from its high estate." Far from it. Politics is being practiced, and with skill and ingenuity, but in a pluralist realm effectively isolated from the traditional channels through which political responsibility is enforced. Policy objectives are still discussed, often in the jargon of bureaucratic and scientific objectivity; alternatives are still weighed, dropped, and adopted. Policies tend to be adopted, however, by oligarchies under no compulsion to recognize the entire range of affected interests. The gamut which proposed policies must run is consequently nonpolitical. The standards by which they are judged are professional ones professionally arrived at; they are organizational imperatives interpreted by officials whose interest lies in the exclusion of competing interests. Policies tend to result from negotiations conducted free from public control in an atmosphere uncorrupted by the amateur citizen. The various codes adopted, as well as the plans rejected, necessarily order the lives of Americans—Americans who will not or cannot avail themselves of the instrumentalities of the state, unaware of the inequality of conditions they perpetuate when they authorize a plurality of private regimes to operate with sovereign force.

9

The Norms of Social Research

Social scientists themselves seem to be caught up in the current of American pluralism. Despite their frequently professed desire to remain purely analytical or hypothetical, an appreciable number of them have in fact helped give theoretical stability and respectability to a technologically harnessed pluralism. How, it is worth inquiring, have they reinforced pluralist institutions, granting them, so to speak, a patent? How have their abstract projections made clear what our concrete institutions have so far left in an undeveloped stage?

Ostensibly objective students of society and politics, they have accepted an undiscussed frame of reference which has the unsought effect of exalting the autonomous group, the functional community, and what is recently going under the name of the homeostatic system. By committing themselves to an analytical model suitable for understanding the behavior of small groups, they have kept themselves from enlarging the scope of their science. Failing to go beyond an attractive image of pluralism, they have treated large groups as if they were small and have, in effect, protected from professional scrutiny a newer, barely understood economic and industrial order. Moreover, insofar as the model which orients their work defines a set of prevailing social relationships as natural, they have unintentionally provided what is nothing less than a criterion for alternative public reforms.

Although we are not compelled to accept the offered analytical model, we are made aware of the cost of ignoring it. To ignore it, we have been told, is to exchange a functional system for one fundamentally incoherent and anarchical. We are free to make our choice. But from a scientific point of view, in any case, the most efficient system is the comprehensively organized one—society defined in terms of the ties between its constituents. These ties give the system unity. Their presence makes it; their absence breaks it. Although the knowledge of social science can be used to plan for play and freedom, to achieve nonconservative ends disrupting the existing social scheme, this cannot be certified as sound by social scientists when they believe that deeply embedded within our social world there is a functional structure, a closed, boundary-maintaining, internally harmonious whole, an ideal—strikingly like the America we know—that lies deeper than mere appearances.

To the extent that the social scientist identifies his search for knowledge with the gradual realization of an ideal deemed immanent in reality, he participates in patterning seemingly random behavior. Of course, his approach may remain purely formal and analytical. When engaged in purely relativistic, comparative analysis, he leaves unsettled what factors specifically impede the attainment of the ideal. Indeed, he will be careful not to offer ideals, acknowledging that what is marginal in one case might well be central in another—depending always on ultimate social purposes. Thereby he leaves open any public discussion about ideals. But the moment he extracts a *substantive* definition of a disequilibrium from the American experience and quietly incorporates it in his analytical scheme, he shuts off discussion—or assumes that the last word has already been said. What constitutes an equilibrium in particular cases is then believed to be settled. Everyone will then simply know what is meant by the characterization of behavior as a departure from "the system in homeostasis." The phrase will be vacuous only to the uninitiated, to those not altogether at home in America and its halls of higher learning.

It would be tedious to show with what readiness deviations from the "homeostatic model" or "the going society" or "the American system" are being identified. They are widely seen as the conflicts and displacements which have been generated by a complex industrial society. Only a deeply prejudiced person, it is made to appear, could fail to see that, whatever our twentieth-century opportunities and goods, the present is really a painful era of individual neuroses, community disruption, complicated politics, and endless factional crises. This "condition" makes the application of social skills, of knowledge about human relations, mandatory. And such knowledge, at its finest, is the product of an instrumental social science.

There being little disagreement about what constitutes the substantive nature of social delinquencies, pathological conditions may be objectively defined, and social science may rightly apply its knowledge and methods to the task of discovering how individuals may be moved with speed and efficiency toward the healthy goal.* It becomes credible to argue that psychologists should "seek to provide a basic science of human thinking, character, skill learning, motives, conduct, etc., which will serve all the sciences of man (e.g., anthropology, sociology, economics, government, education, medicine, etc.) in much the same way and to the same extent that biology now serves the agricultural and medical sciences."[1] So fixed are the ends of government that the social scientist can go to work furnishing the means. "In much the same way" as agronomists and physicians apply the laws of biology to assure productivity and longevity, social scientists might apply those of psychology. The "theorizing" they engage in will be the theorizing not about ends but about means. As Dwight Waldo observed in a 1956 survey, "American political science has not been characterized by works

---

* According to one writer, three "aspects of definition" have been approximately agreed on: (1) "the internal inconsistencies of the [social] unit, as a result of which common objectives are relatively lacking"; (2) "*anomie*, or lack of internal organization, and conflicting social organizations within the units"; and (3) "conflicting rules of behavior" and "conflicts of values." (Edwin H. Sutherland, "Social Pathology," *American Journal of Sociology*, 50 [May 1945], 429–35, 431.)

seeking either to justify or to controvert the political order. Rather, the political order has been 'accepted,' and distinctive American 'political theory' has tended to be concerned with means and methodology."[2]

Knowing the common good, seeing it manifest in America, social scientists are prepared and subsidized to perfect the devices for gaining consensus on it—if need be, by encouraging the influential to promote the practices of social engineering. Understanding their own functions, social therapists or policy scientists are not only studying society in a scientific manner, but are also seeking to make politics itself increasingly scientific. Politics will become infused by science as they will show, in the language of Harold D. Lasswell, "a lively concern . . . for the problem of overcoming the divisive tendencies of modern life and of bringing into existence a more thorough integration of the goals and methods of public and private action."[3] As Hobbes had hoped long ago when he wished his speculations to fall into the hands of a sovereign, social theory and social action can at last coalesce. Without putting its assumptions into question, social science can specify the ties which provide, in practice, for America's unity.

The task of social research is easily defined: it is to identify the social structure and determine what is functional in it. It is, moreover, to gain knowledge of the factors which cause the idle to be engaged, the distracted to be attracted, the weary to be enlisted. It is to search for the conditions of instability, the prerequisites for stability. It is to restore upset balances, resolve conflicts, heal sore spots, facilitate assimilation, and, most important, remove the innumerable blocks to understanding. It can be peremptorily concerned with the reduction of discord, the relief of tension, the softening of competition. Even where this view is opposed, the organization man is expected not to constitutionalize or break up the corporate unit but somehow, while preserving his individuality, to adapt to it. About the prevalent research orientation, the testimony of Robert A. Nisbet is especially instructive because it is offered with genuine sympathy for the work described:

Research projects tend to center increasingly on problems of individual assimilation within groups, classes, and cultures. The astonishing spread of the study of group structure, group dynamics, interpersonal relations, and of associative components in economic and political behavior bears rich testimony to the change that has taken place in recent decades in the type of problem regarded as significant. . . . The social group has replaced the individual as the key concept . . . and it is almost as apt to observe that social *order* has replaced social change as the key problem. Beyond count are the present speculations, theories, and projects focused on the mechanics of group cohesion, structure, function, and the varied processes of assimilation and adjustment. . . .

[This] is now a conservative revolt and is to be seen in those approaches to the study of man where the individual has been replaced by the social group as the central unit of theoretical inquiry and ameliorative action; where organicism and its offspring, functionalism, hold sway in the interpretation of behavior and belief; where there is a dominant interest in themes and patterns of cultural integration, in ritual, role, and tradition, and in the whole range of problems connected with social position and social role.

While the objectives of this "conservative revolt" are analytical, Nisbet concedes that they nevertheless "reflect a set of deep moral urgencies" insofar as they are "given meaning and drive by moral aspirations toward community."[4]

The specific problems which beset the community of men, men whose discomforts have in the past inspired the politician's calling, are to be attacked by what in the broadest sense is a science of public administration, personnel management, or human relations. A "preventive politics" closely allied with "general medicine, psychopathology, physiological psychology, and related disciplines" is to be created. In 1930, Lasswell saw that

the time has come to abandon the assumption that the problem of politics is the problem of promoting discussion among all the interests concerned in a given problem. Discussion frequently complicates social difficulties, for the discussion by far-flung interests arouses a psychology of conflict which produces obstructive, fictitious and irrelevant values. The problem of politics is less to solve conflicts than to prevent them; less to serve as a safety valve for social protest than to apply social energy to the abolition of recurrent sources of strain in society.[5]

A "unified natural science of human life" may well help channel social energy so as to diminish existing strains or demolish their recurrent sources.[6] The late Kurt Lewin, according to one social scientist who has sympathetically commemorated his work, seems to have grasped what is required:

He felt that, if we could but correctly conceptualize the a-historical, situational factors determinative of behavior, then we could manipulate these contemporaneous situational factors and produce the sort of behavior which all persons of good will would desire. If we can but discover the "systematic laws," the laws of the "pure case," *i.e.,* those laws whereby a given "life-space" inevitably produces a given behavior, then we can know how to change persons and groups to remake their behavior according to our heart's desires.[7]

Effective action must spring from a comprehensive view of the social system. Thanks especially to the pioneer work of Mary Parker Follett and Elton Mayo in the areas of private administration, it has become clear that behavior remains inexplicable until an administrative or industrial organization is seen not as a formal, authoritarian unit within which commands pass rationally from top to bottom but as a more amorphous social system of uncharted groups. Because these informal groups manifestly exist, the duly functioning manager must understand them. What must be understood, most specifically, is the extent of irrationality characterizing the behavior of those within the informal subgroupings. The system maintains itself precisely because its components, individual workers, are moved by nonrational impulses. Since their action is primarily emotional reaction, it can be regulated by appropriately touching their emotions, and for this it is essential for the managers to understand the feelings and sentiments of the rank and file at the bottom.[8] The rational, logical table of organization hides what right-minded management must take into account: the irrational bonds between men which bring order to their relations. These ties—sentiments, customs, social codes—guarantee stability.[9] Never recorded (except by anthropologists studying the factory subculture), they are transmitted orally from worker to worker. They are implicitly understood and acted upon. They are the folk mind discerned by the well-trained leader.

Once accepted, this view makes considerations of power or authority superfluous. To maintain the industrial state, what is significant is not any specific allocation of power but instead the prevailing harmony of relations, the efficiency of communications, the cordiality of intercourse. Hence it is far less important to worry about the distribution of power and influence than to perfect the devices by which good feelings can be improved. "Whether or not a group functions in an atmosphere that is hostile or congenial, or whether the production is high or low, depends upon the amount of genuine cooperative participation entirely apart from the parity of power."[10] Since the good manager does not govern, at least not in the scientifically governed state, there can be no justification for checking, opposing, or resenting him. He will have been informed by empirical science that an efficient productive unit can be maintained "only by working through the informal organization. It is only in this area that it is possible to manipulate the mental and emotional processes of people so as to build a harmonious organization. . . . The successful executive therefore cannot rely simply upon his 'power' to get orders carried out. To carry his organization along with him he also needs understanding, skill, and personal influence."[11] Put differently, "the administrator is the guardian or preserver of morale through the function of maintaining a condition of equilibrium which will preserve the social values existing in the cooperative system. Only in this sense does he have 'authority.' "[12]

"In spite of the power of his position," it has been affirmed, "the top executive cannot decide arbitrarily what the organization will be like and how it will function. . . . The skilled executive can, however, use his knowledge of the organization and of his position in it to *permit* the development of an effective whole."[13] What he permits, they want to do anyway—provided they understand. "The essence of democratic leadership," another writer has explained, "is the capacity to influence people to act in ways that they come to realize are good for them."[14] The "central problem of leadership," as the authors of a textbook on American public administration have noted, is the gaining of acceptance of the leader's objectives.[15] "By what means can he persuade his employees to *want* to do what he wants to do?" "How can employees be stimulated to put loyalty to the company above their own self-interest?"

The problem, at least for Americans, is one of means. "By developing an atmosphere in which changes and improvements can be generated from within the organization rather than imposed from above, the skilled executive can eliminate much of the organization's resistance to change without forfeiting any of its stability."[16] Applied science has pointed the way, so that it has in fact become reasonable to conclude from experiments resting on Kurt Lewin's studies that "the more 'democratic' the procedures, the less resistance there is to change, and the greater the productivity."[17] As a result of an experiment conducted in a Virginia pajama manufacturing plant, to cite but one example, it proved possible to overcome worker opposition to changes in production methods "by the use of group meetings for which management effectively communicates the need for [predetermined] change and stimulates group participation in planning the changes."[18] Management expectations are fulfilled "democratically," according to Morris S. Viteles, because the group dynamics work of Lewin and his followers had shown how to

produce not only direct benefits in the form of better results in influencing attitudes, but a feeling of participation on the part of employees in planning programs which can, in itself, contribute to successful achievement in moulding and modifying attitudes and in improving motivation and morale.

Such feelings can be evoked by providing for employee participation in decision-making. Their cooperation "becomes an effective device for lowering resistance to change, and aiding production by lowering the resistance of barriers to the 'goal' of higher output." Of course, undisguised coercion can also produce change. But, says Viteles,

the use of group participation permits smoother "locomotion" to the same "goal" without the creation of "tensions" which may lead to industrial strife. Participation in decision-making in industry is generally viewed as an experience wherein attitudes favorable to change are taken on by the workers. . . .

The potential for industrial strife is lowered, since the change in group perception associated with group participation tends to bring the production "goal" closer to the standard desired by management. Furthermore, "emotionality" is lowered since workers playing the "role" of planners tend to keep discussion at a relatively depersonalized level.[19]

In practice, getting consensus on goals calls for an emphasis not on the mechanism of politics, not on specific institutions or procedures for compromising competing interests, but, far more broadly, on morale, on the "style of living," the "social climate," the spirit pervading the dynamic field. Lewin and his associates provided a concise demonstration of this in an experiment during the Second World War. They tried to discover how best to motivate the students who were using eight of the dining rooms at the State University of Iowa to choose and then eat whole-wheat bread. Lewin verified that in the dining rooms where consumers were *lectured* about the desirability of switching from white to whole-wheat bread and could privately weigh their interests, it was more difficult to induce the change than in the rooms where the leadership "permitted" them to make the change by "voluntary group decision," the leaders and the led assuming, of course, that the overriding wartime goal—a healthy, viable nation—was beyond the scope of any "voluntary" decision.[20]

When there is no doubt about the meaning of the general will, when morale within the field is good, anything within wide biological limits is indeed possible and acceptable. Within the group that gives behavior what is defined as its true socio-psychological meaning, the most painful or unpleasant action can be made palatable. "Under ordinary circumstances," Lewin has pointed out, "an individual will strongly resist an order . . . to eat three dozen unsalted soda crackers. As 'subjects' in an experiment, on the other hand, individuals were found ready to 'take it' without either hesitation or resistance." Enlightened and therefore enthusiastic about the ultimate end, the individual, like the victim of disease who desires life above all, will subordinate all diverting interests. "In the role of patient, for example, the individual permits as 'treatment' by the doctor what would otherwise be vigorously resisted because of bodily pain or social unpleasantness."[21] To break human resistance and smooth man's way, the overriding good must be clarified. To improve the tone of society, men must be moved not to misconstrue their genuine interests. Gardner Murphy has seen fit to observe:

Human relations will almost automatically be bettered if new ways of perceiving one's situation can be made available, not too solemnly, but with zest and humor, through stories, skits, movies, or better still, actual games, parties, work-projects. As the therapist might state the matter, the person must be assisted in a friendly manner to see himself and his associates in an accepting way, parking his defenses and especially his sense of guilt outside the gate. . . .[22]

Such careful assistance will bring the final goal into precise focus, eventually making it possible to rule out all conflicting subjective visions, all conscientious objections. The "facts" will simply be accepted. To lead the good life will be to embrace and be loyal to those identified ultimate objectives which are self-evidently right. When the good life is finally led within the right order, the problems that once terrified men will dissolve, their apparent actuality having been due to misguided imagination and extraneous works. Within the "democratic" group, choices between alternatives will no longer create anxiety, since all alternatives but the fixed goal can be shown to be opposed to the publicly validated common interest.

Once it becomes coordinated, the healthy social organism will move steadily and easily, each of its parts adjusted to every other. It will be free to operate as each member performs its function. The freedom of the parts is assured by the freedom of the whole. When the whole is functioning efficiently, when it is maintaining its poise and integrity, the parts will experience satisfaction. After all, we are told, "freedom is only possible for an individual in so far as he genuinely identifies his own satisfaction with the general well being."[23] It becomes legitimate to counsel, therefore, that "the whole personality must be involved in such a complete way as to make future conduct a spontaneous expression of that involvement."[24] Such involvement is the cornerstone of a wholesome, democratic regime. Democracy will grow naturally from the interpersonal relations experienced in tolerant and generous community living. More specifically, in a community thus prepared to experience democracy, economic leadership will not be irresponsible, as heretofore. The new economic leader, as Gardner Murphy has sketched him, will "understand the democratic process as well as the economic reality"; he will be able to "take hold of his corporation, his board of directors, his stockholders, his workers, his consumers, his public as a wise political leader would take hold, revolutionizing the guidance of his enterprise from within and without. Many of those who talk of the partnership of business and government vaguely grope toward some such conceptions." Perhaps through plebiscites, referendums, and public-opinion polls, everyone will get a due sense of participation and make democracy work.[25]

Man will find his bearings in social action. Integrated, he will achieve fulfillment; enclosed, he will find his freedom. Absorbed and liberated, he will be able to look down on the pathological society which still accommodates conflicts of interests by deliberately leaving a margin for the unadjusted, the disoriented, and the apathetic.

It has been contended here that the proponents of at least one research approach celebrate a specific political order by constructing a formal framework which absorbs alternatives. Their formalism, it has been suggested, is easily come by, for there is widespread agreement on what in fact constitutes a social equilibrium. If these observations are accurate, it would seem that a radically restrictive, illiberal impetus lies at the very center of a considerable part of current social science. To be sure, there is a wholesome diversity of research interests. No single ideal, after all, has been consistently operative to guide all current social science—nor even all the works of the authors mentioned. Highlighting the area in which innumerable projects intersect has meant not being fully appreciative of the various motives and hopes of professional social scientists. This needs all the more emphasis because there has literally been no meeting ground for them: no single headquarters, organization, or journal. There is in fact little convergence, little interdisciplinary work, whatever the long-run tendency. Thus it cannot be validly maintained that the bulk of American social scientists are consciously aiming to construct some specific social order and fit men into it. They would definitely deny favoring the normative pattern which supports a good part of their activities. Indeed, they prefer, probably without exception, a pattern altogether contrary to the one which gives meaning to their work. Surely Lasswell speaks not only for himself when he proclaims his conviction that in America the main accent of the social sciences "will be upon the development of knowledge pertinent to the fuller realization of human dignity."[26] The belief that it is necessary to serve only the cause of the individual is often voiced and always implied. American social scientists, in short, are liberals.

Yet it should be apparent that this liberalism is not relevant to the perspective which gives status and coherence to all of the scientific operations actually proposed or executed during office or laboratory hours. The postulates which provide the basis for a portion of the work in human relations institutes, in research centers, or in the field remain incompatible with or divorced from the ardently expressed interest and worthy motives of social scientists. By consistently adhering to their postulates rather than to their liberal sentiments, they should be able to construct and test an abstract behavioral system of functional, neutral terms which would potentially provide an exhaustive relation of variables. Assuming social forces to be in a state of natural balance, they should have a norm by which to put existing social orders to the test. Contributing to a unified science of means, they should be able to determine how variables might be economically moved toward the norm.

The proper approach to social reality, they assume, will disclose man's most elemental bonds; it will dissolve all peculiarities by revealing them to be harmonious universals. When suitably embraced, what appears as incongruous will disclose itself as congruent. By the familiar procedure of diligent scientific probing, it will be possible to approximate the natural, right, and necessary order of man and his society. Once established and refined, a full set of generalizations will make the real organization of the facts of social and political life intelligible. Constructed according to an adequate theory, man's history will be understood in all its contingencies. Any diversity of circumstances still perceived will then be misperception, a resultant of ignorance, sentiment, or willfulness.

Within the total field, nothing can be exempt from the reach of a naturalistic social science. To produce social change—which is assumed to be the only way to gain social knowledge—the social scientist must rigorously exclude any possible ties with an order presumed to transcend the field he desires to affect. To grant the possibility of autonomy to such a link between the factual and the normative would spoil the integrity of his final position. Of course, individual action is not ignored; it is treated as a significant, because efficacious, function of the all-determinate group structure. Thereby made scientifically commensurable, it cannot threaten to make the state of affairs with which the social scientist is experimentally concerned unmanageable or unpredictable.

This applies even to the social scientist's own prejudices and sentiments. He is called to approach society with sensitivity and self-restraint, to handle the social field with a delicate touch, with his off-duty interests and impulses under control because objectives finding their source somewhere beyond the field would cause the object under investigation to become disturbed. What is required of him is a purgation of preconceptions which check his empathy. Only when he acts free from those ever-diverting ends which transcend the field can the final revelation—the law which does and should order man's behavior—be his; only at this timeless moment when the truth is formulated can he join the stream of humanity and can humanity once again join nature. His finished theory would at last make it possible for him to understand and control every baffling idiosyncrasy, to know that nothing is really detached and unnatural because all the things that matter are buried here and now, concealed more or less deeply in the present state of man's development. The true nature of things is immanent within experience. Nothing stands outside it; no autonomous vagrant spoils its integrity; no independent purpose governs it. Hence a humanistic concern with transhistorical objectives is irresponsible, a distraction from the scientific need to develop timeless hypotheses for the analysis of factual, aimless flux, of motion without beginning or end. Thus, as the future is held to inhere in the past, the ideal blends into the real.

The vision of the well-functioning community in which all is motion and behavior may be a most shadowy one. Yet even those who have not beheld it in its fullness work as if it were the basis of their faith. Not having in fact encountered the immanent harmonious order, they labor as if determined to achieve its incarnation, as if aspiring to give birth to that very state which, though far from realized, is woven into the nature of society and constitutes a system of relations among the perceived disparities. They may proceed to engineer harmony in a given industrial or administrative unit in response to "the mood of the times" or the call issued by those in positions of power. Alternatively, they may insist that some intuited or provided definition of harmony sets up tensions and is therefore not sufficiently inclusive. In any case, if social scientists are not attempting to resolve some practical problem by activating what appears sluggish and by integrating what appears fickle, they are seeking to draft a framework which will ideally encompass all variable, unstable, and disturbing forces—including those embodied in some particular government of the moment.

That analytical research, even when pointedly empirical, should ultimately be forced to employ such a total view for its orientation is actually not surprising, given its initial understanding of social units as self-sufficient wholes. As it feels compelled by sensed conflicts to step back from the minute particulars and enlarge its field of vision, it comes to see that the "real" system must be larger than had originally been suspected. There is always an impinging environment. The specific organization, it becomes evident, must be seen in a progressively broader context. For those few whose vision penetrates all boundaries, there is finally nothing but an undifferentiated whole, the wonderful unity of nineteenth-century German idealism and romanticism. The plurality of previously esteemed parts fades entirely. No valid theory can reveal their distinctiveness, and it becomes unnecessary to consider the possibility of conflict between them. On the contrary, the very institutions—such as parliamentary procedures—which might mediate such conflict must at last be recognized as unscientific expedients, superfluous in the healthy system, obscuring the reality of the underlying order.

Thus whether the research is applied or pure, the assumption of an underlying harmony of parts is placed beyond challenge, and social scientists are steadily led toward a theoretical scheme, a constitutive order, which will finally synthesize all conflicting social units. Their frameworks for political inquiry (to borrow the subtitle of a work by Harold D. Lasswell and Abraham Kaplan) are such as to establish a position from which it appears to be altogether self-evident and unarguable how "expensive" it is to society when variables remain unintegrated, when seemingly novel, unique, idle features are not adjusted, when the individual is not granted due status, or at least the entrancing belief in status. Noting this expense from their special point of vantage, pained by society's inefficient, uneconomical, dysfunctional forces, they delineate or hope for a scientifically objective and morally satisfying theory arranging for individual freedom within a state indulgent toward its constituents. Their manifold models, still incomplete and tentative, imply that man's social order merits allegiance when it fulfills the individual, and hence at once liberates and stabilizes him, by representing his diverse interests. Holding in esteem precisely that communal pattern which manifests the general will, they are consistent in assigning both a scientific and a normative plus to the socialized individual, to man as a selfless, political animal. Paralleling Rousseau's famous plea for "some form of association . . . as a result of which the whole strength of the community will be enlisted for the protection of the person and property of each constituent member, in such a way that each, when united to his fellows, renders obedience to his own will, and remains as free as he was before," reinforcing this ideal, they have come to assume that attributing primacy to the all-embracing social system accords with the very structure of social reality.

Using an approach which values above all its freedom from values, its absolute objectivity, the social scientist can legitimately set up as well as move society. His knowledge lies in his action. As he arranges his state so as to strip it of data—more accurately, pseudo-data—not amenable to incorporation in the body of scientific knowledge, he becomes, to the extent that he is permitted to be successful, its founding father.[27] And since he feels justified in claiming empirically confirmed objectivity for it—for he has, indeed, confirmed it by making it—he may go to work in the public arena, in the legislature and the market place, on the basis of decisive assumptions to which those whose interests and goods are affected by his action have not had to consent—however readily they may in fact acquiesce. He is, after all, fulfilling their inherent will, helping an ideal to realization.

As academic research gives aid to this immanent ideal, adopting it as final norm, converting its hypothesis into positive knowledge, its model into dogma, it implicitly identifies *its* ideal with man's ideal. It offers not an approach but a norm, not a tool for analysis but a theory justifying an existing state of affairs. It offers a system of values which, when all is said and done, vindicates the previously discussed American pluralist experience. More intrestingly, it points up conclusions of which there have so far been only faint intimations.

That a good deal of American social science research has the effect of unwittingly condoning a closed order should not surprise those familiar with the longing of the European founders of sociology for the feudal system. Their bias, too, was antipolitical. They, too, hoped to take things "out of politics." Their quest for reintegration, it will be remembered, had been provoked by the dissolution of the social units associated with the *Ancien Régime* and the atomization of society brought about by the Industrial Revolution. Beginning with Fourier and Comte, their concern was to find clear echoes in the works of all those continental Europeans whose distaste for the politics of liberalism, for civil negotiation between conflicting interests, makes their ultimate conservatism intelligible: Tarde, LeBon, Lombroso, Durkheim, Pareto, and Freud. In the United States—where Burke and Locke could flourish side by side and where it was possible to speak of conserving liberalism—those students of man and society reacting against the French and Industrial Revolutions did not, however, have to search for institutional arrangements modeled on the prerevolutionary social scheme. Nor was any theoretical defense of conservatism forced into existence. Tocqueville rightly anticipated that all advocacy of feudalism, of the hierarchial community, and of a consistent federalism, would remain qualified, inconclusive, and ambiguous—at least to the extent that it would be persuasive.

In a country pervaded by a sweeping, frequently infuriating, all-corrosive liberalism, no creed frankly espousing the establishment or the conservation of a status society was able to take hold. In fact, some of the very students of society who have come closest to embracing a neo-feudalism—Elton Mayo, Mary Parker Follett, and Erich Fromm among others—have all taken pains to repudiate the feudal past. Yet if a frankly conservative rhetoric had to be rejected, a conservative ideology did not. Schemes defeated at the polls, blocked by the legislative process, or blown up by civil war could complacently find their way into the undiscussed premises of social analysis. Having nowhere else to become lodged, they could become the hidden foundation of research. The premises of pluralism, in brief, could become the premises of social science.

It is possible for this to happen only when social scientists are impatient and prematurely conclusive, when they build their conclusions into their initial assumptions. There is nothing inherent in the methods of social science which compels a conservative stand.[28] On the contrary, sound scientific analysis remains forever negative, comparative, relative, and even ironical. It must challenge all settlements, both practical and theoretical. But social analysis betrays a loyalty to an unamendable theory, an ideological commitment, the moment its hypothetical character is neglected, the moment its approach—elevated to become an end itself—is assumed to be embedded in the very nature of social reality or of human history. The orientation for the study of social, political, and economic phenomena then becomes identified with "the real state of affairs."* A pattern of constructs becomes synonymous with the very structure of society.

---

* Studies by American anthropologists are not, it seems, immune to this critique, as David Bidney has shown in his review of their analytical schemes. How these carry the stamp of a characteristically American pluralism is made evident by his discussion of the culturalistic fallacy, that is, the conversion of "an epistemic or methodological abstraction into a distinct ontological entity. . . ." According to Bidney, they make culture "represent an autonomous, superorganic level of reality subject to its own laws and stages of evolution"; and they hold cultural phenomena to be a self-explanatory, closed, homogeneous system. (*Theoretical Anthropology* [New York: Columbia University Press, 1953], pp. 51, 73–74, 77.)

When social scientists identify their analytical models with significant reality, they make it appear credible to hold that certain social arrangements are objectively inefficient. Having converted hypothetical presuppositions into dogma, degrading other possible perspectives and settling for one as final, they make their empirical science the autonomous warrant for reform, authenticating the credentials of science as it is made to work. Their work thus has the effect of securing agreement on the substance of goals not by the method of politics, but by what wrongly seems to be the method of science. Their dogma, of course, remains concealed, forced into the interstices of methodology rather than into the frame of systematic argument. There is an inevitable loss when this happens, for the merits of alternative social orders are not so much undisputed as made the subject of methodological disputes. And because participation in debates about methodological matters is restricted to initiated and accredited professionals—whose language is not common speech—potentially concerned interests are excluded. The perspective by which reality is approached thus tends to settle what, from another point of view, may well be a subject still open to debate. The perspective, in short, becomes doctrinaire.

Such a doctrine may be detected in one significant part of current American academic practice—the part which has found it easy to accommodate itself to an institutionalized pluralism. It can be shown to be both didactic and doctrinaire when it embodies any one of three postulates: (1) that the mechanics of social change are completely determined by interacting groups; (2) that government is nothing but a responsive instrument for stabilizing an equilibrium of competing interests; and (3) that public policy is exclusively a group product. Where it has uncritically reflected an ideology of pluralism, it has accepted it interchangeably as a norm of social health, a model for analysis, and an ideal immanent in reality.

Close to the turn of the century an appreciable number of American political scientists, reacting against philosophical idealism, had hoped to find a more solid comprehension of the political scene than had their legalistic and formalistic predecessors. They sought to deal with observable and preferably countable facts.

Their quest took the form of studies of constitutional conventions, city governments, and the private governments of corporations, interest groups, labor unions, and trade associations. Their studies purported to provide unsentimental reports of what is "really" happening, at least insofar as the stuff of reality was susceptible to what seemed a straightforward positivist approach. In detail, frequently with statistics and charts, they described not the statics but the fascinating and often muddy flow and counterflow of politics. Having shown up statics as fiction, they became progressively more concerned with the dynamic process of politics. While they did not deny the reality of human ideals—surely they were keenly aware of their own—they permitted their studies to circumscribe them. They reduced purposes to the only thing which could count: their measurable impact. Students of political groups therefore tended to treat ideas of justice as potent myths, as efficacious means.[29] And they concerned themselves precisely with the nature of these means, the nature of all means, the nature of power. Assuming power to be the unifying key to politics, they could properly make it the focal point of their work. In the name of realism, they proceeded from the baseline drawn by Arthur F. Bentley's influential *Process of Government* (1908).[30] With Bentley, they could not accept "brain-spooks" or "mind-stuff" as the determinants of political action. They held that the state might at last be really understood by the investigation of palpable activity, by getting the feel of an endless stream of decisions. "Mind-stuff" could still play a role, but only in relation to a continuum of behavior, only as a manifestation of the autonomous, genuinely operative substructure of politics. Thus Charles A. Beard in his study of the basis of politics perceived a substructure of economic groups; Charles E. Merriam embraced an undifferentiated concept of power; and Harold D. Lasswell posited psychological foundations.

This search for the simplest effective foundation of the field of politics, for the most durable constellation of atoms, led readily enough to the employment of the old and fruitful hypothesis of the group nature of society. Social theory had of course always taken cognizance of groups, realizing that to postulate an associational disposition in man explains a great deal of politics and sug-

gests otherwise hidden relationships. A thoroughgoing application
of the hypothesis was therefore perfectly natural. Indeed, ever
since the appearance of Bentley's pioneer work, as Earl Latham
has shown, "American writers have increasingly accepted the view
that the group is the basic political form."[31] This has made it
possible for social scientists to approach man and his ideas as functions of the group, to see him in relation to a total configuration
of social forces, to "understand" him by understanding his group,
and ultimately to reach and activate him by reaching and activating his group. In the field of social psychology it has become possible to conclude empirically that the individual knows the world
and acts within it primarily through his associations, that his associations produce those patterns of knowledge which regulate his
behavior.[32] "These patterns," David B. Truman has written, "are,
or are rapidly becoming, the primary data of the social scientist.
To identify and interpret these uniformities . . . is the most effective approach to understanding a society—or a segment of it such
as its political institutions."[33] Such understanding, it is affirmed,
need not depend on any knowledge of a common good or a public
interest independent of a compromise of group interests. The governmental process can be seen simply as group warfare. Governmental phenomena are a function of groups freely interacting.[34]

The belief that society and politics are best understood by
taking full account of man's affiliations has been entertained so
broadly, fervently, and uncritically that, in application, its instrumental nature has not always remained clear.[35] The casual facility
with which the group hypothesis has come to be handled has made
it easy to see politics as substantially nothing more than a process
of interacting power blocs. As the political process has thereby
been identified with an equilibrium of competing forces, a final
ground for analysis is reached. To fully comprehend the very substance of politics and policy, we learn, is to accept the world of
men, at least the world of Americans, for what it has presumably
been right along: a polity in which groups struggle to gain or
maintain power over one another. This polity is the only polity.
Nothing more profound or less formalistic "really" exists or goes
on. Whatever else may be part of American life, it is private, not

part of public politics, not to be caught in the net woven by the practitioners of group analysis.

As this view becomes the only meaningful one, pluralism is in effect hypostatized. And as the immutable nature of political reality is presumed to be clear, all that remains necessary for its assessment is to extend and deepen one's knowledge of America by the rigorous application of that ultimate conceptual framework which allows one to behold a vibrant pluralism. To know America is to know it as a community within which those who care will struggle fraternally for public power. To have knowledge of America's political process is coincidentally to have knowledge of America's substantive goals as well. What had once been dealt with by an inexact political philosophy concerned with eliciting, juxtaposing, and sifting common opinions—a philosophy aspiring to discriminate between right and wrong conduct—is to become an amoral, natural science of human behavior.

Although the need for such a science has for long been proclaimed in America, with Henry Adams the first to do so systematically, there has until recently been little interest in integrating the overwhelming variety of group studies. Only as innumerable uncoordinated and sometimes intensely personal projects have begun to reveal how colorful and complex our behavior really is has it come to appear imperative to discipline the study of society and politics. This new concern with the unification of research (a concern always meticulously qualified by the caveat that integration should never be "premature") has resulted in a dogged quest for a theoretical system of human behavior, for something like Boyle's general theory of gases. Despite the questions raised about the feasibility or desirability of the integration of techniques, and despite the warnings about a new scholasticism, the interest in developing an architectonic science of human behavior remains undiminished.[36]

It is now hoped (and not for the first time in the history of ideas) to find a substitute for the traditional, and so far always inconclusive, effort of social science to distinguish between the degrees of excellence of social institutions, historical regimes, public policies, or individual doctrines. This allegedly dated emphasis on examining the relative wisdom of alternatives is to be replaced by a stress on the building of a general descriptive theory of social behavior. In line with this, consideration is to be given to the purification of methods and the definition of operational models. Identified by an array of vague labels which significantly suggest the convergence of various disciplines—labels such as functionalism, sociometry, operationalism, equilibrium analysis, topological psychology, social field theory, social geometry, homeostatic model construction, or even socio-psychobiology—truly synthetic knowledge is to be earnestly pursued and, so it would appear, respectably endowed. And because the skeleton of the new science is believed to be embedded in all sound research, whatever is being produced in the social sciences may be confidently drawn on and integrated. Empirical research which happens to be centered on specific problems is to be reviewed for its contributions to a systematic theory. Thus inductive and deductive thought are to merge so that out of variety it may be possible to forge unity.

Such a body of united knowledge, at once empirical and rational, is to give formal expression to relationships between observed phenomena. These phenomena, it is hoped, will be unambiguously linked by a network of logical or quantitative notations. The links, expressing the functions of the data they connect, are to be set forth in functional terms, the only terms able to signify relations. There can be no escape, in fact, from mathematical terminology, for only mathematics is able to designate the relationships between "things" devoid of qualities other than such relationships.

Genuine social knowledge will therefore consist of a framework of unequivocal connections between data. Because terms of "intrinsic" meaning cannot validly become the object of discourse, whatever may appear to be intrinsic must be eliminated. It is necessary to escape the prison of a language which incorporates values, to cease using quality-ascribing adjectives which intriguingly hint at the existence of essentials, to center instead on dynamic processes, on potencies and actualities. As long as ambiguities slip into the framework, as long as dramatic or partially subjective symbols remain potent, the conditions for a natural science of society—one which might make it at last possible to predict the probable results of any variation of data—must be unsatisfied. "One of the great tasks of the value sciences (social sciences) in our day," Harold D. Lasswell and Abraham Kaplan have written, "is to develop a naturalistic treatment of the distinctively human values potential in the social process."[37] To fulfill this task it becomes mandatory to convert subjective value standards into precise indices, to attack all random terms, to eliminate concepts which happen to embody more than the concrete field or laboratory operation for which they stand, and, in short, to make discourse operational. This requires attempting what it is never fully possible to achieve: tying language to action in every particular. Symbols useful when the channels of communications are not clear—when redundancies are required to catch our attention or to overcome troublesome noises on the line—must be extinguished. Freed of emotive terms, a satisfactory language will refer to nothing but those social and political arrangements which have objective existence in what scientific convention defines as the world of real experience. Since every possible condition which surrounds the data-connecting terms will be actually included in the scheme of descriptive statements, all metaphysical assertions subversively hinting at the existence of a realm other than the "operative" will be eliminated. At their best, social scientists will manage to design a thoroughly refined theory untarnished by moral consideration, subjectively felt data, and historical bias—a theory enabling us to grasp the nature of social and political reality in what is presumably the only meaningful way possible.

Recognizing the unrewarding nature of so much of what is being published in the academic journals, discussed by convention panels, and nourished by philanthropic foundations, and recognizing a failure to illuminate the human condition under non-utopian circumstances, some writers have been tempted to characterize social science research at mid-century as compulsive, uncritical, or cynical.[38] Nevertheless, if in the efforts to construct a social and political form there has indeed been a shying away from substance, might this not be due to the belief that concern with substance is irrelevant? Conceivably, the offered work is not anemic and barren, as some of the critics have said, but inconsequential. What keeps it alive is a deeply felt (though innocent) consensus on the "real problems" which makes bother with anything but methods and appearances seem irresponsible. There is tacit agreement on what is substantively economical, functional, progressive, healthy—and therefore just.

It may be precisely this agreement which invites the preoccupation with abstract form, the appreciation and perception of a static order underlying the fluctuations of history. The abstract form, in other words, may be widely identified with what good fortune has granted: the American system. Thus, without further consideration of what it substantively entails, an existing, well-institutionalized pluralism may be equated with a value-neutral science. The social facts unearthed by the appropriate method will happen to coincide with a particular ethic, the one Americans are believed to have cherished right along. Thanks to this most fortunate of coincidences, scientific knowledge of natural facts will reinforce what is indubitably the great American cause. It will consider as irreducible, as beyond analysis and critique, an esteem for the individual, for his material and spiritual goods, and, furthermore, for the institutional order which has traditionally facilitated "self-realization."

Thereby the progressive realization of the scientific ideal will have the effect of approximating what is unarguably the American one as well. If this is the case, there is no lamentable shying away from matters of substance on the part of social science. On the contrary. The substance—vulgarly called "Americanism"—is simply known and accepted. American ideals and American institutions are thus made exempt from that type of analysis which shows other ideals and institutions to be mere rationalizations or weapons. American ideals and institutions have a different status. They are not façades. They, and they alone, are not to be correlated with the power struggle all others disguise.

If social scientists think ideals to be mere functions of an underlying pluralistic order but do not hold that this applies to their own, does not at least one set of ideals, namely theirs, gain the status of objectivity? If values generally are to be subsumed under the new science of society but the specific value system of pluralism is somehow preserved exempt from reduction (as it is when used as final ground for explanation) is this not due to a belief in the *natural* rightness of a pervasive pluralism? The tenet of a normative pluralism, the identification of the common good with the struggle of groups for power, becomes consequently something more than subjective preference. The notion that men find fulfillment in "congenial and creative interpersonal relations" will be viewed interchangeably as natural fact and normative judgment. What is more, the tenet of pluralism will be confidently embraced as an objective good. Whatever situation it happens to describe may then be rightly desired without further reliance on an action-confounding metaphysics. Whatever threatens such a situation will necessarily be objectively undesirable. It will be understood as diseased, regressive, dysfunctional, uneconomical—and therefore unjust. To see this requires no further debate. Why then should social scientists consider the case for American pluralism on the merits? They have scarcely found it necessary to engage in that wholly explicit defense of a pluralistic public order which is about to be reviewed—and which, precisely because it is explicit, is the more easily exposed as deficient.

10

The Case for Devolution

An implicit commitment to a political order like that embraced by at least part of contemporary American social science cannot, of course, constitute an argument in its own behalf. An outspoken and convincing argument is likely to be furnished only by thinkers who are aware of opposition, and hence feel pushed to enlarge their metaphors and engage in polemics. In the United States such an undisguised dialectic, while not absent, is hard to come by. What we tend to find are two positions, both attached to the status quo. One is the all-too-innocent kind provided by the already summarized methodological perspective. The other is the all-too-knowing kind provided by the candidate for office and the lobbyist.

It would make it easier to delineate American pluralist theory if we could ignore these two positions and rely on an American political philosophy. But to obtain a genuinely philosophical statement, one formulated in an encounter with other philosophical statements so as to reveal the excellence of a pluralist order, is no easy matter. It becomes especially difficult because our efforts to deal with public issues have been pre-eminently ideological, designed to impress men, not to make them understand. To be sure, publicists advocating pluralism do not have to be treated as defenders of group interests; indeed, to treat their work as mere ideology and to disallow alternative treatment is to succumb to pluralism. But although we may interpret their effort as one intended to enhance our understanding about what is excellent in politics and not to induce action, it should actually be more instructive first to turn briefly to a body of European theory.

Because its horizon tends to be wider, European theory is far less susceptible to reduction than American thought. It is more likely to partake of the tradition of philosophical discourse, which tends always to amplify the connotations of particular positions—including the position taken by pluralists. Recalling a European background, borrowing its allusions and using its dimensions, should therefore help make explicit what American theory, such as it is, merely suggests.

But there is an even greater justification for comparing American pluralist thought with that of Europe. In Europe, pluralism could become a frankly normative doctrine, for it was not, as in the United States, the self-evidently correct and unquestioned instrument for achieving political order. It was a real moral alternative. Our pluralism, as the preceding chapter has shown, has been axiomatic, and hence overwhelmingly analytical. It arose amidst consensus and never sought to revise our understanding of the ways in which policy can develop. While posing as positive science, it was based on an unconscious adoption of "the functional system." It thereby concealed what the militant pluralism of Europe had to incorporate in both its analyses and its polemics.

Just before the First World War, Europe witnessed a burgeoning of intellectual interest in pluralist institutions—those which had existed in past history, those which were hidden in the present, and those which might yet be achieved.[1] Historical study, systematic analysis of the present, and reformist efforts looking to the future all seemed to march hand in hand toward a revelation of the same truth. Philosophically, the case for pluralism was recognized to rest on two presumably inseparable beliefs: the liberal belief in the rights of the individual and the seemingly correlative belief in the small governmental unit as the necessary foundation for the realization of liberal values. Thus the good state could be identified with the small state. If despite the exercise of prudent statesmanship the state had grown large, expansive, and imperialistic, the appropriate policy would be clear: it would be necessary to institute, within the boundaries of the state, those small collectives which alone preserve the habits of true self-government, which, by making political practices habitual and personal, conserve the goods of politics, the virtues of civility.

These premises made it possible to re-emphasize the pertinence of Aristotle's familiar contention that "if the citizens of a state are to judge and to distribute offices according to merit, then they must know each other's characters. . . ." To those who were to echo Aristotle, it seemed evident that in the large state, judicial decisions and political elections "are manifestly settled at haphazard." Hence in the good state the population would have to be restricted to "the largest number which suffices for the purpose of life, and can be taken in at a single view." It might be recalled that this position was not substantially different from Montesquieu's. He had affirmed in *The Spirit of the Laws* that it was only "natural" for a republic to limit its territory. There appeared excellent reason for this:

In an extensive republic, the public good is sacrificed to a thousand private views; it is subordinate to exceptions and depends on accidents. In a small one, the interest of the public is more obvious, better understood, and more within the reach of every citizen; abuses have less extent, and of course are less protected.[2]

To those in England who were to rely on such reflections it seemed obvious that "abuses" were being widely protected, whether by a philosophy which concealed them, by elites which governed in their own interest, or by unmanaged economic and technological forces. A number of thinkers, prompted by their respect for individual freedom, were aesthetically and morally stirred by what they beheld in their social and industrial environment. They grew indignant over the degrading effects of industrialization, especially its inhuman discipline. They witnessed and documented the development of the concentration of power under cover of a postulated but nonexistent laissez-faire economy which gave lip service to individualism. This economic power they saw falling into the hands of classes who, it seemed to them, performed no positive social function. What is more, they were disturbed by the growth of concentrated political power they saw in German nationalism, state socialism, imperialism, and militarism. Their underlying impulse was to protect the individual against the corrupting influence of monolithic power, against whatever consolidation of force surrounded, entangled, and ultimately destroyed him. Because of the ever-present potential of the abuse of power, they felt that the very possibility of its unified and effective exercise must be made remote. If the existing state was the victim of the dominant class ruling in its own interest, the neutralization of the state became imperative. If it was unrepresentative and irresponsible, so ran the elaborate non sequitur, it had to be fragmented—that is, pluralized.

In behalf of the dignity of the individual person, then, but aware of his fate when unrestrained minorities apply machine power to work and organize the market, two generations of political pluralists attacked the theory which gave an exploitative capitalism its justification. Thus they turned against all theories that bound individuals and groups unqualifiedly to the state, whether the theory defined the state as the embodiment of the general will, as legally omnipotent, or as the highest manifestation of disembodied reason. Rousseau, Bentham, Austin, and Hegel—none of them escaped the onslaught of the pluralists. On the one hand, the pluralists reacted against the liberal utilitarianism which had placed the individual in a social vacuum, abstracting him from all associations and making him the sovereign calculator. In this reaction, they saw nineteenth-century English liberalism as subverting the premises of Locke, as depriving right reason of moral content by permitting the principle of utility to be substituted for the conscience of man. The door was opened to statism, they realized, the moment Bentham introduced his sovereign legislator, the moment Austin had positive law replace the law of nature. And on the other hand, their reaction was not only against the atomized (and all-too-quickly reintegrated) society envisaged by English liberalism but also against continental idealism, in particular the

Hegelian doctrine that no matter what power permeated the real state it could give but a glimmer of the ideal.

Exposing the pretentions of German idealism, the Austinian theory of sovereignty, and Spencer's rationale for a laissez-faire state, the English pluralists sought to direct attention to the social reality and the political facts which philosophy (as well as jurisprudence) had generally begun to blur. They found philosophy not so much syntactically incredible or even morally shocking as untouched by reference to recent historical experience. The prevalent abstractions seemed artificial and contrived. To be sure, English pluralism itself was not disengaged from metaphysics. It was not free from the moral drive to lend individual rights some sort of a theoretical foundation, to provide functional representation for the organizations which the liberal state—assuming that all interests, after all, are harmonious—threatens to absorb. Yet it was a sense of the unreality of philosophy, especially as it found expression in what was later to be identified as historicism, that made it desirable to be deliberately naïve and see through some of the offered categories. The result was a revolt against established forms and fictions, especially the fiction of "sovereignty." The English pluralists, trying to hold fast to political reality, hoping to find a basis for neglected interests, aspired towards a theory founded on the observed facts of man's political life. Bentham, Bagehot, and Wallas had dug through a layer of customary forms to locate a psychological substructure; and Maitland, Figgis, Tawney, Barker, Lindsay, Laski, and Cole found an associational one. They all did so by concentrating on a plurality of groups which emerged as soon as one inquired which social units in fact aroused and commanded the individual's interests and loyalties. And the modern state, it turned out, was seldom among these. Neither the positive nor the negative state ever provided genuine satisfaction. Men were far more inclined, it was recognized, to feel obligated by their church, their club, or their union than by the sovereign state. And against these groups, the state failed again and again to prevail. Did not the labor unions engaging in the French postal strike of 1908, the South Wales miners' strike of 1915, or the Norwegian general strike of 1916 actually share in sovereignty? Did not the policies of the churches affect the real constitution of society? Conflicts between groups and the state were not consistently resolved in favor of the state. Groups preserved prerogatives, fought the state, modified it, parceled it out. Rousseau's, Austin's, and Hegel's theories were all jeopardized by the facts—facts which pluralists, given their orientation, not only discovered but also appreciated. Thus their case was to be at once historical and moral, empirical and normative. What truly existed—or more accurately, what existed incipiently—was fortunately as it should be. All that remained for political theory thus inspired was to stress and nurture what was incipient, what the liberal state had unjustly relegated to the periphery either because, like the church, it represented the old, vanquished enemy, or because, like the trade union, it represented new and completely unrecognized needs.

This general position was given unintended support on the continent by the scholarship of Otto Gierke. Ironically, his work was a contribution to German nationalism, to the effort to revive ideas and institutions native to Germany and to repudiate the "alien" doctrines of Roman law. Roman law had treated the corporation as a legal personality which owed its existence exclusively to state action. Against this view, Gierke urged that the corporation, having flowered without state aid on German soil, must be an irreducible entity, not a creature of the law, not a fictitious personality made or unmade at the pleasure of the state. It was a living organization with its own will, its own collective consciousness. While there was no need to react against Roman law in England, Maitland found an application for Gierke's ideas. Prodded by Gierke's research, Maitland was induced to refer to the state as only one of a number of associations, and one, furthermore, with no right to pre-eminence. Thus Gierke's work, while not attacking the doctrine of state sovereignty, could provide the background for perceiving the natural autonomy, and therefore the natural rights, of a plurality of unrecognized or disparaged associations. It became possible to use his doctrines, as did Figgis, to vindicate the group rights of the church or, as did Laski and Cole, to defend existing economic groupings. Thus if group and state were ever to come into conflict, the question of whom to obey could be an open one: man has variable functions, and he may well side with the group which truly represents him against the state.

The belief in the representative nature of the group, as opposed to the state, was based on the premise that the associations which men had freely established would always enlist their interests, that functional corporations, as R. H. Tawney had it, would be governed by professionalized, socially responsible managements. By this means, a merely formal freedom for citizens in the state at large could become concrete freedom for individuals. Giving men freedom where it mattered—within the association they obviously valued, the functional society which encompassed their day-to-day economic and productive relations—they could be counted on to participate enthusiastically in politics. Under whatever label it went—industrial democracy, economic federalism, functional corporatism, or guild socialism—the new confederation of self-regulating, harmoniously coexisting groups would replace the old monist state. The old state would be transformed into a coordinating authority, taking cognizance of concurrent group majorities and then minimally responding in their behalf. Sound public policy would emerge without positive state action. At best, the state would be a public service corporation.

A full theoretical treatment of the state as a public service corporation was given in France by Léon Duguit.[3] Chiefly interested in defining the basis of law and unconcerned about individualism, Duguit had observed his country's assumption of responsibility toward the community through its system of administrative courts. He had seen the state not as the source of law but as a servant of the community. Its dictates were imperative only by virtue of a legal fiction. Realistically seen, pluralistic social forces made public enactments possible. While there were some in all regimes who, as a matter of fact, did exercise governmental public service functions, they did so, Duguit insisted, under law which itself expressed that underlying social solidarity by which governments arise in the first place.

However much Duguit remained a captive of idealism—just as Laski was to remain attached to T. H. Green—the idea of state sovereignty was foreign to his thought. In this, the English pluralists, who were also ready to deny the state that primacy which idealist theory had postulated, could join him. After all, they had seen that individuals respond to various subnational associations, regions, and productive units. They, too, found sovereignty divisible and allegiance to the state contingent and qualified. They concluded what American statesmanship—insisting on bills of rights, on a separation of powers, and on federalism—had concluded more than a century before. They affirmed that the state could have no inherent natural right (1) to impose upon its power-wielding competitors or (2) to oblige individuals to obey state dictates for the sole reason that these dictates found their source in the state.

There is a familiar but still telling sequel. The English pluralists had taken a fresh look at society in the name of realism; yet there was a point at which they ceased being analytical. Having denied validity to the doctrine of monolithic sovereignty with their appeal to the facts of associational life, they abandoned analysis and tended to see an independent reality in those groups to which the individual actually gave his loyalty. These groups, so it seemed, truly represented his purposes and functions, realized his values, and thus made his freedom concrete. Into this reality they did not probe. Moreover, the pluralists' belief in a society of confederated groups rested on the implicit notion of a common interest—at a minimum, an interest in the maintenance of groups. Such ideas as common good, community interest, or general will were rejected, but they could not be wholly dispensed with. Since the essence of the political process was conceived of as a purposeful adjustment and reconciliation of group policies, a common purpose as well as an effective helping hand had to be posited. When Cole and Laski conscientiously desired to move forward to refurbished constitutions, it became clear that the state simply could not be escaped. To communicate the reality of the matter without postulating a purposive state proved to be excessively ponderous in theory and inexpedient in practice.

English pluralist theory had deprived the state of power and delimited the role of government in terms which American thinkers have seldom felt impelled to employ. In the New World, there seemed no need to argue affirmatively, radically, and consistently for the reduction of state power. The state as a plurality of competing power centers emerged as if predestined by nature. Public-spirited men, in basic agreement, would merely have to debate alternative ways of implementing the mandate. Once fundamentals were duly grasped with the certainty of a John Adams, who could solemnly avow that there were two classes in every society "because God has laid in the Constitution and course of nature, the foundation of the distinction,"[4] political philosophy was hardly necessary to justify a social and political system. Explorers, pamphleteers, preachers, publicists, lawyers, and statesmen believed it unnecessary to discuss the substantive purposes of government. Although this may have served American practice reasonably well, it has also made American theory notably contradictory or vague—as has been noted rather gleefully by those who permit themselves to assume that second-rate theory must lead to first-rate government.

While American institutions have remained unmistakably effective, one of the conditions for first-rate political speculation was missing. As American political practice has been manifestly healthy, political thought has been stunted, as if deprived of the opportunity to develop and shine by the absence of any serious philosophical or societal pressure which might compel thinkers to spell out the final purposes for which institutions ought to be effective.

What ultimately pressed Europeans to furnish fully developed theories of pluralism is easily seen: a historical situation which left the individual at the mercy of the sovereign state and a corresponding theory which sought to justify this situation. But while such a situation (the sovereign state versus the unaffiliated individual) could galvanize a counteroffensive in Europe, it could hardly affect Americans. It depended on a concept of the state wholly alien to an environment in which consensus about constitutional limitations and associational prerogatives was so general (except during the Civil War period, which *did* produce something like political philosophy) that a seemingly natural balance between private groups and public government could be maintained with relative ease. What was articulated by nature, it seemed, did not require articulation in learned volumes.

A pluralist theory defending the excellence of a system of social balances was likely to develop only when theoretical props seemed necessary, only when the system which placed seemingly natural limits on the power of the state to act was felt to be weak, and only when specific groups felt threatened by a single-purpose, unified state apparatus. Insofar as America's pluralist order has actually been a vigorous one and the monolithic state but the bogey of extreme right or left wing individualists, there has always been an air of unreality about American theories of pluralism. The monistic state militantly denounced by American pluralists bears little resemblance to the American state we know. Thus as their positive plea seems superfluous (don't we already possess, with surfeit, what they cry for?), their negative one appears strikingly European in character. They argue in the European tradition, against the European state, against European theories. And they are at a loss to find the rhetoric able to touch Americans who have generally experienced the state not as an idealized embodiment of the public will but as the broker of competing wills. Their arguments do not really take hold; their "theories" appear only as another variant of things as they naturally are. At best, they enable us to appreciate the familiar. At worst, they put our critical sensibilities to rest.

The pluralist plea, at least until the present day, has seldom been a direct defense of social variety and cultural diversity. More characteristically it has been addressed to means, not ends, and has recommended institutional devices which might produce the conditions for individuality. Clearly, one of these implementing institutions has been the geographical division of governmental power —federalism. The other and overlapping one has been the more complicated division of governmental power based on the various economic functions of individuals—best known as functionalism.

The argument for federalism could also defend functionalism as long as the residents of geographical regions had roughly the same economic interests. With Locke, it was then possible to up-

hold liberty, property, and land in the same breath. It is easy today
to forget the dogmatic nature of Jefferson's original commitment
to land and the men who worked it, Jefferson himself having found
his early views ultimately inexpedient. Not so much offering an
argument as categorically affirming his faith, Jefferson wrote in
1783 that

> Those who labour in the earth are the chosen people of God, if ever he
> had a chosen people, whose breasts he has made his peculiar deposit for
> substantial and genuine virtue. It is the focus in which he keeps alive
> that sacred fire, which otherwise might escape from the face of the earth.
> Corruption of morals . . . is the mark set on those, who not looking up
> to heaven, to their own soil and industry, as does the husbandman, for
> their subsistence, depend for it on the casualties and caprice of customers.
> Dependence begs subservience and venality, suffocates the germ of virtue,
> and prepares fit tools for the designs of ambition. . . . Generally speak-
> ing, the proportion which the aggregate of the other classes of citizens
> bears in any state to that of its husbandmen is the proportion of its
> unsound to its healthy parts, and is a good enough barometer whereby to
> measure its degree of corruption. While we have land to labour then,
> let us never wish to see our citizens occupied at a work-bench. . . .[5]

Jefferson considered American society upright and free insofar
as it was noncommercial and nonindustrial. "I think," he wrote
to Madison, "our governments will remain virtuous for many cen-
turies; as long as there shall be vacant lands in any part of America.
When they get piled upon one another in large cities, as in Europe,
they will become corrupt as in Europe." Cities, Jefferson was sure,
were "pestilential to the morals, the health and the liberties of
man." Let the industrial worker—and with him both his manners
and his principles—remain in Europe.[6] With the French Physiocrats, Jefferson knew that whatever is good for agriculture is good
for the country, that whatever hurts agriculture offends the di-
vinely ordained order of nature. But whereas the Physiocrats based
their beliefs on a testable proposition, maintaining that agricultural pursuits are instrumental in providing what man values and
that no other activity produces wealth, Jefferson saw agriculture
as the very embodiment of public and private virtue. It was for
him not merely one possible source of wealth but the fulfillment
of absolute morality.

In taking this stand, Jefferson and those who agreed with him could feel that they were vindicating not some special vested interest but the common good. After all, toward the end of the eighteenth century, not only the common man but ninety per cent of all Americans, common or uncommon, were farmers. "The great Business of the Continent," Franklin could rightly proclaim in the 1780's, "is Agriculture."[7] To champion virtue and democracy was therefore to champion agriculture. And this entailed holding to the barest minimum all public power which might collectivize the world's freest citizen, the independent American yeoman.

Given a community of free farmers, there is no reason for permitting power to become concentrated. Whatever common tasks there may be—and within the domestic realm they will be few—dispersal of governmental power will not make it impossible to carry them out effectively. Right-minded and most probably like-minded individuals will spontaneously pursue the common interest. Governmental power may be sharply divided up if, as Jefferson believed, all agencies of government draw their authority from a fundamentally homogeneous people, especially a people isolated from the troubles of Europe. Since their interests do not conflict, dividing the power of their agents will not make for inefficient governmental operations.[8] Thus a thoroughgoing decentralization of governmental power will automatically make for that minimum of social control which is all that is essential. The separate states, the readily available governmental form, will be, in Jefferson's terms, the "true barriers of our liberty." Close to the people, they are likely to be controlled by the people, who are the source of all legitimate power.[9]

This, of course, is one of the main currents of American thought, another variant of which may be found in the writings of John Taylor of Caroline County, Virginia:

The more power is condensed, the more pernicious it becomes. Divided only into three departments, such as king, lords and commons, it can easily coalesce, plunder and oppress. The more it is divided, the farther it recedes from the class of evil moral beings. By a vast number of divisions, applied to that portion of power, bestowed on their government by the people of the United States; and by retaining in their own hands a great portion unbestowed, with a power of controlling the portion given; the coalescence of political power, always fatal to civil liberty, is obstructed. Small dividends are not as liable to ambition and avarice, as great dividends. Self interest can only be controlled by keeping out of its hands the arms with which it has universally enslaved the general interest.[10]

And for Taylor it followed that the potential oppressor could be disarmed only if one-fourth of the states would have the right to veto any proposed change in the balance between the nation and the states. To him, constitutionalism meant a federal system maintained by the kind of "concurrent majority" which Calhoun was later to insist on. Whatever positive power to govern there was, it was to devolve on nothing but a majority which had previously concurred.

With a far greater emphasis on what Taylor left implicit—the ultimate objective of preserving private rights—Madison argued in *Federalist* papers No. 10 and No. 51 for extending the size of the country and thereby admitting a complex plurality of interests. These, he attested, would certainly help provide the diversification which makes it unlikely for a united majority to abrogate private rights. Madison's concern here was not, of course, with freezing a specific set of institutions. The doctrine of federalism was only a means for safeguarding not primarily states or associations, but individuals. To be sure, the plea for private rights was made in terms of a case for federalism; but this was only to be expected, for each of the states could be seen as a homogeneous unit, giving full expression to the interests it incorporated. As long as that was true, all that needed to be done to secure government by the consent of the governed was to resolve, as the states themselves did in the conventions called to ratify the Constitution, that whatever power had not been expressly delegated to the new national government was to be "reassumed" by the states, and the people thereof.

At bottom, the undiscussed question about a possible alternative *form* of government was always whether it would frustrate efforts to alienate the inalienable rights of men. It was the belief in the primacy of this standard which finally caused Jefferson to back down. In 1816 he asked Benjamin Rush "whether an opinion founded in the circumstances of that day [and here he is referring to 1785] can be fairly applied to those of the present"; perhaps, he noted, independence now required more than an egalitarian agrarianism. If Europe's hierarchical order could not be relied on as the workshop of America, perhaps agrarianism would have to be augmented on American soil.[11] Whatever his apprehensions, Jefferson as President was prepared to accept an ideal of a commonwealth as a balance of commercial, industrial, and agricultural interests.

This was no passing ideal. Calhoun, with motives not substantially different from Jefferson's, sought to preserve a national balance, "to unite the most opposite and conflicting interests, and to blend the whole into one common attachment to the country," thereby achieving "patriotism, nationality, harmony, and a struggle only for supremacy in promoting the common good of the whole."[12] On the eve of the war between the states, he conceived sectional independence as perfectly compatible with a viable nationalism; indeed, he considered such independence a prerequisite. But by the time Calhoun submitted his brief for the rights of the section, the doctrines he advanced were bound to be jarred by social reality. By then, it was clear to those who subscribed to the philosophy of the Declaration of Independence that the slave economy of the South had alienated a whole set of private rights. Moreover, since the philosophical foundation for Calhoun's formula for constitutionally protecting the Southern economy was the belief in private rights and, pushed further, in the incommensurability of the individual, it seemed scarcely necessary to make a reasoned response to the proposals he advanced. As William Lloyd Garrison was driven to say, "Argument is demanded—to prove what?"[13] If Calhoun argued in behalf of a self-contained section which would "take care of its own" and at best guarantee "proportional equality," he also argued for limited government which might give those whose interests were at stake a real opportunity to affect policy. There was no way, as Louis Hartz has exposed the embarrassment, to restrict the thrust of his case for constitutional government. Self-seeking men—and Calhoun conceded that nature planted some such everywhere—cannot be trusted, he said, to enact the common good. Their drives must be checked. Their power must be opposed by countervailing power. For Calhoun it inexorably followed that a sound constitution had to secure to each of the great sections the right to veto the acts of the national government. Because only the national government was likely to treat unequals as if they were equals, it alone needed to be curbed. To check the nationwide numerical majority, which was compelled by nature to obey its interests and attempt the exploitation of the Southern minority, the national government would have to be so constituted that when interests clashed no specific major interest could possibly be deprived of the right to reject national programs. No national interest, whatever that might come to mean, could be invoked to justify breaking through the section's borders and meddling in its internal affairs.

But the very mystique which Calhoun denied to the nation, he was ready to bestow on the sections. To him it was obvious, and this is the crucial point, that each of the geographical sections—cemented by historical experience, natural resources, and modes of production—fully expressed specific interests. That he was wrong in attributing homogeneity to the sections does not affect his premise: groups demonstrably united in interests and aspirations should be granted unqualified representation at the national level. History made it easy, of course, for the Senator from South Carolina to confuse his nation's sections with homogeneous groups expressing all the interests of their individual members. Hence to him the section triumphant could simply appear to be the individual triumphant as well.

Yet, in identifying one with the other, Calhoun responded to an impulse in no sense peculiar. Throughout the nineteenth century and well into the twentieth, that "general equality of conditions" which had impressed Tocqueville during the Jacksonian era made it altogether reasonable to link a commitment to private rights with the institution of government at the grass roots. Self-government meant local government. That link was bound to become anachronistic with the emergence, after the Civil War, of those industrial giants which Charles Francis Adams, writing in 1871 after his return from England, saw as transforming the power structure of America. The new corporations, he reported,

have declared war, negotiated peace, reduced courts, legislatures, and sovereign States to an unqualified obedience to their will, disturbed trade, agitated currency, imposed taxes, and, boldly setting both laws and public opinion at defiance, have freely exercised many other attributes of sovereignty. . . . All this they wielded in practical independence of the control both of government and of individuals. . . .[14]

That this is hyperbole does not matter. Mere belief in the wickedness of the trusts gave an edge to the effort to revivify the images of an earlier, simpler, and more comprehensible polity. It seemed obvious that men were being dwarfed by industrial giants, indeed, by industrialism itself. This notion gave force to the proposals— proposals Rexford Tugwell acted on as late as the early days of the New Deal—for reconstructing and revitalizing the diminutive state, the self-sufficient community in which labor might be meaningful and life intelligible.[15] The land, even the vacant city lot, could be seen as the salvation of the worker hit by an exploitative capitalism. "Back to the soil" and "back to the land" became watchwords as early as 1885.[16] By 1907, Bolton Hall's *Three Acres and Liberty* became a best seller. There was abundant practical advice on "how to cut loose from the city." And there were the fumbling, well-intentioned efforts to make a success of new agricultural communities. But there was decidedly no literature in America to parallel Hilaire Belloc's sustained anticapitalist paean to the rustic simplicity of the Middle Ages.[17] Not until the group of self-styled Southern Agrarians decided to take their stand at Vanderbilt University in 1930 did something like a program emerge. But the most telling part of their stand turned out to be not their plan for the redistribution of property and power but their subsidiary indictment of modern life as sterile, coarse, and flat. Thus their reaction, though elegant enough, was basically an irrelevant one: they repudiated not only an emergent social order but a technological one as well.[18] By the time the agrarians published *Who Owns America?* (1936), the New Deal had made their economic policy eccentric and otiose.

What always gave force to agrarian slogans, programs, and even movements was the evident conflict between the legacy of Jeffersonian individualism and the new industrial concentration and nationalization. And if bigness threatened, smallness seemed the appropriate response.

Such a response was not likely to be stated coherently in a country providing equal opportunities, free competition, and open frontiers. Every really consistent case for provincialism, especially when it pretended to be based on an awareness of American conditions, was guaranteed to inspire the sarcasm of an H. L. Mencken. It could not help but sound irresponsible, outlandish, or simply wild. Thus it has been tempting for many thoughtful Americans to turn hopefully to whoever might respond systematically to totalitarian bigness. Erich Fromm, a transplanted European, seemed to fill this need in the 1950's.[19] He had been induced by a European background to apply a Marxist framework to what he felt certain was the problem of contemporary America. Contemporary European history, especially German totalitarianism, had made him sensitive to the social diseases afflicting the individual. Analyzing the modern world in 1941, Fromm generalized that whereas man in the feudal society of the Middle Ages had been unfree but secure he is now free but insecure. Whereas he had been "rooted in a structuralized whole" which gave life meaning, he is now disassociated, bewildered, and anxious. Western man, Fromm maintained, had been

freed *from* the bondage of economic and political ties . . . which used to give him security and a feeling of belonging. . . . He is threatened by powerful suprapersonal forces, capital and the market. His relationship to his fellow men . . . has become hostile and estranged; he is free— that is, he is alone, isolated, threatened. . . . Paradise is lost.[20]

For Fromm, the American is altogether a part of this picture. In the United States, too, the individual's sense of powerlessness grows as he is frightened and made to feel insignificant by a cluster of intimidating collectivities: large corporations, big unions, uncontrollable economic forces, political machines, and metropolitan communities.[21] But Fromm continued where other commentators stopped—by adding that it is not necessary to pay this price for a healthy individualism. Genuine love and meaningful work are still possible. America need not succumb to totalitarianism. We can and must imbue man with a new faith in the possibility of individual spontaneity and alter the material conditions of life. We must provide "a planned economy that represents the planned and concerted effort of society as such."

When Fromm became specific, what looked like an espousal of statism readily turned into something more American. To create what he called *The Sane Society* (1955) and to enable man to regain autonomy, he advised his readers to live up to "a socialist vision which is centered around the idea of workers' participation and co-management, on decentralization and on the concrete function of man in the working process. . . ." It is essential, he contended, to rejuvenate a democratic pluralism, to transcend the bureaucratic state, to reintroduce the principle of the miniature community by organizing "the whole population into small groups of say five hundred people. . . ." The members of these social cells are to debate public issues on the basis of information supplied by some "politically independent" corporation, one composed of personalities "whose outstanding achievements and moral integrity are beyond doubt. . . ." These virtuous leaders, to be sure, will "differ in their political views, but it can be assumed that they could agree reasonably on what is to be considered objective information about facts." In this group of incorruptibles, then, we would find "the true 'House of Commons' " which, in cooperation with a house of representatives and an executive establishment, will make the policies and institutions of Western society at long last sane and orderly.

One can best appreciate the somewhat heady "communitarianism" of Fromm's new order by discerning its underlying pattern—a neat array of complementary, objective needs laid out by nature. It is this alone which ultimately justifies not only the outlawing of such commercialism as compels individuals to desire what they do not rightly need but also, and more important, the scrapping of machinery which hinders continuous participation in the making of political decisions. The present-day difficulty, it would seem, is that once the citizen has voted, "he has abdicated his political will"; he can "do little except vote at the next election, which gives him a chance to continue his representative in office or 'to throw the rascals out.' "[22]

According to Fromm, a society depending on such constitutionalism cannot rationalize man's ways of production, distribution, and consumption. As he had already made clear in *Escape from Freedom*, mass participation in public affairs is imperative. Because the formal act of voting is insufficient, political rights must be extended to the economic sphere. The individual must be fully involved in all processes determining his life; he must become politically involved "in his daily activity, in his work, and in his relations to others." Collaboration, not conflict, will govern these relations. Where there is popular participation, there is no need for discrimination or regulation. The ideal society is one "in which the individual is not subordinated to or manipulated by any power outside himself, be it the State or the economic machine. . . ."[23]

Having turned away from political reality, especially American political reality, Fromm insensibly clarified what Americans have either expressed far more awkwardly or else managed to sublimate. He envisaged a community which, as Lewis Mumford has intoned again and again, would be "human" in scale. In the midst of the ugliness of industrial civilization, such a community, according to Ralph Borsodi, would constitute an oasis of genuine friendship, beauty, and intelligence. It would not, as Baker Brownell poignantly described it, force individuals to divide their labor and leave the land. The rural life based on a rural economy would ineluctably produce the sane culture.[24]

In an earlier day, a generation of muckrakers and Progressives had given this vision a distinctively political foundation. Less enamored with Arcadia, but confident that an activated citizenry would do right, they had predicted that government would cease to be oppressive when brought close to the people. The cure for the evils of democracy—city bosses and government by corporations—was more democracy. "Democracy," said John Dewey, "must begin at home."[25] What could seem incisive as late as the 20's, however, appeared as dated by the time Samuel Seabury argued in 1950 for "a decentralization and redistribution of the public power." Seabury's objectives were the unimpeachable American ones: he hoped that "personalities, groups and commonwealths may, without state obstruction or interference, develop their present and potential capacities. . . ." But all he could constructively suggest was that "industrial government should be self-government and should find its expression outside the state through voluntary agencies of labor, capitalists, and consumers operating under a New Federalism within which representation should be accorded upon a functional basis."[26]

These miscellaneous searches for a world at once simpler and richer found concentrated expression in the work of a remarkable American thinker and woman of action, Mary Parker Follett.[27] She so amply anticipated and quietly influenced a newer vision of the good society that a review of her own writings should help expose some of the ramifications of the case for devolution which were later to become blurred. Her work, especially *The New State: Group Organization the Solution of Popular Government* (1918) and *Creative Experience* (1924), succeeds in pulling together and in Americanizing a host of attempts to come to grips with the organizational forms of modern life. At the same time, it establishes a connection with the more current efforts to demote the political state, to unchain a plurality of corporations and grant autonomy to the economy.

Employing the terms of both pluralism and idealism, Follett proposed a redefinition of the democratic state. Although she shared the temper of the Progressive era, she felt that a genuinely progressive solution to the prevailing social and economic maladministration should depend not on new political devices but on a grass-roots, face-to-face approach. And this required the deliberate development of a complex federation of groups within which the individual person, intimately touched, would achieve wholeness.

These themes found more detailed and less hortatory application in her posthumous papers collected in *Dynamic Administra-*

tion.[28] Here she addressed herself primarily to industrial administration and business management, convinced that business was one field in which leaders were consciously leading and, what is more, managing manageable social units. Where business governed, thought and action could coalesce; the reflective study of the political process could fruitfully mesh with the political process itself. Above all, here were usable laboratories as well as the precondition for a science of means: agreement on ends.

From her contacts and observations in the world of business she derived support for insights which are now all but commonplaces. Thus behind the façade of the traditional table of organization she made out a complex, informal, and unplanned structure. She questioned the notion of human organizations as rational hierarchies of power. To this view she opposed her theory of the necessary diffusion of authority, a theory springing from her moral sensibilities as well as from the observation that decisions are never isolated actions but dynamic processes. She cut through rigid organizational forms to their peculiar human constituents whose fundamental needs, irrational reactions, and concealed motives she sought to understand and order.

While her preoccupation was always with the small, manageable group, she displayed a far broader interest in bringing order into the whole of man's estate. Distressed by social disorganization, she constructed her case for the new state on the basis of what she diagnosed as the unhealthy condition of the modern world. She therefore felt called on to prescribe a new order, one which would rest on objective "laws of association." These laws, when finally known, would constitute both the science of man's behavior and the proper foundation of society.[29]

Man's true community, she maintained, results not from the mere addition of individual wills but from their interpenetration. At the same time, she felt no need to give the group a social mind or a corporate soul. Her postulates kept her from having to attribute autonomy to collectives, for she assumed axiomatically—and this was crucial to her outlook—that particulars *naturally* fit together to make a whole, that special interests become the general interest without abstraction, as a matter of course.[30]

Hence she found it easy to appreciate variety and conflict.* Only through differences, she knew, could new values be created. One's peculiarities could somehow be contributed to a common cause without the need to make compromises. Such contributions would not mean giving up anything that really matters; they would mean participation in the creation of something new within which conflicting forces have been comfortably accommodated. Private interests are thus elevated to form a group will. This will is sound, for it takes account of all interests. The process by which it is formed makes it possible to consider the facts rationally. It will automatically dissipate controversy, yielding solutions to specific problems. Factual situations contain their inner imperative, and all one must do is "discover the law of the situation and obey that."[31]

Yet while most of us still fail to recognize that facts are facts and that the accommodation of interests requires no force, some groups have come to understand that their own wants are truly those of the public. For example, New York City real estate interests, Follett related, have changed their attitudes: "Moralists used to tell us that the only path of progress was to make people willing to give up their own interests for the sake of others. But this is not what our real estate men are doing. They are coming to see that their interests are in the long run coincident with the interests of all the other members of the city." This vision is generally evident in the world of business. Competition is being replaced by mutual help. Farsighted companies, Follett wrote approvingly in 1918, permit cooperation to occupy a larger and larger place.

Should a residue of conflict between the aspirations of business and those of society remain,

* No doubt, too, her innocent optimism helped. She gave a number of revealing instances to show how, without any compromise whatever, syntheses can be effected. For example, when in a library she desired a window closed and another reader wanted it open, they jointly hit on a solution satisfactory to both: opening a window in a connected adjacent room. Or, to use a more instructive instance, when the interests of a husband who liked motoring and his wife who liked walking came in conflict, integration was achieved when he hit on the solution of tiring her by playing tennis. (See Follett, *Creative Experience*, pp. 157–62.)

the public will of a particular community may have to be educated to appreciate certain standards. That is exactly what is going to make business management a profession: to realize that it is responsible to something higher than the public will of a community, that its service to the public does not lie wholly in obeying the public.[32]

Follett deplored that this "responsibility to something higher" had not yet been met by important groups in the community. Thus the realm of labor-management relations was still governed by the "false psychology" of compromise and concession, false because "real harmony can be obtained only by an integration of 'antagonistic' interests. . . ." There is a need, she wrote, for "non-partisan groups for the begetting, the bringing into being, of common ideas, a common purpose and a collective will." This active convergence of interests can be achieved only by new modes of association through which all particular wills can interact. Only then, when "a scientific technique of evolving the will of the people" has been offered, can it be said that "every man *is* the state at every moment. . . ."[33]

To enable the collective will to express itself, Follett, with the utopian's fondness for homely specificity, recommended the organization of voters in non-partisan neighborhood and occupational groups. Such groups, she affirmed, will produce common purposes and an exhilarating spirit of mutual confidence; vigorously extended, they will provide the basis not for a reconstituted medievalism but for a new federalism.[34]

The new federalism was to be a blend of (1) the political pluralism of Barker, Figgis, Croly, Laski, and Duguit and (2) the "new psychology" which teaches the fallacy of distinguishing between subjective and objective, which shows that all is ultimately one. Based on correct psychological insights, this federalism proceeds from multiplicity to unity.[35] Properly conceived, it is not one in which the central power imposes its will upon the parts. It is rather a whole of interacting parts moving jointly in a common direction on the basis of shared facts and joint experiences.

This system cannot be brought into being, however, by the coercive action of a governing elite. "The most essential thing to remember about government is that control must be generated by the activity which is to be controlled. Therefore in industry, in cooperative undertakings, in government, control must begin as far back in the process as possible, else . . . we shall have power over instead of power with."[36] The organ of control must be a fully responsive register of public sensibilities. The exercise of power must be diffuse, soft, and—if the term "power" is used in its conventional sense—unnecessary. For all this, it is evident that Follett was not so unrealistic as to allow us to dispense with impersonal managerial teams to keep social movements moving. It remains their task to set a pleasing mood for agreements, to motivate activity, productivity, and industry by making it subjectively enjoyable. They remain truly the custodians of good order, providing the incentives, probing, testing, interviewing, getting everyone engaged and involved, seeking to live up to Follett's unargued but still arguable insight that "management is the fundamental element in industry."[37]

At its best, a science of management would comprehend the industrial field as a whole, would understand the behavior of all its interacting parts, and would thus see into the future. But, she wrote,

anticipation will not mean forecasting alone, it will mean more than predicting. It will mean more than meeting the next situation; it will mean making the next situation. . . . I cannot therefore wholly agree with those historians who say that the study of history should help us predict situations; it should do more than this—it should help us create situations.[38]

Follett made no claim, of course, that this state in which man's prophecies could be made to fulfill themselves, in which the ideal future could be forced into the corrupt present, had ever been brought into being. Nor did she claim to know how to institute this state of affairs most efficiently. She was certain, however, that not only a firm will but also an informed mind was required, and the necessary information, when Follett wrote, was not easy to come by. "The greatest need of today is a keen, analytical, objective study of human relations," she believed. And since social science was not being helpful, she relied on the world of business. "I find so many business men who are willing to try experiments," she said in 1926.[39] Ultimately, though, she knew that the social scientist, whatever his guise, would have to go to work. He would have to intervene actively "in industry and business, in legislative committees and administrative commissions, in trade unions and shop committees and joint boards of control, in athletic committees and college faculties, in our families, in parliamentary cabinets and international conferences." Anticipating social anthropologists, industrial psychologists, and plant sociologists, Follett urged that social science, to find out what is possible, be rousingly experimental, bothering not with the meaning of business but with its productivity, not with the legitimacy of power but with its extension, not with the ends of the state but with its vitality.[40]

Follett's real orientation—her assumption of natural social harmony and the role she consequently assigned to politics—was obscured by her enthusiastic valuation, so easily reached in her case, of conflict; it was obscured by her emphasis on an individualism seemingly fully expressed and fully realized within the state. To her, this state is not contrived to liberate individual human energies: it is quite spontaneously constituted to do so. It is not an artifice in perpetual need of statesmanship to maintain its authority, but rather a closed system, a smoothly functioning body in homeostasis. Its human constituents have value to the extent that the state enchants and absorbs them, giving them their true freedom by satisfying their real will. Such a wholesome equilibrium of private desire and public interest may be instituted by a social science relying on tested hypotheses. When these are energetically applied by the sensitive investigator who discovers social dislocations, they will reveal as well as create the coherency of the natural world. To fit self-interested, unpredictable, or playful men into the reality disclosed becomes then only a technical problem to be patiently solved by those prepared to handle individuals and their sundry beliefs.

Clearly, Mary Parker Follett did not push on to argue for such a regime. And what is more important, her repeatedly expressed concern for human dignity would in practice have been no mean impediment to the realization of an illiberal society. Yet when one seeks to draw together all of her preoccupations—(1) her genuine affection for the values of the pluralistic community, (2) her anxious awareness of existing tensions and displacements, (3) her interest in developing an objective general organizational theory, (4) her belief in an ultimate balance of human roles and purposes, of man's interests and values, and (5) her determination to identify individual freedom with a fully functional social order—when one seeks to make a meaningful compound of these, one becomes aware of an ideal which has remained submerged in the work of other American thinkers, of the dangerous confusions inherent in the pluralism of even the most dedicated humanitarians.

It had been Mary Parker Follett's insight during the early part of the century that a workable pluralism presupposed the unifying force provided by idealist philosophy. Although, in contrast to the English pluralists, she would not willingly go the way Hegel had pointed—toward the monist state—she had no qualms about accepting an idealist dialectic. Since this dialectic has always had the tendency to push its more impatient proponents toward some final synthesis, she was surely on treacherous ground. But it did give her case a dimension not to be found in the works of those other Americans who, challenged by a new economy, were also to speculate about desirable public policy. Thus their plea for an autonomous plurality of corporations, or for a self-regulating economy, was at once more shallow and innocent. They remained oblivious to the statist implications of idealism. They failed to see that the effectiveness and authority they were denying the state would merely become attached to the nominally private structure of power. They did not so much plead for less politics as for transferring politics from the public to the more estimable corporate realm. For the unsentimental, so they alleged, this was the only alternative. If it is true (and who can deny it?) that there is no way back to the shores of Walden Pond, to the Oneida community, to the family-size farm, to the village grocery, to the private law practice, to the long ballot, or even to the greenbelt towns of the Resettlement Administration, we will have to place our future in corporate hands. And if analysis could show that such a trust has not been misplaced in the past, there will be all the more reason to make the transfer with confidence.

It was David E. Lilienthal who, after the Second World War, followed through what his earlier zest for administrative decentralization had intimated.[41] The autonomy he had previously been prepared to bestow on a government-group partnership in the Tennessee Valley, he was now ready to grant a corporate economy. In his *TVA: Democracy on the March* (1944) he had alleged that genuine planning for common purposes required policy making by a coalition of functionally represented power blocs.[42] His respect for the realities of power was not to change. In rousing terms, he asserted in 1952 that big business is essential for national security, resource conservation, efficient distribution, and maximum productivity. He discussed the hazards of big business only to dismiss each in turn. He was clearly pleased by the prospects of a new corporatism and little concerned about its possible corruption in the absence of external checks.

For those who worried despite such assurance, it remained to make the system attractive not on a rhetorical but on an analytical plane. And for this John Kenneth Galbraith was better equipped than a public administrator. He clearly saw that neither wartime productivity nor postwar affluence could really be attributed to small-scale enterprises and price competition. The economy surged and expanded despite its noncompetitive management by a limited number of large-scale concerns. For this state of affairs, Galbraith provided a reasoned apologia.[43] Progress, he wrote, depended on monopoly; research and technical development are the natural rewards accruing to market power. But such power need not discomfit anyone, for big business always found itself troubled by such outsiders as organized labor or a united front of retailers. The danger to individual freedom was averted by a system in which admittedly powerful economic groups felicitously generated countervailing ones. Excess profits, it seemed, always were an inspiration and incentive to the disorganized. Of course Galbraith could not have offered this as an exhaustive description of the facts. After all, there could be no question that some of the power blocs in apparent opposition were in fact amiably working together. All kinds of convenient partnerships—between banking and manufacturing, union and management, business and government—secured an economy more tranquil than Galbraith's model. For Galbraith, it was an ideal to work for—if need be, with the positive help of public government.

But not all proponents of a new corporatism were to be so directly normative. Adolf A. Berle, Jr., built his case on an empirical foundation.[44] He maintained that the corporation is not primarily a creature of the law, a juristic personality. It exercises power independent of state power. It has, "*de facto* at least, invaded the political sphere and has become in fact, if not in theory, a quasi-governing agency." Its power is both highly concentrated and extraordinarily extensive. "American political thought has been frightened, and corporations themselves have been frightened, at any suggestion that they might emerge as political institutions in their own and separate right." But facts are facts. Corporate power, "though limited, is in large measure absolute."[45] Corporate management cannot and should not escape its duty to plan for the good life of the community.[46] How are we to guide the desires of corporate management which exercises *de facto* public power? "If corporations are to make industrial plans, what are the criteria for these plans? If they are to make gifts to support philanthropy, what kind of philanthropy shall they support? If they are trustees for the community, what kind of community interests do they forward?"[47] Berle sharpened his questions by noting that since corporations need no longer rely on the capital market to finance themselves, public opinion exercised through the capital market has become an unreliable check on corporate power. Nor are consumer preferences effective; prices can be administered by the corporation. Fortunately history itself, aided by nature, provides inhibitions and guidelines. History has shown that corporations will conscientiously seek to anticipate public reaction before it finds expression in legislation. They tend to be responsive even to latent community feelings. Furthermore, corporate concentrates, as Berle called them, are poised to exploit one another's errors, thus putting all on their guard.

But beyond this, another force is operative, and it may put

our minds at rest. It would seem that "absolute power in any form of organization is commonly accompanied by the emergence of countervailing power. . . ." Despite the similar language, Galbraith's concept is given a different meaning. "Deep in human consciousness is embedded the assumption that somewhere, somehow, there is a higher law which imposes itself in time on princes and powers and institutions of this terrestrial earth." This restraining force is in the very nature of things, manifest in the undefined philosophy of management. To alert this corporate conscience to injustices, there must be corporation-sponsored procedures allowing the victim of quasi-governmental policy their day in court. And for the corporate courts there must be a "body of doctrine," a "referent of responsibility," to orient decisions. Whoever was to formulate this doctrine and ensure its enforcement, it was not to be the state. "In the coming 'City of God,' " Berle prophesied solemnly, "the state is not to be the dominant factor."[48] In his *Power without Purpose* (1959), Berle asserted that the lords temporal, to use his own characterization of corporate management, would be effectively curbed both by the lords spiritual and by an indomitable force for right in the very nature of man. The economic order, he maintained, would be "accountable" to an admittedly imponderable "public consensus," one articulated by "our spiritual élite." Although he assumed a separation of the economic and the political—a separation he indeed recommended where it did not exist—he remained aware of the inextricable mixture of economic and political power, noting that "the views of leaders of the business community unquestionably enter forcefully into the consensus and their application of its doctrine is part of public opinion. . . ." Although fully aware of this, his trust in the progressive character of American capitalism remained untouched.[49]

Whereas Berle's statements were diffident, urbanely qualified and indirect, those by others were confident and ebullient. Thus Lilienthal had simply liked things the way they stood, certain that they must be, or perhaps should be, the way he saw them:

Our top industrial leadership has assumed . . . not only responsibility for production itself, but for a whole range of the social and political problems which are to be found in a modern industrialized nation. In short, there has been a revolution in the nature of active responsibility of Big Business. The president of a large company is now responsible to practically everybody![50]

There is no need to be troubled by the lack of checks on a system operating so beneficently. As the most fastidious economic analysis could somehow be made to show, it provides what the public surely wants: not state-enforced competition for its own sake but rather industrial productivity, corporate performance, and an affluent society.[51] For these presumed ends of the economy, "workable" competition is good enough. What we care about, after all, is not the power structure or the organizational character of the market. We are not ultimately concerned with how business happens to be situated vis-à-vis the public agencies with which it deals or the private persons whose needs it satisfies. Its power to manipulate consumer needs, to discipline its constituents, to emasculate the dictates of the state are all irrelevant. What we really want is performance in the public interest. What we ideally expect of the economy is maximum technological development, unceasing production, and a constantly rising level of material welfare.[52]

Judged by this ideal, policy is sound if it duly rewards output and growth, rise in per capita income, ability to gain ever-renewed consumer favor, "innovation," and "dynamism." Policy is not properly concerned with the relations between the parts of the economy, the way its components divide or share power. Nor is it concerned with the process by which the consumer makes his choice. There is no reason to consider state control of consumption, the regulation of the content of leisure, or—the very thought is painful—methods for developing the practice of civic virtue. "The alternative use of the resources which a wealthy community appears to use frivolously," Galbraith could explain, "will always be in other employments."[53] A sound policy leaves well enough alone. What counts is results.[54]

Thus we can dispense with debating the purposes of the political state or the seemingly private goods of the risk-taking, predatory individual. For the discipline of economics at least, individual and state are discredited entities. We must consequently evolve a policy accommodating neither the individual nor the state, but rather the vast middle stratum of large-scale economic groups. Public power may justly devolve upon them. They turn out to be the promise of American life: they are what an agrarian economy had been to Jefferson, what a confederated nation had been to Calhoun, and what a Golden West had been to generations moved by a myth of uncorrupted pastoral simplicity.

The new corporatism must be welcomed not because anyone exalts bigness as such but because the fulfillment of ideal expectations is tacitly attributed to the economy. This is done not after engaging in political philosophy or public debate; it is posited by the science of economics. Its key terms—growth, results, productivity, output, performance, workability—all refer to undiscussed and probably most agreeable ends. And economics, remaining a purely instrumental but far from dismal science, can insist that to will these wholesome ends is to will the means; to will the products of an advanced technology is to will a plurality of large-scale firms, a pluralism of elites. The proposition that the large-scale firm is the veritable embodiment of efficiency (a proposition more frequently affirmed than demonstrated) coincidentally supports the doctrine. Its mainstay is the conviction that a network of corporate giants fortuitously provides the only type of competition which, given the assumed expectations, is truly workable.

Accepting as "goods" what the workable system produces, having faith in an economy whose corporate members are embodiments of rectitude, we need not withhold sovereign power from the economy. That we should only minimally interfere with it was, in fact, an early postulate of Franklin D. Roosevelt's.[55] To maintain the welfare of American citizens, he said in 1933,

requires the regulation of such balance among productive processes as will tend to a stabilization of the structure of business. That such balance ought to be maintained by cooperation within business itself goes without saying. It is my hope that interference of government to bring about such a stabilization can be kept at a minimum. . . .

He may have felt what John Knox Jessup was to imply in 1952: that the old balance between the domains of economics and politics never really existed. "Any President who wants to run a prosperous country," Jessup declared, "depends on the corporation at least as much as—probably more than—the corporation depends on him. His dependence is not unlike that of King John on the landed barons. . . ."[56] An archaic federal system should give way to a new corporatism. There is no need to direct corporate enterprise to achieve public purposes. Acting responsibly and in concord, corporations themselves, to echo the words of Calhoun, will maintain a national balance, giving us "patriotism, nationality, harmony, and a struggle only for supremacy in promoting the common good of the whole."

Nor is it necessary any longer to exclude the labor union from this vision. Management's autocratic control of the work force, as Stuart Chase has seen it, had constituted the first stage in the history of labor-management relations. The second stage is marked by conflict. The final one is ushered in when management and labor "begin to see the fundamental unity of their interests," when "it is no longer a question of 'capital' dealing with 'labor,' but of management and labor dealing with stockholders, consumers and the public."[57] The union is essential, Frank Tannenbaum has proclaimed, for it is a conservative force in society. "It is a social and ethical system, not merely an economic one. It is concerned with the whole man." It seeks to make "the daily task coterminous with the good life," motivated not by the desire for increased wages but by the worker's need for "security, justice, freedom, and faith." It should therefore conceive of itself "as exercising a necessary moral role for the whole of society, and this moral role includes the economic, political, social and other interests of man." Should it fail, Tannenbaum warned, the leviathan state will imperiously provide for the public welfare. To frustrate the state, the business corporation and the labor union will have to "become one corporate group and cease to be a house divided and seemingly at war." When at last the worker has learned to identify his "lifelong interests with the fortunes of the industry in which his lot happens to be cast," when "the system of 'estates' now being developed" will have been established, the promise of the Industrial Revolution will have been fulfilled.[58] It remains the task of statesmanship to keep the emergent forces always in balance, to strengthen the weak and weaken the strong, and thus to attain a "working equilibrium." This task, but no additional ones, befits the world Tannenbaum has beheld—one "which seems to be going nowhere, and which seems to have no all-dominant philosophy or faith, no impassioned ideal that drives it beyond human reason and beyond human frailty. . . ." Leadership, we are told, consists solely in balancing interests, in guaranteeing peaceful friction, endless growth, and perpetual dynamism.[59]

That such leadership is properly the function not of traditional statesmanship, as Tannenbaum holds, but of a science of social engineering unconcerned with the merits of alternative ends was shown by Elton Mayo and his coworkers in the 1930's and the 1940's. There is no need today to review their much applauded, as much deplored, and extensively popularized efforts except to indicate how Mayo came to the realization that real politics is public administration, that real statesmanship is industrial management.

Modern society, as Mayo believed before he joined the Harvard Business School, is radically out of balance: individuals and groups, incapable of communicating effectively, are in wasteful conflict. Clinical investigation of man's industrial setting exposes what has always rankled industrial managers: widespread mobility, irritability, unsteadiness, fatigue, absenteeism, irregularity, and, above all, misunderstanding. The disease of which these are the symptoms has resulted from misguided attempts to produce social health by "political regulation."[60] Mayo granted that the state can record and enforce an existing moral settlement. But he would not permit it to take the lead in changing it.[61] Regulation of conduct by public authority conflicts with the facts of human nature; it is based on the scientifically false notion that human interests conflict. Worse, it introduces "politically-manufactured and irrelevant passions" into the public arena, thereby making men emotional, suspicious, and aware of their differences. Such politics cannot be the basis of good government. Today's problems are technical ones. They must be treated in conformity with the real needs of industrial man.[62]

Without our knowing it, according to Mayo, our needs are already being satisfied through nonpolitical industrial organizations. Industries are happily "learning to regard themselves as social functions rather than sources of merely national wealth, and are already experimenting in the direction of extra-political or world-wide organization." As they work for the common good, that is, as they cease to conceive of themselves as mere profit-making mechanisms and become responsive to the community, the governmental apparatus proves itself to be extraneous. Hence it becomes superfluous for public bodies to mediate interests. Courts of arbitration or collective bargaining are pointless. They can never bring about a condition of wholehearted cooperation.[63] They imply the need for concessions and for reservations, whereas the institutions of the healthy society imply that undisturbed individuals, having no special interests, can contribute their all and hold nothing back.

As our economic enterprises are arranged today, we have no choice but to waste our emotions by displaying feelings of opposition. Yet our hostilities are due not to our special interests but to the failure of the existing political order to give our real selves an opportunity to unfold. Present methods for resolving differences have caused our interests "to harden . . . into emotional antagonisms, instead of developing the rival conceptions, both defective, into mutual understanding." Only by this dialectic can "progressive rationalization" be achieved.[64]

Mayo did not believe that such a dialectic creates syntheses by virtue of its inherent rightness. It is not self-propelled. While he frowned on political procedures for the realization of the right order, he recognized the need to employ the specialist who, as an agent of rationality, can induce proper motivation. This specialist will have to "stand outside the situation he is studying." With the confidence given him by his knowledge of scientific administration, he will keep aloof. He will understand "the human-social facts for what they actually are, unfettered by his own emotion or prejudice." Conscious of "the biological and social facts involved in social organization and control," he will know that the proper concern of political discussion is not so much the question of who should govern, of the legitimacy of authority, as it is the question of whether those in effective control are objective, whether they are "aware of the problems—physiological, personal, social, and technical—involved in a situation both technical and human." Alert to the ends of management, informed by a scientific sociology and psychology, knowing how "to receive communications from others and to respond to the attitudes and ideas of others in such fashion as to promote congenial participation in a common task," he will be prepared to exercise his skill so as to forge fraternal bonds.[65]

By controlled experimentation he will aid in the progressive unification of society while at the same time building the body of a social science. This quest requires not an understanding of history by a reflective intellect but the will to participate. The human relations expert knows that until social science, in Mayo's phrase, "walks into adventure," there can be no genuine progress. And just as chemists no longer quote the alchemists, so can he jettison "Aristotle, Plato, Machiavelli, and the books of other authors."[66] To achieve the mastery of human affairs experimentally, he must be taught how to "secure the effective participation and coopera- tion of everyone," how "to help society to unanimity," how to provide for "the maintenance of spontaneous cooperation."[67] It seemed evident to Mayo that human relations was not being taught well. The universities overvalue a host of subjects which fatally attract the otherwise able student, offering "philosophy, litera- ture, sociology, law, economics, and—God save us all—government." They fail, above all, to develop the student's "manipulative ca- pacity."[68] To release the energy of individuals, an elite of human relations specialists must be equipped with the knowledge—ad- mittedly not yet complete—of "how systematically to set about the task of inducing various groups and nations to collaborate in the task of civilization." They must know how to reduce the conflict between worker and employer, between industry and industry, between nation and nation, certain that any ideal which aims at less than this will surely produce social catastrophe.[69]

This imperative applies not only to the industrial state, extensive as that is, but also to other areas of human life. It is relevant to the totality of the "existing situation, both within the national boundaries and as between nations. . . ."[70] In fact, the collapse of Western civilization is inescapable unless we "develop a better *élite* than we can at present show in public, private, or academic life." Being enlightened about the nature of the social equilibrium, this elite must clarify the goals of work, the true objectives of industry. As long as the mass of men are confused about objectives, they will remain unbalanced, undependable, and irresponsible. The elite must realize that this lack of balance can be correlated, as Mayo disclosed experimentally, with the worker's failure to share the interests of the industrial company. So far, the goals of management have remained unaccepted because of management's own failure to communicate. The worker has not yet been given "sufficient understanding of his work situation. . . ." Because he finds it difficult to be enthusiastic about an end he can but dimly see, he must be enlightened. This will make him balanced, steady, and hence productive. "The physiologists," Mayo remembered, "have found that work can continue to be performed only in a 'steady state.'" And if "that steady state is achieved, 'the exercise can be carried on indefinitely.'"[71]

Having assumed that within modern industry man is indeed unsteady—as evidenced by his fatigue, his absence from the job, or his low output—Mayo set himself the task of discovering what forces outside the individual cause his instability. To that end he managed the now familiar experiments at Western Electric's Hawthorne plant.[72] From these classic experiments he concluded that mobility, absenteeism, stalling, and restricted output can be overcome most effectively by improved understanding. When all involved in industrial production understand their goal, they will work to their physical utmost. Altruistically, they will do their duty. Vehicles of motion, they will be movement manifest. Since they are not calculating animals whose work is stifled by rationalistic weighing of alternative purposes, no *specific* end need be furnished to keep them enthusiastic and active. Indeed, an incandescent vision of purposeless productivity, like Sorel's great myth, will remain blinding and unanalyzed. Accurately speaking, they do not understand their activity, for they are not above it. Their rationality is immanent in their action. When they sense this unreflectively, fully living their productive lives, they will be happy, satisfied creatures. To the extent that they are submerged in the *élan vital*, they will lead the perfect life.

For the rational individual, immersion in an "industrial reality" is to be complete. Fortuitously, neither industrial reality nor the social will imposes burdens which might justify the individual's resistance, for what he really wants and what is asked of him coincide. As a matter of both fact and norm, only one compulsion is and should be operative in a social group: the "inner compulsion to think and act in a way that is socially acceptable. . . ." In all preindustrial communities, and presumably in the good state, "the situation is not . . . that the society exercises a powerful compulsion on the individual; on the contrary, the social code and the desires of the individual are, for all practical purposes, identical. Every member of the group participates in social activities because it is his chief desire to do so."[73]

Such coordination is to be found in the ideal democracy, democracy defined as that form of government in which "the central and peripheral authorities supplement and complete each other—logical and purposive control from above, spontaneous and cooperative control from below.[74] In the true democracy, the individual will labor without restraints, with full spontaneity and commitment. It will be possible for him "to feel, as he works, that his work is socially necessary." He will recognize that he only deceives himself when thinking that he has ideas of his own because in fact "they all originate in the social and professional tradition of the community to which he belongs."[75] United with others, enlisted to give his all, he will find no *reason* for resentments. In the perfect society, Mayo wrote, enlisting Edith Cavell's words to suit his purposes, " 'patriotism is not enough; we must have no hatred or bitterness towards anyone.' "[76] Those individuals who persist in showing their misunderstanding by being irritated and by engaging in argument must expose themselves to necessary therapy. The treatment for the agitator will have to differ from that for the agitated; but its final aim must be to harness all in the great task "to help society to unanimity."

Those who formulated a theory of the exemplary state as one within which public authority would devolve on a plurality of groups were initially concerned with individual freedom, with private rights. Postulating the kind of voluntary, representative, interest-satisfying association which enables individuals to find fulfillment, they hoped that the public realm would become synonymous with the realm in which a plurality of groups would naturally complement one another. For this public realm, little government would be necessary. Its limited role would be to preserve that balance which, at best, would always emerge spontaneously without political help. The resultant natural equilibrium, its parts in amiable competition with one another, could be granted independence. Expressing the fundamental harmony of its constituents, it would not have to be forced to depend on either the sovereign individual or the sovereign state.

To translate this ideal into practice under modern conditions, it became evident, the fundamental unity which pluralist theory had assumed to exist would not be self-enforcing. The immanent natural order—in the face of unnatural and hence intolerable conflict—would have to be energetically instituted. To the extent that group anarchy is discerned as intolerable or that a massive cry for order is heard, the end of policy would have to be the establishment of order. Policy then would have to aim at integration so as to restore the health of the body politic.

When the singular aim of policy is to integrate what is disintegrated, to make healthy what is diseased, we no longer need the statesman for suggesting, considering, and mediating alternative ends. Instead, we enlist the technician to move men as painlessly as possible toward health. Thus the logic of publicists as well as social scientists who sought to have public authority devolve on society as a confederation of groups was to drive them, insofar as they were rigorous, to a theory of an elite-governed society. When they were unequivocal and conclusive, they had to accept the need for a benevolent autocracy. They knew that as long as groups threatened to act in human history—as long as groups would serve conflicting individual purposes, responsive to the callings and whims of men who begged to differ—it would always remain necessary to have social pathologists and social therapists on hand. Yet, for the thoroughgoing advocate of pluralism, they would not merely be on hand; they would rightly be at the very center of society because they alone, ever sensitive to nature's dictates, could diagnose disease and restore health.

Part Two: The Conflict Within Pluralism

Liberté, Égalité, *and* Fraternité *are* all *parts of the democrat's creed. They are all necessary to him and they all more or less contradict each other. The democrat's task is to maintain a tense balance between the three.*

—H. Mark Roelofs, THE TENSIONS OF CITIZENSHIP (1957)

When men receive legacies under new conditions of society, they are more prone to try to adjust their circumstances so that the bequest may be applied than to abandon their inheritance.

—Robert C. Wood, SUBURBIA: ITS PEOPLE AND
THEIR POLITICS (1959)

11

The Challenge of Individualism

The principal driving impulse behind American pluralism has always been our commitment to uphold the dignity of the individual person. How is it possible, then, for the assumptions of pluralism to find expression in political and economic institutions, in a research orientation, and even in the polemics of publicists, all of which work against individualism? Individualism alone could never have justified the case for the autonomous corporation, the pervasive adoption of the research norm of equilibrium, or the plea for the single-purpose society. A peculiarly delimiting interpretation of our modern environment had to play its part. If today our pluralism has in effect contributed to the degradation of the individual, we can explain this only by noting how we have misinterpreted or simply ignored the present character of our public order.

The fact is that the proponents of pluralism, deeply perturbed by historical trends, arrived at their position because they saw that some of the alternative ways in which individual freedom might be rescued and restored could not possibly be workable, given the conditions of modern life. They saw that an ascendant industrialism, a prevailing legal order, and a capitalistic economy tended to make their ideal of the free individual irrelevant. Reacting against the institutions made legitimate by an atomistic conception of the body politic, they were driven to prescribe or to practice alternative forms of social therapy, hoping to heal what to them were self-evident sore spots. The temptation to reorganize productive units in the image of the guild, to redesign communities in the image of the village, or to reform the social system in the image of the "functional" regime became virtually irresistible—especially when the modern era was apocalyptically perceived as obviously dysfunctional, burdened by groups in conflict and individuals in despair.

Yet in its unanticipated, practical consequences, the remedy tended to be so effective as to subdue the very moral impulse which had initially stimulated both politicians and students of politics. Their starting point, we know, had never been society. They were all individualistic, attempting always to qualify the nineteenth-century claim that the last word had been said about society and the economy, that the last alternative had been reconciled. In this they were at one with traditional liberalism. When they added an egalitarian note by granting the right to pursue happiness to all men—thus compounding individual rights and popular rule—they accepted Locke's democratization of liberalism. When they opposed the artificial narrowing of the individual's horizon, they accepted Rousseau's understanding of man as an unfinished, indefinable creature with a limitless potential for development.

Today, the very standard provided by their basic individualistic concern must automatically jeopardize that institutionally embodied, academically rationalized, or bluntly defended pluralism which has been described so far. Nevertheless, our pluralism has generally escaped systematic critique. The reasons are understandable enough. As a creed, it has been so implicit in our thinking that the discrepancy between our experience and our desires could remain concealed. Even at the risk of repetition, it is important that this discrepancy be made fully explicit.

The empirical investigations dealing with the flow and counterflow of pressure between and within large-scale interest groups—

investigations which have been so extensively relied on in the previous section—were not planned, of course, to endanger either the social organization or the political theory of pluralism. Their authors never presumed to transform the theory that postulates the associational nature of society, recognizes the autonomy and consequent rights of associations, and denies the state the rank idealist defenders of sovereignty had assigned to it. Still, to the extent that the primacy of the individual person remains a political ideal, the facts disclosed by the research relied on in the preceding part of this book must seriously challenge the faith in the naturally harmonious relations between and within groups. They must challenge a faith which supports the beliefs (1) that the good society is merely a confederation of self-regulating groups; (2) that the unrepresentative exercise of all governmental power is frustrated by the dispersal of public authorities; (3) that a just public policy is simply the automatic result of the clash of group interests, the result of the free play of pressure politics; and (4) that the central government's proper role is to discern and act upon no more than a common denominator of concurrence between groups. Faith in the durable soundness of these tenets is responsible for the incongruity at the very heart of pluralism.

The actual political behavior of business, labor, farm, and professional groups has generally failed to effect a modification of these tenets. The evidence, however, should be clear. Examination of the reality upon which political pluralism allegedly rests—namely, the homogeneous group at once liberating and fulfilling its members—has indicated in detail that large-scale organizations do not provide the institutions for the adequate representation of individual interests. We know that as variations in individual interests become manifest within organizations, the organization's leadership, secure in its tenure and intent on surviving, will find it expedient to permit them free expression—and that this will be done in the name of the public interest. By muffling dissent and repressing factionalism, it will enforce unanimity of outlook and policy. The individual member of an organization will be kept in line by a variety of sanctions, ranging from subtle social boycott to the systematic denial of access to tangible rewards, whether these be dividends, profits, promotions, pensions, patents, bonuses, or the unguided use of leisure. Furthermore, entry into the group may be made difficult and withdrawal impractical.

Even more is involved. The demand of traditional pluralist theory for individual participation in the policy-forming process through primary groups has been made sentimental by modern organizational conditions. When we accept these conditions, it becomes meaningless to exhort individuals to share in making the decisions of their organizations. What, after all, are "their" groups in a highly industrial, hierarchically organized, thoroughly interdependent, and pre-eminently urban society? Few are the neighborhoods which successfully contain the individual's manifold interests, and those few which remain are increasingly more quaint and less viable. Nor is the business firm the cohesive, single-purpose unit able to give the individual a sense of fulfillment. The union to which he pays his dues, the so-called voluntary association whose membership card he carries, the professional guild which serves him, the political party whose "member" he seems to be—none of these are the primary groups which were so close to the hearts of all pluralists because they were said to arouse the individual's sense of loyalty, to make a legitimate claim on his time, and to induce him to participate. If primary single-interest groups are fading out of the social picture, if large-scale, multiple-interest associations are taking their place, it is quixotic to expect individual participation in the policy-forming process. It is naïve to plead for less political apathy; in the final analysis, the apathy of the mass of men is but a function of technological advance. When public policy is made at all, it emerges from the quite concerned participation of competing oligarchies. To this fact, traditional pluralist theory does not pretend to do justice, for all of its empirical sources and most of its sentiments antedate the modern industrial, economic, and organizational revolutions.

It has become evident that the irresponsible use of power to penalize action within groups and mobility between them must once again raise the very question which had set the advocates of pluralism to speculating in the first place: How, in a necessarily complex industrial society, can human energies be effectively liberated? How can the realization of individual goals be promoted without somehow intimidating those groups which men do require to succeed in even their smallest enterprises? How can responsible representation of individual interests be assured? How can insensitivity, or excessive sensitivity, to the welfare of the citizen of the modern state be effectively curbed?

Recognizing the continuing pertinence of these questions some contemporary thinkers have merely demonstrated the fundamental irrelevance of their reflections to the American scene. They have urged a "return" to laissez-faire, to the liberalism of Jacksonian democracy and Manchester economics. Every other road, they have insisted, leads to serfdom. In at least one important respect, this liberalism is hard to distinguish from pluralism, since it too maintains that society, when emancipated from the necessarily abusive power of government, is spontaneously good and therefore best administered, if at all, by untrained, well-disposed bureaucrats.

The American theory discussed in the previous chapter urged no such return to undiluted individualism and a laissez-faire state. But although it was unwilling to retreat, it was not able to advance. It simply could not transcend the form and substance of pluralism. Its advocates, often hoping to say more than had already been said, continually fell back on pluralism, embracing it the more fervently the less it yielded what it promised. Fromm, Follett, Tannenbaum, Lilienthal, and Mayo all celebrated the wholesome pluralist community, quietly approving or stridently urging the diffusion of power to make policy, crying for a new "democratization" of government, inventively delineating various forms of mass participation in politics: "economic democracy," "functional representation," or "decentralization of administration."

But here, too—as pluralism becomes imaginative and ready to escape the grip of the past—empirical studies have not ceased to put theory into jeopardy; they have instead merely sharpened the questions further. Thus it has been shown that weaving interest groups into the fabric of the state will in practice remove the distinction between society and government, between critic and ruler, thereby weakening the responsibility of those in power. Moreover, it will promote responsiveness not to the variety of conflicting interests on the scene but only to the most potent among them.

As Lloyd H. Fisher observed in his study of the California harvest labor market, the argument for delegating decision-making power to local bodies in regions where conflicts of interest are involved—and particularly where such conflicts have resulted in the triumph of one of the parties—simply overlooks the need to keep justice aloof and blind lest she be ineluctably drawn to respond to the best organized and most powerful group. Only when there is a homogeneity of interests, Fisher showed, is the experience of "the local area a safer guide than the remote intelligence of a Washington bureau." He conceded that the local resident is "more sensitive to local problems and is, therefore, a better judge of what is feasible than the federal bureaucrat or the briefly commissioned circuit-riding lawyer, clergyman, or professor"; yet he added that such sensitivity, when institutionalized in decentralized public authorities, tends to make the power to formulate policy the property of the few, to confirm existing power relationships, to support the strongest of various interests to the exclusion of others.[1] Philip Selznick reinforced this theme by noting in his study of the TVA that drawing interest groups into the state in the name of grass-roots democracy is likely to produce coalitions which will monopolize the power to legislate. It should not be necessary at this point to examine various efforts to atomize government so as to liberate the individual and enable him to make free political and economic policy choices; it is enough to recall that in practice, these efforts have generally resulted in surrendering the individual to whatever fate existing corporate groups have successfully conspired to arrange for him. Decentralizing governmental power, liquidating it, "giving it back to the people," has not strengthened the hand of the individual. Instead, it has simply exposed him to other, nonpublic forms of coercion.[2]

But an unqualified pluralism is most damaged by the evidence which vitiates Madison's claim that individual rights are secure and arbitrary inequalities diminished when private interests are encouraged to proliferate. The possibility of effectively pulling various interests together, of somehow making the cotton farmer of Georgia see eye to eye with the cotton farmer of California, has been amply demonstrated. Madison's hope that, although "factious leaders may kindle a flame within their particular states,

[they] will be unable to spread a general conflagration through the other states" is misplaced in an industrial society united by open and closed television circuits, by the opinion-manipulating equipment at the disposal of "factious leaders"; it is as misplaced as David Hume's belief, on which Madison relied, that in the large country "the parts are so distant and remote, that it is very difficult, either by intrigue, prejudice, or passion, to hurry [the people] into any measures against the public interest."[3] The notion that there are natural limits to the power of numerical majorities has been discredited by our success in modifying and removing the natural obstacles which at one time had imposed the limits. If public authorities respect the boundaries between states, as the Constitution bids them to, private authorities are under no such compulsion. The large private organization, as Grant McConnell's study of the American Farm Bureau Federation has revealed, can organize widely separated constituencies and ignore the legal boundaries contrived to inhibit public politicians. Under such conditions, the states—which are invariably at a competitive disadvantage, being compelled to succumb to high bidders—are unable to achieve those high liberal purposes which allegedly justify their existence.[4]

That the organs of state government are more amenable to private pressure than those of the national government is widely acknowledged. "The relations of business with state and local machines," according to V. O. Key, Jr., "have been so intimate that business could block much legislation in the sphere of state power. . . . A characteristic of the federal system seems to be that entrenched interests in the long run can better protect themselves in dealing with state legislatures than with Congress or with federal administrators."[5] At the state level, pressures are less likely to be canceled out by countervailing pressures. Resistance to pressure is more likely to be penalized. Private and public interests therefore find it easy to embrace one another.

It is true that when no one within a state (not excluding tourists, nonvoters, and misfits) is discomfited by such an embrace, when a state's actual and potential citizenry is truly homogeneous and as much of one mind and one interest as Madison could have assumed, there is little cause for attempting to extricate the public instrumentalities of government. It then becomes perfectly plausible to consider such a state, as Justice Holmes did, as an insulated chamber in which to pursue social experiments, a laboratory in which variables, by suitable legislation, might be stabilized to achieve agreed-upon ends.

Yet today Montana is no more simply "the copper interests" than Nevada is "the gambling and silver interests." There are always the managers and the managed, the young and the old, those still seeking and those who have settled down. In one way or another, all public action elevates or depresses them—and does so unequally. Once the inherently discriminatory character of all affirmative policy is recognized, we may rightly question every private exercise of public power. To give private groups public functions is to sanction their immunity to the criteria of responsibility we are committed to apply to public groups. In a constitutional regime, there is the expectation—based on a rationale yet to be discussed—that those who exercise public power will be directly or indirectly responsive to more than one dominant private interest, that they will be institutionally compelled to consider the variety of individual aspirations.

Such a variety can be all too effectively unified by private groups commanding economic power centers situated outside the political system. By taking politics out of decisions, by engulfing the decentralized governmental unit, they betray that part of the liberal creed which insists on the autonomy of the public order and the general will. Politics is displaced precisely as public and private orders are permitted to fuse. In the resulting mergers of personnel and of hopes, one of the cornerstones of liberalism is exposed to corrosion: individualism, as empirical studies have shown, is simply unrealizable in a society which fails to distribute public power equally. Sharing public power may, certainly, be undesirable, impracticable, or imprudent on the ground that there are higher goods—the leisure, the privacy, and the freedom obtainable only from illiberal, hierarchical, undemocratic organizations. Yet is it not true that when such illiberal organizations in fact govern, when we fail to aim at a roughly equal distribution of public power, the response to the plea for pluralism will demolish individualism?

In *The Federalist,* No. 51, Madison expressed the hope that the individual in America would be guarded against the oppression of his governors and against his own presumptuous groups. This hope is being frustrated as pluralism runs its course under modern conditions, when private law-making groups operate under color of public ones—or, conversely, when public instrumentalities are obliged to find their sole source of support in private ones. To allow public policy to be shaped only by such a pluralism is to present a radical challenge to the ultimate aspirations of pluralism itself.

If nothing but the theory and practice so far reviewed could be relied on to frame a practical response to this challenge, the reformer's task would be hopeless. However, a pervasive but still muted ambiguity characterizes America's traditional institutions, the research into them, and the philosophy justifying them. It is possible to uncover, clarify, and elaborate a nonpluralist thesis embedded in the dialectic of the American tradition, and thereby bring a measure of rationality to the inconsistencies and equivocations so amply built into American pluralism.

Part Three: The Transcendence of Pluralism

And no man putteth new wine into old bottles; else the new wine will burst the bottles, and be spilled, and the bottles shall perish. But new wine must be put into new bottles; and both are preserved.

—Luke 5:36–38

The nations of our time cannot prevent the conditions of men from becoming equal, but it depends upon themselves whether the principle of equality is to lead them to servitude or freedom, to knowledge or barbarism, to prosperity or wretchedness.

—Alexis de Tocqueville, DEMOCRACY IN AMERICA (1840)

12

The Articulation of American Statism

A simplistic, unexamined belief in the good society as a plurality of self-rectifying groups acts today as the sole theoretical shield for the existing complex of our associations and for a considerable part of our academic research. While this belief discredits the extremes of anarchy and totalitarianism, it implies no specific allocation of governmental power; it can be as generously hospitable toward the small group with a single interest as toward the leviathan with many. Welcoming such a wide spread of possibilities, the theory of pluralism seems vacuously formalistic and relativistic. To be sure, it is firmly grounded in the belief that the individual person ought to be free. And freedom, say the believers in pluralism, is not license. But to give content to this assurance, to erase the impression of mere formalism and relativism, the theory of pluralism would have to point to something more substantial than individual freedom. American pluralists themselves, however, have never delineated anything more with any degree of consistency. Instead, they have relied on an inarticulate common experience. It is this consensus which has actually inhibited and shaped individualism, and kept our public action from being as innocent as our pluralist ideology. Even if inarticulate, a theory is latent in our habits, procedures, and institutions.

Should we desire to provide a rational, theoretical challenge to the enclosure of the individual by contemporary associations, we might look for guidance, then, to that part of our experience which has so far remained undiscussed. Here we might find, in ill-defined forms, the relevant substantive standard for the orientation and reorientation of public policy; a unified, coherent, nonpluralist position might be found embedded in at least some of the very practices of American constitutionalism. Moreover, we may even discover a few outvoted, outnumbered, or outmaneuvered apologists for a conception of the state as more than the adjuster of manifest group interests.

While past defenses of the pre-eminent, nonpluralist state may be viewed by us today as if they somehow existed in patent opposition to American pluralism, there is in our history no salient dialectic, no dramatic encounter of fundamentally alternative positions. The very individuals quoted as defending group invulnerability in the form of federalism, decentralization, or corporatism can be drawn on to show how well they really understood overriding national needs, how they were prepared to make use of the sovereign, positive, group-destructive state. Political conduct and its justifications have often been a mere matter of approach, form, emphasis, and style. But even style has consequences, especially today when so much of the material with which statesmen must work is unalterably given.

To react responsibly to the pressures of given technological and organizational forces, we are compelled to make distinctions, even seemingly trivial ones. We are constrained to watch for style in the advocacy, formulation, and execution of policy. And as we review our past in an attempt to formulate a rational stand, drawing on a selected part of our amorphous history, we may properly be grateful that the equivocations of dead statesmen free our hands.

Although the American state as unified and positive is just as inchoate as the previously discussed theory of American pluralism, it is nevertheless discernible. It does intimate the persistence of efforts to accord legitimacy to a state which can effectively cope with an emergent economic order. If it is incomplete, at least it does point the way to completion.* Unrefined and undeveloped, it has always been decked out when it was expedient to serve specific purposes: the purchase of Louisiana, the establishment of public education, the emancipation of slaves, the disposal of "over-age" destroyers, the "seizure" of steel companies, or—as used even by Calvin Coolidge—the striking down of a veterans' bonus. Disturbed by ascending social and economic forces, we may at last feel called upon to refine, systematize, and articulate such a theory, to give it underpinnings which would integrate the valid components of both pluralism and statism, thereby assuring at once a more secure grounding for state action and a transcending of a confusing, tedious, and anachronistic debate between increasingly illiberal liberals and increasingly unconservative conservatives.

Again and again, the starting point for such a theory has been the recognition, clearly set forth by Burke, that a strong government is not the only source of injustice, that a feeble government which gives free rein to factious nongovernmental groups may be just as oppressive.[1] There has been a perennial recognition, in the apt words of a contemporary political theorist, Thomas I. Cook, of "that ethical universalism without which libertarian diversity becomes destructive or is sacrificed at last to an imposed absolutism."[2] It is this universalism that John Adams sought to join to the power of the state. "When cunning and force united are balanced against cunning and force united," Adams wrote, "reason must be armed to mediate between them." By itself, reason will not produce agreement between the leaders of factions. "Nothing short of an independent power . . . can keep them within bounds. It is the interest and the policy of the people for their own safety always to erect and maintain such a power. . . ."[3]

---

* It might be noted that there were no second acts in the lives of Hamilton (the most sustained advocate of the unified state) and Thoreau (the most sustained advocate of anarchism). Had they lived longer, would not America have given them the familiar choice of (1) modifying their programs, (2) using an oblique rhetoric such as Veblen's, (3) becoming silent or going into exile?

In *The Federalist*, No. 23, Hamilton made clear that where such a power was legitimately vested, it must be commensurate to the tasks which call for its exercise:

A government, the constitution of which renders it unfit to be trusted with all the powers which a free people *ought to delegate to any government,* would be an unsafe and improper depository of the NATIONAL INTEREST. Wherever THESE can with propriety be confided, coincident powers may safely accompany them.

The powers which "a free people ought to delegate to any government," those which serve the purposes of the union,

ought to exist without limitation, *because it is impossible to foresee or define the extent and variety of national exigencies, or the correspondent extent and variety of the means which may be necessary to satisfy them.* The circumstances that endanger the safety of nations are infinite, and for this reason no constitutional shackles can wisely be imposed on the power to which the care of it is committed. This power ought to be co-extensive with all the possible combinations of such circumstances. . . .

Responding to Washington's request for an opinion on the constitutionality of chartering a national bank, Hamilton wrote in 1791 that the power to incorporate, as a "general principle," is

inherent in the very *definition* of government, and *essential* to every step of the progress to be made by that of the United States, namely: That every power vested in a government is in its nature *sovereign,* and includes, by *force* of the *term,* a right to employ all the *means* requisite and fairly applicable to the attainment of the *ends* of such power, and which are not precluded by restrictions and exceptions specified in the Constitution, or not immoral, or not contrary to the *essential ends* of political society.[4]

That the institution of federalism was no bar to this followed for Hamilton from the "axiom" that where sovereign power had been granted, it was "by force of the term" supreme.[5] Hamilton had no doubt about the need for "one General Government" with complete sovereignty, for "two sovereignties cannot exist within the same limits." Failing to confer "a degree of power commensurate to the end, would be to violate the most obvious rules of prudence and propriety, and improvidently to trust the great interests of the nation to hands which are disabled from managing them with vigor and success."⁶ Hamilton considered such power properly lodged in the executive. In *The Federalist,* No. 70, he determined to defend "energy in the Executive" as

essential to the protection of the community against foreign attacks; it is not less essential to the steady administration of the laws; to the protection of property against those irregular and high-handed combinations which sometimes interrupt the ordinary course of justice; to the security of liberty against the enterprises and assaults of ambition, of faction, and of anarchy.

As a matter of fact, we have relied on the doctrine of inherent powers of government to protect the constitutional order throughout American history. Admittedly, an explicit dependence on inherent powers has seemed appropriate only in our foreign relations, when we have confronted other sovereign nations.⁷ But we have always been prepared to define governmental power during crises, to cope with depressions, riots, subversion, and real or threatened war. In the words of the Supreme Court, we have never lightly assumed "that in matters requiring national action, a power which must belong to and somewhere reside in every civilized government is not to be found."⁸ We seem to have known that the power of a state is inherently coextensive with the undefinable conditions which call for its exercise, and that its exercise under such conditions conforms to the spirit, if not to the letter, of the Constitution. Such knowledge enabled Lincoln to argue that a limb— a constitutional safeguard—might have to be sacrificed to save the life of the constitutional order. In far less extreme terms, other Presidents have permitted their words to reflect the record of executive and legislative action.*

Though in practice we have not hesitated to rely on a reservoir

---

* "The nation," wrote Herbert Hoover, "must protect its people from catastrophes beyond their control. . . . Child labor, health, sweated labor, old age, and housing are but part of our social responsibilities." Whether individuals, private groups, the states, or the federal government should assume such responsibilities depended, he said, on who could effectively meet the crisis. But he added that the federal government was, in any event, "the final reservoir of national strength." (*The Challenge to Liberty* [New York: Scribner, 1934], p. 295; see also pp. 158–59.)

of positive power in the state, we have had few advocates or philosophers who would formulate anything like a consistent doctrine
to justify reliance on it. Under the influence of European historicism, a number of thinkers, it is true, did free themselves from a
laissez-faire fixation. Touched by German idealism and romanticism, Henry Carter Adams, Richard T. Ely, Josiah Royce, Mary
Parker Follett, and others reacted systematically against the negative state.[9] More generally, toward the end of the nineteenth century a number of clergymen, economists, sociologists, and political
scientists opposed the identification of a ruthlessly competitive
individualism with the natural order of things. Washington Gladden, Josiah Strong, John R. Commons, Henry Demarest Lloyd,
Woodrow Wilson, W. W. Willoughby—all of them recognized the
positive social-welfare function of the state.[10] But while they, with
John Adams, might speak of the state as an agency independent
of the factious groups which sustain it, they could not bring themselves to outline a coherent plan for public action. Edward Bellamy's fictionalized treatment excepted, they came to no conclusions.*

Various self-conscious conservative thinkers, to be sure, somehow located specific institutions through which American traditions might be preserved. But they found nothing stable to cling
to. When they did manage to identify some suprapolitical institution which could preserve liberal politics, they exposed themselves
as either unrealistic or ineffectual. Thus Henry Adams, half in
desperation, wrote his brother Charles that

what we want is a *school*. We want a national set of young men like ourselves or better, to start new influences not only in politics, but in literature, in law, in society, and throughout the whole social organism of the
country—a national school of our own generation.[11]

Brooks Adams, who was certainly more radical in his analysis of

---

* One might carry an image of Henry George as violating the consistently antistatist upshot of American thought. But he was acclimated
like all the others: he hoped without irony that by means of his program
society would "approach the ideal of Jeffersonian democracy, the promised land of Herbert Spencer, the abolition of government." (*Progress
and Poverty* [New York: R. Schalkenbach, 1955], pp. 455–56.)

American industrial capitalism, thought it ultimately best to support the training of an elite of liberally educated generalists, a new class of administrators. Education, he said, would enable an antiquated government to realize America's destiny. Irving Babbitt was more specific but no more convincing. He placed his faith first in the "inner check," then in the Senate, and ultimately in the majority of the Supreme Court. In 1914, Walter Lippmann thought that drift could be mastered by the new kind of business managers who "stand outside the higgling of the market" and could be trained to assume the responsibilities of stewardship.[12] Herbert Croly promised a great deal more.. He had indeed managed to call for the staffing of a Fourth Department of the government by an elite of social engineers. But by the time he placed his whole case before the readers of the *New Republic*, he was back in the American fold: in 1922 he exulted in small groupism and saw the local clergy rejuvenating the nation by working through America's neighborhoods.[13]

While our rhetoric, then, always turned out to be contradictory and thin, there nevertheless were Americans determined to maintain that the government has the plenary authority, the inherent power, to act in behalf of individuals. Their argument expressed an opposition to laissez-faire, an unwillingness to accept as adequate public policy what merely happened to emerge from group combat. And it could also be pushed ahead to become a plea for developing civic leadership more discerning than the *de facto* groups in society, a plea for training an educated managerial cadre. Thus there has been an inadvertent alliance of progressives who wanted more energetic government and of conservatives who wanted the energy concentrated in a governing elite. But whatever the orientation of those who supported the power of the state, whether it was progressive or conservative, it was always suffused by uncertainty, indecisiveness, and ingenuousness. No case for public action managed to sound clear or ring true.

The twisting thought of Herbert Croly merits a closer look here, for if Croly is an important figure, it is precisely for his innocent inconclusiveness. Because the conditions for popular appeal and political success are beginning to change, he may today challenge us to spell out what he left abbreviated. He may compel us to acknowledge the paramount role of the state as an instrument for the creation of private well-being. Irritated by his ambivalence, we can perhaps make respectable what he, as well as the thinkers on his right and left, have always found so hard to respect that they either lost heart or preferred to be appealing and successful.

Shortly after the closing of the American frontier, at least as Frederick Jackson Turner had dated it, Croly sought to rouse Americans so that they might purposefully fulfill the promise of American life. Since the virgin West could no longer furnish the ground for the good society, it was necessary to turn inward and backward, to rely not on the untamed wilderness but on the American tradition.[14] The promise America might yet fulfill was being denied, Croly affirmed, not by an ever-expanding industrial civilization but by the failure of the privately controlled economy, allied with city bosses, to distribute the national surplus so that the lives of individuals might be enriched. He argued that adherence to one part of the American creed, uncontrolled private enterprise, would frustrate the realization of another, the qualitative enrichment of individuals. Distinguishing between two traditional creeds, Croly saw individualism as both more fundamental and more threatened. Exploited wage earners, he feared, might destroy individualism by irrationally marching under the banner of equality. To preserve individualism, he called for rational, deliberate state action.

Having carried the argument thus far, Croly abruptly came to conclusions which can find their justification only in the ultimate conviction that state and individual are one. Although he so evidently cleared the way for the positive state, he failed to vindicate devices by which the domain of the private might fight off the domain of the public, by which competing private claims might be mediated. On the contrary, he wanted the individual to be politicized, to become loyal to the nation, to blend with the idealized state. De-emphasizing political and civil rights, Croly would have the whole community pursue the all-inclusive ideal. What became essential to him was a common exaltation of Americanism as a new nationalism. Americanism, joyously embraced, would naturally guarantee the highest qualitative enrichment of individuals as they dedicated themselves to the national enterprise. In America, individualism and nationalism would happily fuse.[15]

Thus Croly succumbed to an Americanism in which all would naturally go well. It is as if he could not bring himself to make his plea for conscious, public control of economic forces without falling victim to the very American past which he counseled his fellow progressives to transcend. Departing from the pervasive individualistic ideal of America, he espoused a national socialism. The sole justification for this was his inarticulate premise that, at least in America, there would be no genuine difference: individualism and socialism would come to the same thing. Just as an unseen, beneficent hand would make the social good emerge whenever individuals pursue their private interests, so it would likewise make the social good emerge when the state pursues the national interest. The nation's leader, at once heroic and saintly (as Croly himself phrased it), could be trusted to embody the popular will.

When this Nietzschean vision later made Croly uncomfortable, he simply placed his faith in popular democracy. It then became possible for him to make explicit what he had merely implied: a distaste for traditional American politics. He proceeded to condemn the checks imposed by federal and state constitutions, which he thought impeded the positive action necessary to save America from those who used private power irresponsibly. The centralized leadership which Croly had at first thought necessary was now found to be replaceable by mass participation in government, by a revitalized, genuinely fraternal regime which would learn to dispense with the two-party system.

Whatever constructive plan his analysis of a freely drifting economy demanded, Croly would not provide it. He drove Americans to realize its need, but then left a blank. It is true that he filled the blank, but his "contributions" turned out to be no more than a variant of Americanism. Having distinguished between individualism and a policy of laissez-faire, Croly called for state action to preserve individualism. Yet in doing so, he found himself unable to summon up anything but a ringing nationalism. Other Americans, it is true, could not even make his initial distinction. They identified individualism with local autonomy, federalism, and pluralism. But one conviction all have had in common, and to this day our theorists continue to share it: an unexamined belief in social harmony. Once this agreement is challenged, however, it may become possible both to rely on the distinction upheld by Croly and to escape the hold of the past. We should then be able to spell out and accept the theoretical plan he almost gave us.

The concrete practices and the specific policies of American government express our determination to strengthen the state for protecting individuals against groups far more effectively than our half-hearted, circumspect rhetoric has done. Recovering and then reconsidering what has been normatively central to the constitutionalism we have actually practiced should therefore give sharper point to a theory for dealing responsibly with the problems of contemporary society.

Although it would be gratuitous to furnish still another review of governmental practices in the United States (there are, after all, textbooks aplenty), it may yet be worth while to mark out at least one set of relevant practices in order to move to the center what our rhetoric has made to appear marginal. Some of our political processes might thereby be exposed as being indispensable to achieve the purposes for which they were designed. Others might emerge as less necessary. We may possibly learn which of our institutions carry the proper credentials.

One difficulty besetting the search for a normative pattern in American institutions is evident. Strip away the façade of orderly procedures, and all that seems to stand revealed is a confusion of intricately connected reflexes spasmodically articulated in public law. It appears that all that can be confidently asserted is that innumerable discrete gestures, appeals, petitions, maneuvers, and bargains somehow coalesce to form public policy which, in turn, rewards or penalizes the very individuals and groups instrumental in shaping it. It seems easy to conclude, therefore, that the objective observer can do no more than register the pressure of quantities of power. And these, since all is never said and done, can yield no meaning.

But perhaps a somewhat less exhaustive analysis of what appears to be a boundless decision-making continuum may enable us to perceive some public ends after all. It may enable us to recall that we have instituted governmental devices and effectuated policy to create, revitalize, or simply maintain the procedural rights of individuals. Indeed, the whole of our constitutional order may be seen in these terms, and in these terms exclusively. When we have been concerned with the rights not of individuals but of groups—whether the groups happen to have been the states, religious orders, business partnerships, or craft unions—the rationale for this concern has been the conviction that for all practical purposes the groups and their membership were one and the same. The group was each and every member writ large. Believing the group to be homogeneously united in its purpose, we could then content ourselves with regulating its external relations, its impact not on its own membership but on other groups in society. But when we somehow felt that its membership was heterogeneous, of divided loyalty, we have recurrently regulated, though often with hesitation, its internal policy-making and policy-enforcing procedures. We have employed the arm of public government to keep procedural rights alive—to guarantee old ones and, when an altered environment called for innovation, to promote new ones.

These general propositions are not hard to illustrate. We have traditionally recognized the rights of individuals and the rights of their homogeneous groups by seeking to ensure the inconclusiveness of all specific public enactments, hoping thereby to provide individuals and their groups the opportunity to shape and reshape policies. This has been achieved by means of a party system through which immoderate interests are moderated, accommodated, or neutralized. It has, furthermore, been achieved by dividing power between the states and the nation and by distributing it, at the national level, among legislative, administrative, and judicial agencies made mutually suspicious because each has derived its power from a different economic, geographical, or ideological sector of society. Nor is this all. Within the formal branches of government themselves, rivalries have been deeply implanted.

Congress—itself divided—has been fragmented into nearly 300 committees and subcommittees headed by those who, thanks to the seniority rule, represent stable minorities. The executive establishment has been so shattered organizationally that the unity of even particular bureaus is often superficial, concealing myriad internal partisan alignments. Thus the bureaucracy no less than the Congress has been so constituted as to account for and represent specific interests.[16] And although it has rarely been considered from this point of view, the judiciary, too, has been so structured that its decisions cannot help but register the variety of values and demands voiced by individuals whose views are presumed to differ. As the members of courts come to their conclusions, which remain always subject to review, they are compelled to consider uncountable alternatives, being affected not only by the contestants before them but also by *amici curiae,* their law clerks, argumentative and dissenting brethren, and contributors to law reviews.

This division of authority and work—so well built into the structure and processes of government—has been encouraged, in the words of Justice Brandeis, "not to promote efficiency but to preclude the exercise of arbitrary power."[17] Rivalry within and between the branches (not to mention the states) has helped eliminate the merely personal element from congressional, executive, or judicial legislation. The determination to keep things this way should explain the persistent emphasis in legislation itself on the procedural rights which individuals and their groups may use to affect the policy-making process. It is an emphasis which has paradoxically remained even in statutes jeopardizing a tradition of civil liberty.*

* Thus the Internal Security Act of 1950 which empowers the President to proclaim an emergency and subsequently authorizes his Attorney General to detain any person "as to whom there is reasonable ground to believe" that he will "probably" engage in espionage or sabotage was so burdened by procedural guarantees as to make its practical workability doubtful. The price for passing the Act—a price which ironically had to be paid by liberal members of Congress—was its emasculation. (See Cornelius P. Cotter and J. Malcolm Smith, "An American Paradox: The Emergency Detention Act of 1950," *Journal of Politics,* 19 [February 1957], 20–33.)

The way policy is deflected from concern with substantive liberty and compelled to focus on procedural rights is probably best reflected in the work of the Supreme Court. Despite the cries of those critics of the Court who perennially charge it with reading a substantive higher law into the Constitution, the Court's work can be interpreted not as an effort to enact Herbert Spencer's *Social Statics* or Lord Keynes's *General Theory* but rather as a continuous effort to see that in the public realm individuals are sustained in what are ultimately their civil rights. As Robert G. McCloskey has pointed out, it is noteworthy that the

most effective and far-reaching substantive check on governmental power yet devised in our legal system [namely, the due process clauses of the Constitution] entered the Constitution through a door marked "procedure." . . . Indeed a careful examination of legal decisions in the heyday of the due process clause suggests that what later students have called "substantive due process" was in the minds of the judges more like a widened concept of procedure. Surely they almost never admitted frankly that they were weighing the objectives of governmental policy rather than the manner of its accomplishment, and they tirelessly probed challenged legislation to discover elements which would smack of procedural irregularity.[18]

"Procedural due process," Justice Jackson has said, "is more elemental and less flexible than substantive due process. It yields less to time, varies less with conditions and defers much less to legislative judgment."[19] What is substantively achieved will be sound—provided always that procedural safeguards are present. In Jackson's words,

Procedural fairness and regularity are of the indispensable essence of liberty. Severe substantive laws can be endured if they are fairly and impartially applied. Indeed, if put to the choice, one might well prefer to live under Soviet substantive law applied in good faith by our common-law procedures than under our substantive law enforced by Soviet procedural practices.

The implicit faith here is that fastidious adherence to the variable demands of "procedural due process" will effectively nullify substantively unjust action. Following this premise, the Court can be seen as performing its proper role by doing no more than voiding what is inimical to the operation of a constitutional regime, unblocking stoppages in the democratic process, promoting, more constructively, the kind of public spirit and individual character essential for the maintenance of constitutionalism.[20] It can be seen as functioning properly when it resolves, in the language of Albert A. Mavrinac, "to encourage the technique of self-government by agreement" while preventing "the transformation of American government into something positive, something making decisions for the good of the community apart from the articulate interests of the country," thus keeping government "a place where agreements are facilitated and not an independent source of value judgments about the proper conduct of social arrangements."[21] Moreover, it can be seen as functioning at its very best when, taking advantage of opportunities provided by a tired chief executive and an unstable national legislature, it acts affirmatively, responding to latent, inchoate, and undeveloped interests, actually striking down "government by agreement" because, as in the Segregation Cases, it judges such agreement to rest on too parochial a base, because it believes a specific community affected by some private agreement is larger than the parties to it acknowledge.

It should be accepted at this point that the American system of government, at its best, though not consistently in fact, is fundamentally so constituted as to produce public policies aimed at upholding procedural rights in the public sphere—whether this sphere is economic or political. Significantly, it will uphold them even when a convenient mythology conceals the public character of what we, still under the soothing spell of a preindustrial era, fondly think of as an inviolate private domain. Thus fully recognizing the public character of large-scale associations—business corporations, labor unions, agricultural groups, professional guilds, or proselytizing sects—we have in fact regulated their external and internal conduct. Whether the official source of regulation has been the legislature, the executive, or the judiciary, whether it has been the national government or one of the states, regulation has touched groups in their dual aspects: (1) they have been regulated insofar as their policies affected the nonmember, that is, the outsider who might be a member of other groups or who might independently enter the public arena as consumer or as citizen; and

(2) they have been regulated insofar as their domestic affairs assumed a public character. Because we still see such public action as aimed not at protecting procedural rights but as intended to destroy or secure substantive benefits, the historical record bears retracing.

The early and far-reaching role played by the states has only recently been uncovered and highlighted by scholarly research.[22] Subsidizing economic expansion, the states not only promoted industrial and agricultural activity but at the same time imposed checks on those organizational forms which emerged in response to the ever-expanding application of machine power to work. Even before the Civil War, the privilege of incorporating an enterprise had been conditioned on accepting specified restrictions as to purpose, size, and business practices. Counterbalancing corporate power, the states aided agriculture, protected workers, and, more significantly, assumed responsibilities for public education, individual health, and social welfare. In disregard of Spencer and Sumner, they protected the unfit, the underprivileged, and the ill-informed. They regulated liquor, outlawed obscene literature, prohibited gambling, restricted prize fighting, and, at least in the State of Iowa, subjected to fine and imprisonment persons who manufactured, sold, or gave away either cigarettes or cigarette paper. Moreover, they sought to provide for the future welfare of their citizens by seeking to conserve natural resources. It is worth recalling, too, that before the turn of the century they had established commissions to supervise the distribution of gas and electricity, the underwriting of insurance, the cost and routes of transportation, the extraction of coal, the use of convict labor, and the negotiation of contracts. Where monopoly did appear desirable it either fell totally under public control (by 1896, over half of all city water works were publicly owned) or became subject to regulation. When the first federal antitrust law was passed in 1890, 21 of the states and territories had already proscribed practices conducive to monopoly.[23]

At the national level, public pressure steadily disciplined enterprises which threatened to reach monopoly strength, whether they had done so by mergers, price discriminations, or agreements to bar the entry of rival firms. The impulse behind American antitrust policy—as far back, indeed, as the act establishing the Interstate Commerce Commission—was essentially the desire either to prevent the emergence of all nonpublic monopoly or to impose public controls on economies it seemed socially wasteful to break up. Private practices which could be shown to have future anticompetitive effects were simply pronounced "unfair," and hence illegal. Even legislation which tolerated some forms of price discrimination (the Patman Act) or which permitted a manufacturer to fix retail sales prices (the Miller-Tydings Act) conformed to the underlying standard: it was presumed to benefit individual consumers by re-creating a balance upset by business grown excessively big and predatory. It needs no stressing today that major labor legislation has been similarly oriented. The strengthening of labor and the weakening of management is presumed to protect the consumer, as are the legislative efforts to prevent featherbedding, union-management collusion, or union monopoly over the labor force.

When such restrictive economic practices have nevertheless seemed somehow socially desirable, when monopolistic operation has been deemed essential to gain public objectives, the government has bluntly stepped in and directly assumed responsibility for safeguarding consumer interests. During the Second World War, to cite but one instance, the Office of Price Administration exercised to the utmost its power to enact various social values, to indulge or frustrate various public needs, and to determine the fate of economic groups.* Recognizing an absence of competition

---

* In his study of OPA rationing, Victor A. Thompson has pointed out how the government's seemingly technical decisions were in fact value judgments. Thus it seemed merely a technical decision when the OPA's Gasoline Eligibility Committee denied specific benefits to clergymen who traveled to maintain the organization of their church but granted them to others. The Committee's decision to restrict extra gasoline allotments to community-centered clergymen who were linked with their congregations was actually based on a view of the church not as purveyor of truth but as useful social organization. To obtain a preferred ration from the Committee "was, by and large, a reward for being considered important by the committee, or a bribe to get people into, and to keep them in, preferred activities." (*The Regulatory Process in OPA Rationing* [New York: King's Crown Press, 1950], pp. 133–34.)

or an imperative need for a product, the government has not only controlled prices but, as in the field of atomic energy development, production as well.

If the economic market was to be controlled, this was because the political one was assumed to be properly free. The only justification for constraining the individual as a hard-bargaining producer and consumer was that publicly imposed restraints would contribute to making his antecedent freedom as a citizen authentic. Hence as a citizen he could always count on governmental protection against monopoly in the political market. Thoroughly confounding the economic and the political, such protection has meant far more than safeguarding his right to vote, supervising elections, or regulating lobbying. It has meant maintaining his right to be informed, whether on labor disputes or religious matters, in the face of threats to restrict it by his state government or by private groups.[24] He therefore could successfully call on public agencies to protect his opportunity to take part in politics as an individual at once psychologically at ease (a measure of psychological comfort being provided, for example, by social security legislation), physically well (by such legislation as provides for meat inspection), fully or at least fairly employed (by fiscal policy and fair-employment legislation), politically informed (by policed television channels), and sufficiently educated to mark his ballot in secret. Those prepared to aid his education—publishers, non-profit foundations, and schools—have been exempted from innumerable burdens. Both the libelling of groups and the mislabelling of products have been publicly proscribed. Upholding him as a citizen—preserving his impulse toward moderation by reducing his anxieties—the government has pried open not only political clubs but also economic associations.[25] And when the national interest, clarified by international pressure, could be identified with that of virtually all citizens, the government has imperiously imposed on even the most potent of private associations. Although it is true, as Berle has maintained, that corporations exercise power by "cultivating personal relations with the proper officials in government both in America and abroad" and thereby become actual parties to economic treaties,[26] the United States government has again and again remained autonomous, not the instrument of a plurality of large-scale associations, but their master.[27]

If a consistent, central theme is to be found in our behavior, it would seem that by public action we have sought to eliminate every kind of privately sponsored penalization of the individual which could not be reasonably expected to enlarge his freedom. Employing a multitude of regulatory devices, we have sought to give him the greatest possible freedom by preventing every monopolization of the economic and political markets. In times of crisis—especially international crisis, when his very survival has been at stake—we have made him into the dispossessed, naked individual wholly the subject of the sovereign state. But more usually, we have cherished him as an individual of many parts: as producer, as consumer, or as a person activated by some private vision of a social, vocational, or spiritual good. However penetrating and indeed repressive it has sometimes been, public action has attempted to support him in these various roles.

It is this pervasive foundation of policy which can be shown to have sanctioned what has so far remained undiscussed: the regulation of the clearly internal political affairs of groups. Our concern with procedural rights initially demanded no more than the regulation of the external relations of groups, that is, instances in which they exercised power over the rest of the community, over citizens and groups outside. This seemed sufficient as long as the objectives of groups and the objectives of their individual members were rightly felt to coincide. But as their objectives became manifold, courts and legislatures proceeded to regulate their internal affairs as well, assuming that when groups, by virtue of the authority vested in them, begin to absorb the individual in all of his aspects and to make him dependent and subservient, they lose their private character.

To see this rationale for regulation is not to ignore a record of governmental intervention on the basis of other guiding assumptions. The American judiciary certainly preferred to think in terms of contractual obligations. If the courts affected the internal affairs of groups, this was generally only because they were determined to uphold a contract between a member and his asso-

ciation, granting him equitable relief when the association violated its own constitution and laws.[28] As long as the association's
own prescribed formalities were observed, the courts would not,
on this premise, interfere—and it mattered little whether the organization was a single-purpose one like a golf club or a multipurpose one like a medical association.[29]

Yet by holding that organizations, when vested with public
authority, must comply with national standards of procedural
fairness, American courts have had occasion to push harder. It
has been held that to the extent that organizations act as a state
might act, they may not do what the Fourteenth Amendment forbids a state to do: that is, discrimination may not be arbitrary.
The provisions of the Fourteenth Amendment, the United States
Supreme Court said as early as 1913, are addressed not only to the
several states "but also to every person, whether natural or juridi-
cal, who is the respository of state power. By this construction the
reach of the Amendment is shown to be coextensive with any exercise by a state of power, in whatever form exerted."[30] While this
dictum has not consistently informed American courts, it has been
at the base of innumerable decisions.[31] Because a closed-shop agreement gives a union a public character, it cannot claim, the Supreme
Court of California has maintained, "the same freedom from legal
restraint enjoyed by golf clubs or fraternal associations. Its asserted
right to choose its own members does not merely relate to social
relations; it affects the fundamental right to work for a living."[32]
On the same ground, the Supreme Court of Illinois would not
sustain a law authorizing master plumbers to decide who could
enter their trade. Under the law, said this Court, "the licensed
plumber is in full and absolute control of the situation, a private
citizen exercising a power under the protection of the State which
the State cannot lawfully exercise, i.e., the arbitrary denial to a
citizen of his inherent and inalienable right to engage in a legitimate activity by his own free will and choice."[33] Recognizing the
public character given unions by federal legislation, the United
States Supreme Court has treated the seemingly private discriminatory practices of unions as public ones. Although not insisting
(at least so far) that a union must open its doors, the Supreme

Court has demanded that all workers within a craft constituting a bargaining unit be equally represented.[34] Nor have professional guilds escaped: national standards of procedural fairness have been imposed on bar associations arbitrarily discriminating against would-be members.[35]

The regulation of the internal affairs of groups by statute rather than by case law has of course been far more extensive, and its orienting principle—the desirability of positive, even anticipatory, protection of procedural rights—has allowed legislatures greater scope. Thus there has been a steady increase in state and national legislation dealing with the relation between unions and their members. The states have persistently regulated unions in regard to their policies of admission, dues, elections, and financial reports.[36] At the national level, the Taft-Hartley Act (1947), as the first statute specifically regulating internal union conduct, denied the use of the National Labor Relations Board to unions failing to meet specified requirements. Unions were required to file detailed financial reports with the Secretary of Labor and to provide, when called on, information about dues and officer salaries for the rank and file. They were required, furthermore, to have their officers file a non-Communist affidavit.[37] The principle here is no different from the one that operates when the government, as a condition for doing business with it, demands the display of an equal-economic-opportunity poster. Nor are the internal affairs of industrial firms—of airlines, meat-packers, oil-producers, aircraft manufacturers, and thousands of others—any the less affected when the national government, under a series of executive orders, insists on nondiscriminatory employment practices among those enterprises with whom its procuring agencies negotiate contracts.

The relations among those who are functionally members of business corporations, whatever image they may have of themselves, have not escaped regulation either. The Securities and Exchange Commission requirement to make disclosures about corporation finances for the benefit of investors is but one example. The seemingly closed corporation has perhaps been even more intimately touched by efforts to protect such rights as those of automobile dealers. Rhode Island has empowered an administrative board to hear appeals from the rulings of manufacturers who have revoked dealer franchises. Recognized by the Supreme Court as representing an integral part of a national system of distribution,[38] dealers have in fact been granted the right to force manufacturers to act "in good faith" in franchise revocation proceedings.[39]

Although the pattern of governmental action remains unclear,* property rights as well as personal rights have been vindicated in an expanding field of equity jurisdiction. Moreover, the internal affairs of groups have been subjected to steady if casual supervision, which has been increasingly based on the assumption that inchoate public expectations cannot be satisfied by *ad hoc* intervention. Thus the government has been driven not only to deal with consummated private action but also to become continuously involved in it. In at least one dramatic case—the court-sponsored "monitoring" of the Teamsters' Union—it has attempted not merely to check the substantive results of the decision-making process of a labor organization but to supervise the process itself. The involvement could scarcely be greater.

A look back on this record of governmental action may seem to lead to the conclusion that the political has steadily gained on the economic, and the public on the private. Yet this vision of the growth of governmental power must be qualified by an awareness of the capacity of the private sector to deal with skill, ingenuity, and frequent success with the political one. When the issues have been joined—as some believed they were in 1932—the pre-eminence of the public sector, it is true, has always seemed imminent. But at the same time our view of what was truly and forever constitutional served to deflect public action. Despite America's involve-

---

* In 1958, the Supreme Court refused to grant *certiorari* in a suit brought by a number of screen writers and actors who had been blacklisted by the motion picture industry after they had pleaded the Fifth Amendment. The motion picture companies were sustained by the Supreme Court of California: the petitioners, they claimed successfully, had not suffered a remediable wrong and hence had no case. The United States Supreme Court granted *certiorari*—and then changed its mind, Justice Douglas dissenting from the *per curiam* opinion. (*Wilson v. Loew's, Inc.*, 355 U.S. 597 [1958].)

ment in a demanding, intruding, and tension-ridden world, the triumph of the public has always been partial and has never lasted. The notion of government-business partnership, although it became closely identified with the Eisenhower administration, was after all in no way strange to the practice of the New Deal.

Nevertheless, the underlying norm for orienting public action, the stress on proceduralism, has not essentially changed, as has become evident from the foregoing summary of institutional prohibitions on the self-seeking group. All these prohibitions have emerged from the area of procedure. Enforcing continuous responsibility to actual and potential interests, ensuring the perpetual review of policies—indeed, making "review" the key term—they have been accepted in order to keep the private from prevailing in public. Cumulatively, they have defined what, in public, should constitute fair play, seemly conduct, decent behavior, and right action. They can be seen as an ideal operative whenever public power is exercised. Of course they do not always exist, and there has never been anything automatic about their emergence and application.[40] But they do constitute a normative theme.

Aware of this underlying ideal, we should be able to see clearly that some of our practices are well chosen to keep arbitrary public power in fetters while others are extraneous. We should then be able to jettison those constitutional conventions that have imposed excessive burdens on the body politic. If we wish, therefore, to frustrate tyrannical forces, "to break and control the violence of factions," we ought to feel called on to reconsider the plethora of checks and balances which can, should the cry to eliminate governmental apathy or deadlock ever be born of desperation, lead a people to cheer unfettered action outside the constitutional order. Should that time come, review will no longer be possible.

13

Standards for Public Action

Before reacting constructively to the recent forms assumed by political pluralism, we might well steady ourselves by reinterpreting the fundamental standard which has guided a good part of our public action in the past. Systematically formulated, it might then serve as the basis for specific reforms of government—nominally private government as well as traditionally public government.

Of course, we may feel that in case of real need—whenever the forces which shape our lives really get out of hand—it should always be easy to invoke a rationale for state action. Yet neither American theory nor American practice actually provides a ready-made, unequivocal guide. In the past, it has always seemed sufficient to argue for liberty, and no more. Free men, it seemed clear, could and would use their common reason to discover an objective foundation upon which to order whatever life was left free from restraint. An impersonal natural law, disclosed by the exercise of man's reason and enforced by his conscience, would duly discipline individual freedom. Assuming this, Jefferson could rightly place his faith in the people: "Independence," he wrote, "can be trusted nowhere but with the people in the mass. They are inherently independent of all but moral law."[1] Counting on the universality and efficacy of such a moral law, those who accepted the American Constitution did not have to concern themselves with a social theory regulating man's private conduct. They could afford to concentrate exclusively on perfecting a political system which would hold the power of public government to that minimum essential for the survival of all.

The criterion of survival emerges as inadequate, however, the moment we are confronted by a social order which obviously survives and prospers even though we have reason to doubt its excellence. What standards for state regulation of private groups and private lives are then available? In point of fact, we seem to have none.

Innocent, at least so far, of revolutionary crisis and social catastrophe, always prepared to absorb radical and reactionary responses to them, we have not been obliged to provide ourselves with a theoretical justification for state action. On the contrary, it has often been fashionable to insist in a pleasantly Burkean tone that the very success of the English-speaking people with ambiguous constitutions and nonideological party systems has made attempts to be specific about underlying principles pretentious, if not dangerous. And it has been hinted that our failure to base programs on a clear theory of liberal constitutionalism may be fortunate: the owl of Minerva supposedly awakens only after the shades of night have fallen.

It is certainly true that insofar as the American political tradition has relied on nothing but the individualist component of liberal theory—most strongly repudiating the social theory of Rousseau, the one liberal who seemed most aware of man's need for community ties—it has lacked a rationale for the use of public authority, the exercise of governmental control, and, ultimately, the imposition of martial law. This has been true even where there has been such consensus, as in the case for military service, as to indicate an unconscious acceptance of an inarticulate social theory. Our general libertarian bent has consistently prevented a theoretical acceptance of a stratified, hierarchical, corporative social structure. At the same time, however, it has kept us from reconciling ourselves to the inequalities and discipline required by such a system.

We remain unreconciled to any scheme which might do more than make the world safe for individualism. Unable to furnish the standard to judge needed policies, theoretically disallowing it altogether, a liberalism which has depended on an undifferentiated individualism has been compelled consequently to embrace purely pragmatic tests. And when these, upon analysis, do not dissolve into meaninglessness, they presuppose that very consensus which a doctrinaire individualism rejects.

This embarrassment to a liberalism without a social theory tends always to be exposed in liberalism's moments of triumph. Thus the one-sidedness of liberalism has stood revealed whenever the revolutionary forces deriving their support from it successfully overthrew such arbitrary restraints—mercantilism, organized religion, a landed order—as hindered the release of individual energies. The nature that was then invited to run its course (conveniently depicted in metaphors provided by Charles Darwin) proved to be surprisingly restrictive and oppressive, assuming the forms of liberal capitalism, urban housing barracks, and demagogic politics, assuming the forms of mass war, mass organization, and mass culture. The resultant community, characterized by tension, conflict, insecurity, unintelligibility, and consequent frustration, was scarcely a community at all, as utopian socialists, Marxists, and Victorian conservatives alike perceived. If it was nonetheless tolerable in practice, this was due not to anything explained by the rationalism and individualism of the Enlightenment but to a series of happy accidents. Industrialization and an exploitable frontier were able to produce a surfeit of riches making generosity easy; the acquisitive instinct could become blunted; careers could become open to talent; Herbert Spencer's social statics could fail (even prior to Justice Holmes's dissents) to dictate the scope of economic practice and state regulation; finally, a labor movement could find it possible to get under way.

Yet these practical responses to social needs unfilled by older institutions were again and again accompanied if not by a sense of guilt at least by a feeling that true liberalism was thereby betrayed. It seemed impossible in the United States to provide a cogent rationalization for private or state action which would modify a policy of laissez-faire. The rhetoric of individualism could remain dominant in the market of ideas even when we were to be faced by the challenge implicit in the existence of a European social order which, because it lacked the attributes of a genuine community, provoked totalitarian leaders to use force to achieve cohesion, provoking them to manipulate men by exploiting their need for communion and self-sacrifice. To be sure, this challenge has been brought home to Americans aroused by war abroad or made sensitive to institutional developments at home. But relying only on an uncomplicated libertarian ideal, we have had no good reason for becoming perturbed by an emerging contradiction in the institutions it supports. As if in strictest accordance with our ideal aspirations, we have allowed the formation of two types of ultimately antagonistic regimes: (1) the public-spirited, nominally private, oligarchically governed association, and (2) the constitutional state organized so as to be positively mindful of conflicting constituent interests. The parallel growth of both types could be tolerated since their final moral justification was believed to rest on their supposed capacity to enhance worthy ends of the individual. The reason for making a fetish of laissez-faire and thereby encouraging the leviathan association is the same, after all, as the one for using the state as sovereign interventionist agency. In both cases, we have sought to safeguard individual rights. Whenever we have been forced to recognize that despite their common origin these two types of regime were destined to clash, whenever we have become aware of the conflict in sovereignties, we have been prone either to curse bigness and counsel the return to the simple, manageable community or else to bless bigness and counsel the move toward some form of statism. In this twofold reaction—a reaction so far always too extreme and hence "un-American"—what we have habitually failed to perceive is that we need not dispense with the criteria for determining the limits to both public tolerance of private action and private tolerance of public action.

It is clear, of course, why we should shy away from articulating a standard: we suspect its doctrinal character, priding ourselves, as Tocqueville first observed, on being able to survive without theoretical dogma. Yet this confidence in our ability to melt down all systematically stated positions has always struck us as unjustified during times of crisis when new institutions have emerged. Consequently, while we have ignored or denied the need for tests and formulas, we have nevertheless persisted in searching for them. Indeed, our entire intellectual history might well be seen as little more than a record of this search.

The seemingly insurmountable difficulty in this quest is that on native ground we have never been able to find a footing somewhere short of individualism. We have invariably concluded with a veneration of "freedom of opportunity," "the pursuit of happiness," and "liberty against government." But because times of trouble have always kept this essentially radical conclusion from holding good for very long, it may merit another look—especially when conflicts are so deep and sustained as to invite their premature, final, and hence pernicious resolution.

On restating the theory of liberal constitutionalism so as to give a meaningful context to individualism, it is well to begin with an obvious proposition: no group of constitution makers can rightly insist on final knowledge of any principle which might challenge the individual's claim to develop what he affirms is natural to him. Those who take issue with this proposition and advocate political inequality defend themselves by holding that the rulers of a republic of unequals would always remain generous in their treatment of the lower social orders. Yet because history moves so consistently in contradiction to this notion, we are compelled to treat individual persons as equals whenever they enter the political arena—provided we respect them as unique, ultimate, and incommensurable. Lacking confidence in the sustained benevolence of rulers and being unable to formulate a lasting principle which would permit us to force men to engage in civil negotiations as superiors and inferiors, as masters and slaves, such inequalities as we do impose must gain the consent of all—in practice, of concerned majorities. And such consent must be perennially revocable so that all individuals will retain, as a matter of principle, their political equality. This principle cannot be the object of bargaining in the liberal society.

As we deprive individuals of the freedom to achieve their various ends, we must consequently recognize their equal claim to be free—free not as members of society but as men, not as integrated creatures but as free agents. The liberal order, thus conceived, may safely be an all-inclusive one, charitable even toward the radical dissenter. For it postulates every human personality as ultimately elusive and provides that a true community will never take *final* account of anything else.

The weighty presence of this norm—an unrestricted, equalitarian individualism—cannot, however, give positive direction to the social energies liberated by industrialism. While it will proscribe specific programs, it cannot prescribe them. It is a monolithic postulate, not a political ethic. It cannot serve us when we wish to cope with the problems that take shape whenever men exercise power and act as representatives of others. Not decked out to justify one regime as opposed to another, it merely points with insistence at man—the discrete, private, existential entity. Nonetheless, during every historical period such pointing—whether it is that of the Athenians, the Stoics, the Church Fathers, or the thinkers of the Enlightenment—will always entail more than a respect for the incommensurable dignity of the human personality, more than a glorification of freedom. "Freedom exists in being independent," Voltaire said, "in being independent from everything but law." The belief in the need to liberate human potentialities of indefinite range and diversity did not keep Rousseau from pleading for a civil religion. Indeed, even a case for legalized slavery might well follow, as it did for Aristotle, from the conviction that for the sake of the happiness of the individual, virtuous men should govern, that education and leisure for sound political judgment cannot be equally available to all. In short, the norm of individualism, implemented and fortified under changing conditions, can call forth all kinds of laws. While these may enlarge the individual's capacity for action, they may also diminish it—a circumstance anticipated by all but the most out-raged of anarchists.

Yet the actual content of the law affecting the individual is but rarely defined by those in earnest about liberating him. It seems unnecessary to bother with definitions when a specific historical environment is so blatantly repressive that the appropriate reform appears to be self-evident. In times of total oppression, the cry "Liberty!" seems sufficient. Thus a widespread sense of outrage, a cry generated by historical conditions, is simply counted on to supply the necessary plan for social reform automatically. The specific historical environment in which the liberal preaches the gospel of individualism does give his sermon specific social rami-fications. But the moment the protest is lifted out of its context, it fails to provide positive direction. Thus outside of its eight-eenth-century setting, the great liberal outcry of Voltaire, Rous-seau, Diderot, and Paine sounds frenetic. Actually, of course, these thinkers knew that their affirmations were anything but aimless. Seeing freedom as a warrant for countering the oppres-sive forces of economic theory and practice, of aesthetics and art, of theology and religion, seeing it as opportunity and capacity for continuous individual initiative, they knew they were pro-viding social formulas containing and orienting their basic revo-lutionary impulse. Still, their individualistic stance alone, which was negative, critical, and destructive, could not yield social theory. To the extent that they created an institutional or moral vacuum, men were bound to abhor it, naturally preferring a holy terror to an unholy anarchy. And when they filled the vacuum they had created, they themselves recognized the need to go beyond their individualistic sentiments. They drafted blueprints for a new social or moral order, one which a new generation of liberals, drawing on the very impulse which galvanized the old, might challenge.

Precisely because a pristine, uncomplicated liberalism is fun-damentally and irrepressibly corrosive, it is necessarily incomplete. It fails on two counts, furnishing neither a social nor a moral con-text for individual action. While such contexts have always been recognized as essential to human life, it remains to articulate this recognition anew, to suggest how a physical community on the one hand and a moral order on the other are both integral parts of individualism.

To deny the bonds of community is ultimately to make liberalism inadequate in terms of its own goals. Society is the very grounding for the moral freedom on which liberalism insists. Without an economic community, man cannot hold his own. He requires social support to keep himself upright and civilized. "Individuals who are not bound together in associations, whether domestic, economic, religious, political, artistic, or educational, are monstrosities," John Dewey has rightly said.[2] Man depends on associations for the instruments, the concepts, the sheer factual information to give substance to his potential rationality. Without a stake in a viable community, he would be compelled to weigh all alternative policies, to be forever engaged in exercising his moral judgment. To feel drawn into a process which puts every governmental policy to the test is to invite exhaustion, frustrating the natural development of personal interests and sensibilities. Society as a going concern is thus the very basis for man's reason and autonomy, giving his beliefs continuity by protecting his capacity to formulate them against an ever-fluctuating environment. The need for society becomes all the more evident when natural forces which encroach on his independence threaten to assume prominence, when in order to remain free he may desperately call on society to help him stabilize his existence.

Given a shielded area in which his loves and hates may flow freely, the individual may discover himself, gaining an essential point of departure and an ultimate basis for coming to grips with his environment; he may then express himself to those with whom he shares, at a minimum, a community of symbols, a community without which his artistic, scientific, or religious metaphors would fall flat. If it is precisely such a communal base which makes the zeal of the iconoclast meaningful, pluralist theorists were emphatically right in showing that individualism as a dogma so weakens the members of society that they cannot effectively resist coercive state power. Unless human impulses are steadied by at least some attachments and engagements, they will run free and dissipate their strength; the harpooner, Melville reminds us, requires rest in order to use his dart with the greatest efficiency. This, in the final analysis, justifies the doctrine of the French physiocrats that only the individual's own land protects him against ecclesiastical organization. It backs Aristotle's insistence on the citizen's right to leisure and Locke's insistence on man's right to property. And it no less justifies the right to belong, the right to group citizenship. Both property and groups, however various their forms, may be real in that sense, both being man's real estate, more durable and fundamental than persons, making possible the clustering of loyalties and memories, the nurturing of interests, the rooting and cultivation of human faculties. To keep men from being exasperated and bewildered, there must be some established landmarks and precedents. There must be a commitment to the previously experienced and the customary, to the organically related rather than the contrived and artificial, to the habitual and prevailing rather than the purified and ideological. Without a social base, there is no place to incarnate and realize the abstract ideals of individual men, no ground on which to make familiar and lovable the great disembodied abstractions of rationalism, the awesome universals of freedom and order. To remain unintegrated, man requires the opportunity as well as the locale for making the ineffable specific, for placing and articulating the transcendental.

He requires more than his individuality even when, with seeming self-reliance, he sets out to oppose society. What is more, it is not likely that he can long retain his integrity while observing the rites of external conformity. Should he hope to resist those psychological conflicts which destroy effective individuality, should he hope to repudiate the deceptions, disaffections, and alienations demanded by the large-scale social organization, he will not be helped by counsel that tells him to be at once the individualist and the organization man. In short, the individual must be able to act in a fraternal setting which supports him psychologically and authenticates his intimate experiences.

The actual substance of this fraternal setting, however variable, will stand revealed whenever men are up against it, especially when the life of the whole of society is threatened. In some areas, the threat is general and permanent: it is in the very nature of man whose propensity for cupidity—as Augustinian theology, Hobbesian political theory, and Freudian social psychology all agree—is ever present. In other areas the threat is specific and transient: military pressures, acts of God, uncontrolled technological or economic forces. In such critical cases, individuals, in order to remain such, will adjust themselves, surrender freedom to society because they find their freedom intolerable or undesirable. They will let the facts determine values. At such times, "the logic of the situation" fixes substantive social goals, and the entire machinery of government can be brought to bear on society. The refusal to pay taxes or contribute blood, the refusal to participate in politics, the refusal to abstain from profiteering, striking, and dissenting—these can be officially penalized.

It is true that such "objective conditions" remain generally undefined, that men may be unaware of the extent of the area of "common" sense and "natural" assent, that only emergency and crisis expose the depth of their social consensus. Still, however ignorant men choose to remain about their social base, it is indispensable for the realization of the indeterminate values of individualism.

The very indeterminate nature of these values points to the second dilemma of a liberalism wholly identified with individualism. The predicament grows out of our recognition that a moral order is rationally indispensable and that, at the same time, any determinate order must be rejected. But the problem posed is not insurmountable. What applies to a communal base applies no less to the moral order: thirst is appeased by many drinks. The fact that we need order in principle does not require that we embrace any specific one with finality.

The perennially troublesome fact, troublesome for those espousing individualism, at least, is that the search for a realm of ends in reference to which men might order their lives tends to lead to specific conclusions. Such conclusions amount to an ordering of private life which is not, of course, merely self-regarding. Every *use* of freedom is socially relevant. Seemingly private action will shape the lives of others; it will necessarily affect their individuality, and necessarily make something more of liberalism than sheer individualism. This added dimension of individualism will certainly provoke members of society who insist that not every ordering of freedom is of equal validity and that therefore some will merit public support above others. But to give them support— that is, to ask all members of society to support some particular order, to use public means to establish a private order—is to give them that stability and finality which is challenged by the individualist component of liberalism. Thus we are led to perceive that the moment liberals want more than freedom, the moment they determine to be good for something, the door is opened to an illiberal regime which indeed establishes order.

But is it really possible to keep this door closed? If individualism is not a sufficient doctrine for individuals as members of society—as it is not, all modern existentialists to the contrary—the state must enter some areas which individualistic liberals seek to seal off. Compulsions to secure individual freedom are unavoidable. Some invasion of privacy, some blending of state and church, is inescapable. However much we may aspire to prevent the establishment of a public order, we are incapable of preventing it as long as we arrive at conclusions about the good life. As the history of the relation between church and state in the United States reveals, we cry for separation and countenance fusion.

It is true that we can avoid addressing ourselves to the question of what makes for the good life whenever life itself is at stake. In such times survival might serve as standard to determine the degree of permissible individualism and disorder. Yet we will always reject this standard when we have reason to feel that more than survival is in fact possible, that nature can provide us with an excess. We then ask what it is that ought to survive, and hope it will be a public order which is substantively good, not merely one which maximizes disorder. Privately, we know that freedom is not the highest social good; personally, we want others not merely to be free but free for certain good ends. And hence we will not allow freedom to be the touchstone for setting the limits of state power in specific instances. Thus we are impelled as private persons to inquire into the substantive nature of the just order. Rejecting a

merely formal definition of freedom as the absence of effective restraints, we ask for what definitive ends public power is to be
exercised, in behalf of what determinate goods, in reference to
what absolute standard of excellence. Only certain knowledge of
such a standard, so it would seem, will enable us to order freedom.

Yet any particular claim to final knowledge of the best regime
is pretentious. It is noteworthy that the conclusiveness of Plato's
great effort is contradicted by the inconclusiveness inherent in the
dialectical method he employed. Because men cannot have final
knowledge of the good, or at least could not safely communicate it
if they did, we must tolerate various interpretations of the good
life, of what is substantively the best regime. This must be done
not because there is no final moral order (a question we may privately treat but publicly ignore) but rather because man's grasp
is limited. Publicly, we must permit a variable content to a moral
order not because we doubt the existence of an absolutely true one,
as Locke would have us do, but because we must partially distrust
the men who testify about its nature. And such toleration of the
various interpretations of the good life or the best regime entails
curbing all efforts which would put an end to variety, which would
socialize or politicize the realm of personal fulfillment.

The liberal order must leave some things unsettled so that within it man is free to roam, to speculate about the ideal city, to articulate and communicate multiple loyalties. He is not altogether
obligated to serve the established social system and not forced to
be wholly responsive to its impact upon him—not even at election
time. In this order, he will not always take his part or play his role,
and, without proclaiming refusal, he might well fail to stand up
and be counted. He may be idle.

And thus he may be considered free. Assumed to transcend
biological circumstance, economic contingency, and temporal culture, he is, in this view, an ontological postulate, an autonomous,
causally efficient agent. His work and action, consequently, are
given dignity by something other than some hypostatized Truth,
Elite, Race, Destiny, or Class.

This conception of freedom does not deny a common good.
It merely insists that all efforts to determine the nature of the
common good must take the individual's own concerns as point

of departure. Common sense is first of all individual sense. Common knowledge is first of all individual knowledge, or individual conscience. Thus man is seen as self-willed, as disposed to make independent valuations, choices conceivably opposed to those customary ones his contemporaries may label natural selections. Self-directed, he has moral freedom: he naturally seeks ends in accord with his conception of the rational good. Obedient to his own nature, indifferent to authorizations granted by experts, he freely directs his will and his interests not to satisfy prevailing codes but to strive for ideal objectives. This freedom cannot ultimately be upheld on utilitarian grounds, on the assumption that when the individual goes it alone he will providentially tend to benefit society; for even a society which draws no benefit from those who are left to enrich their private selves still derives its own justification precisely from an objective moral order standing above the secular one. Alternatively, such a society is synonymous with simple, incommensurable force.

Policy within the liberal public order, then, will (1) take its bearings from the respect for the individual's will to engage in moral action, (2) provide the physical and moral ground on which this will can be exercised by allowing for meaningful alternatives, and (3) recognize that private conduct is ultimately always public action of some sort. Taking care, initially, to guard man's privacy, to keep his freedom from being defined, it must subsequently frustrate him when he deprives his fellow citizens of the opportunity to pursue their private goods.

But beyond this, policy must guard the associational bases which help secure the individual's freedom, which keep the preoccupations that most concern him from becoming objects of public controversy, compromise, and infringement. To remove these preoccupations from the public arena requires providing ground for them in the private one, nourishing a plurality of vocational, economic, cultural, geographical, and philanthropic associations. Not compelled to enter the struggle for governmental power, these associations will pursue their own interests. As their membership overlaps, cutting across even economic barriers, society is solidified while the interests of its members can remain fluid and various.

To preserve such a working balance of cohesion and diversity it seemed sufficient, at least at one time, to read a right of association into the First Amendment and to recognize, with Madison, the need to multiply individual interests by extending the size of the country, by incorporating diverse regions and hence diverse economic pursuits. Such diversity, while by no means eliminated through technologically achieved integration and standardization, is increasingly hard to come by. The admission of Hawaii and Alaska to statehood, for example, surely enriches American interests. But it scarcely shakes the prevailing patterns of private control of work and leisure. Nor is the systematic introduction of alien elements through immigration likely to be significant. Not only is the resistance to a more liberal immigration policy considerable, but it is also probable that those who may gain admission have gladly made prior adjustments to some stereotype of Americanism which all but cancels their eccentricities. What remains, then, as the alternative means for filling Madison's prescription is the fostering of eccentricity, autonomy, and independence at home, furnishing domestic ground on which diverse interests will flourish.

Doing so in practice demands taxing all to give to the obviously needy what they must have simply to subsist. This has become orthodox doctrine. The difficulties arise when we are pressed to extend this justification for distributing wealth. It is hard to recognize the wisdom of *not* providing a fixed selection of material goods. Making all members of society fare well after their basic needs are satisfied, providing collective welfare, tends to impel us, for the sake of economy, to administer our programs in a standardized manner, thereby threatening to damage human sensibilities. What grows only in diversity and solitude, fenced off and shaded, is difficult to plan for by a solicitous apparatus for uniform public welfare. Too impatient to comprehend the complex ways in which the individual shapes and expresses himself, administrators are only too ready to come to his aid, to provide him with well-tested, socially authenticated tools for self-help. Specific in their plans for his welfare, they may impose involuntary solitude as readily as involuntary communion, tending to identify the range of their imagination with the range of his.

Society can effectively do no more than permit the *release* of cultural energies. To do more is to keep them from operating constructively. What must ultimately be furnished, therefore, are the material, physical conditions permitting the individual to cultivate himself, should he so choose. Alone, in search of retreat and recreation, he is most vulnerable of all—and at the same time in great need of indirect aid. What may serve him best, therefore, are exchangeable goods—like currency. The problem of public policy is to keep him free in his leisure-time quests. It is to prevent the standardization of leisure, the patterning of freedom.

If this is recognized as a problem, it becomes justifiable to legislate so as to restrict whatever groups stand to profit by the regimentation of an ever-expanding private life. Such restriction would mean nothing less than providing individuals and their associations with alternative opportunities for structuring their spare time, for making something of their leisure—even though this be at public expense. While it is desirable, it is not indispensable to have private enterprise compete to satisfy these diverse needs. Man can pursue the good at a public beach as well as a private one—provided always he is not more crowded than he wants to be.

Of course, practical problems inevitably arise when men's goals, and the associations they form to realize them, come into conflict. These conflicts cannot be solved by affirming the need for an all-pervasive social pluralism, the consequent civil right to enter and depart from social establishments, and the seemingly ultimate right to unconditional privacy. Socially, we must still be concerned with the substance of man's private life, with the character of his liberty. The impact of his action on society forces society to consider what he is after, and, if need be, to frustrate him. Under what conditions is it justified in doing so?

Society cannot be indifferent to individual ends; it cannot accept a merely formal definition of freedom, as opposed to one which substantively specifies its quality and aim. A formal definition has often appeared acceptable on either of two grounds: that men naturally use their freedom toward good ends, or that how men use it will not matter to society. Neither of these grounds, we know, can hold. There may, however, be a more weighty justification for providing a merely formal definition: the conviction that a substantive one is so well understood and so widely acted upon in practice that we need not be particularly specific in stating it. It is not that men will naturally use their freedom toward good ends or that society may be indifferent toward what they do when left alone. Rather, it is that they are in fact made to think and act virtuously by existing institutions. Yet from a social point of view, we are not likely to be satisfied with this, either. We have rightly begun to suspect the assumption underlying Adam Smith's great argument for capitalism, that it is possible to arrange social institutions in such a way as "to direct vanity to proper objects." We have begun to doubt the possibility of enlisting man's selfish drives to achieve the public good through an arrangement which makes the good attractive to those drives. Consequently we are again forced to consider it essential to train the will to pursue the good, and to pursue it courageously, consistently, and resolutely. Even if we merely insist that we might achieve this negatively by freeing men of the temptations and compulsions to do wrong, we are not confident, despite our sentiments, about the capacity of our present nongovernmental institutions to instill public virtue voluntarily. We feel, especially when survival is threatened, that the various personal and institutional interpretations of the public good do not generate the kind of patriotism necessary to maintain public order. We doubt man's willingness to transcend self-interest; we do not believe that he will naturally identify his self-interest with the public interest; and we suspect finally that the practices of his associations for culture and profit will not direct his own interests toward public interests. And entertaining doubts, we are prepared to introduce an illiberal regime. How can we check this tendency?

A pure formalism leaves us dissatisfied. Yet promoting or instilling something else will not do either. We might, as we have done before, place our faith in the progressive results of education and enlightenment, trusting that where there is knowledge and light there will be wisdom and goodness. We might—but not with justifiable confidence. What we can reasonably do, however, is to reinforce the ever-possible coincidence that the right-minded will also be the free, that men graced by public virtue will coincidentally have public power. Although there is no way of finally assuring this, no way which is safe, there is a guiding principle, none the worse for being formal: the only way to preserve a community prepared to cope with emergencies by bending the will of individuals toward common purposes and yet resolved to protect individual rights is by maintaining conflicting absolutes in a state of balance. This calls for a conception of the best possible state not merely as one which has managed to strike some balance or another but—and this is crucial—as one which assures the possibility that a balance may again and again be struck under varying circumstances, during times of prosperity as well as of misfortune.

Because the setting of such a balance is necessarily public business, because it should be an expression of the most generalized will, it becomes intolerable to permit private groups to set it with finality. And it becomes insidious as well as intolerable to permit public groups to emerge as shields for private ones. That private groups, not to mention individuals, should pressure for what they believe to be in the public interest goes without saying. It is incumbent on them, and in their own interest, to judge the state in reference to their own needs and hopes. The good man is indeed obliged to judge the goodness of the state. But public bodies—regulatory agencies, legislatures, courts—need not feel thus obliged. They need do no more than make private judgment and private action a genuine possibility. This may require the strongest kind of a state and the most extensive public works—but not a state *defining* the pursuit and content of happiness. On the contrary, none of the postulates which have at various times been identified as absolutely essential to liberalism can rightly receive state support.

Liberals cannot expect the state to subscribe to any of these postulates—including the belief in the inevitability of progress. The notion of progress is especially tenacious; it seems to be the one "essential" of liberalism which has tended to remain after all others have faded under pressure of skeptical analysis. The belief that progress follows naturally once institutional impediments are removed seems absolutely necessary to a liberalism (1) which denies that values can be grounded in metaphysics, (2) which has lost faith in the authority of the human conscience, (3) which is not confident that right reason reveals universals, and (4) which cannot subscribe to the absolutes expressed in natural law. To escape subjective relativism—to escape linking values to Spirits of the Times, to climates of opinion, to triumphant historical forces, to popular majorities, or to potent minorities—a liberalism which has proudly emancipated itself from metaphysics, conscience, right reason, and natural law seems driven to embrace the idea of progress and argue for adjusting institutions to the progressive historical process. The problem this poses is obvious: the individuals who are freed from the restraints of an ineffective metaphysics or a man-interpreted natural law are delivered into the hands of the historical process—or, more accurately, into the hands of those who happen to have the power of interpreting and ordering the historical process. And interpretation—even interpretation by the scientist using the methods of a naturalistic, empirical science— is ordering. It is experimental reconstruction, the relentless disciplining of the object under investigation. If this is true, even those liberals who have divested themselves of every assumption of eighteenth-century liberalism except a residual belief in progress are confronted by alternative orders and the need to justify them. To subscribe to natural progress is no escape.

All that is possible, then, is not to permit final acceptance of any public solution to the problem of which alternative public order is just. For this denial we require institutions assuring irresolution, and emphatically not a school of philosophy. The only public philosophy we do need is one which surely does not deserve the name, for it is wholly negative. An affirmative philosophy which specifies what order of goods is just, must always be deflected by us the moment it begins to become effective in the public sphere—no matter how much consensus there may be on it. To permit it to become potent, to provide it with the power of the state, is in fact to permit it to become untrue to what must be its own assumption—namely, that autonomous men cannot help but embrace the good.

To insist that state power may not support the goods private men seek to make public is not to deflate the power of the state. A state encouraging men to press their various claims, none of which can be seen as ultimate, must have the supreme power to create and preserve the balance among them. And since this power will not spontaneously radiate from man's nonpolitical behavior, there must always be sufficient public power to realize whatever balance may be called for. Here Reinhold Niebuhr's position is wholly to the point. Social life, he has said, will not develop an ideal balance unless it is consciously managed. It will not, of itself,

develop perfect equilibria of power. Its capricious disproportions of power generate various forms of domination and enslavement. Human society therefore requires a conscious control and manipulation of the various equilibria which exist in it. There must be an organizing centre within a given field of social vitalities. This centre must arbitrate con-flicts from a more impartial perspective than is available to any party of a given conflict; it must manage and manipulate the processes of mutual support so that the tensions inherent in them will not erupt into conflict; it must coerce submission . . . whenever the instruments of arbitrating and composing conflict do not suffice; and finally it must seek to redress the disproportions of power by conscious shifts of the balances whenever they make for injustice.[3]

The effort to prevent the institutionalization of injustice must originate in a center of power at least partially protected from the pleasures and displeasures of those whose lives are affected by its decisions. "Between father and son," Yves R. Simon has written, "unity is too close for justice to obtain in the purity of its distinctive essence . . . for justice implies otherness."[4] Insofar as we cannot rely on the good will of the parties whose interests conflict, we require the central organization of public power—which alone makes it possible for men to pursue the good as they behold it.

Thus an integral liberal theory postulates as essential (1) a variable social base, (2) a variable moral order, and (3) a state which provides for the continuity of these variations, which provides for the maintenance of a changeable, moving equilibrium. These elements derive their title exclusively from the respect for the eminence of the human personality. However unrecognized, they inhere in individualism. Without them, individualism is barren.

The dilemma of individualism masquerading as full-bodied political theory—so sharply sensed by Rousseau and so effectively exploited by totalitarian dictators—should be obvious enough: such a theory insists on the primacy of the individual but is always confronted by the individual's need for society and compulsion. In the absence of compulsion, men cannot be free and in the absence of freedom the individualist vision becomes irrelevant. Deprived of his moral freedom when socialized and yet helpless when alone, man is necessarily in a state of tension. This tension has traditionally instigated speculation about the appropriateness of specific institutions for bringing order to what is no less than the human condition. Such order, however, invariably meant the renewed limitation of individuals, the politicizing and integrating of citizens. The knowledge that to realize man's nature it is normatively indispensable to preserve a conception of both the autonomous person and of the directing community, of both individual freedom and social security, shapes a dilemma which, short of an all-too-holy synthesis beyond human understanding, cannot be resolved.

But this does not mean that the tension-relieving institutions men construct and polemicists justify are beyond assessing. It remains possible to assess them in reference to their compatibility with the principles of constitutionalism. It is the characteristic and principled insistence of constitutionalism to provide no secular solution for the fate which is inescapably the human one. Constitutionalism achieves in practice what liberalism demands in theory—it frustrates the realization of all abstract ideals, resting, as Acton's view of American federalism clarifies, on "momentary suspensions of war between opposite principles, neither of which could prevail."[5] At some cost, it institutionally preserves the suspense, the risk, and the tragedy of man's condition.

Precisely to the extent that human ideals become institutionally identified and fixed—as, for example, in the form of the American federal system—they must come into conflict with the norm of constitutionalism. They impose a settled order upon an unsettled community. This may suggest that some institutions are in principle more "constitutional," while others are clearly less so. But like liberalism, constitutionalism has no *specific* institutional implications. Essentially, it makes men aware of a situation, bids them to beware, and induces them to minimal action. It compels no more than an awareness of the undesirability—from the point of view of an ideal liberalism—of the pervasive social control of human life. It insists precisely on the degree of control, and no more, that is necessary to preserve an indeterminate, free area.

What policies to adopt and what restrictions to impose for realizing a maximum of freedom can consequently always remain a practical question tolerating many answers. In a dynamic society, the answers will depend on prevailing conditions, and to provide answers is to date them. What we know empirically and hypothetically about human behavior can always, in practice, be enlisted to maximize individuality and freedom. Priorities may be rationally assigned to various possible, functionally equivalent policies. Recognizing the need for self-esteem as the basis for genuine individuality, for example, we might foster the institutions which generate it. But what the plan consists of cannot be specified once and for all. It must always rest on an assessment of political contingencies, on weighing and balancing the variety of existing power blocs, on that kind of sympathetic understanding of actual and latent power alignments which the statesman, by definition, brings to the sphere of politics. It is his role to discover and to promote the proper balance of liberty and coercion, whether he uses the rhetoric and office of the senator, the judge, or the administrator. Holding off all final answers, he may preserve the alternative ideals for which men in fact struggle, preserve them not as concrete manifestations but as myths and symbols.

To keep men from being wholly satisfied by social plans is no easy matter, as those responsible for the enforcement of the suspension of hostilities (and these are our politicians, if not our ultimate statesmen) are always compelled to recognize. To maintain the norm of constitutionalism, to preserve a perpetual state of irresolution, requires leaving the precious things of the spirit untouched and unsettled, permitting men to be guided by socially unharnessed curiosity, keeping the state, as Roger Williams had preached, from enforcing morality and piety.

It is precisely the institution of constitutionalism which can brace the liberal legislator who is troubled by the need to touch and settle matters of the spirit, to put curiosity into social harness, to use the power of the state to enforce morality and piety. By what principles might his conduct be made legitimate? How, in practice, might such principles conserve liberalism? How can the norms of constitutionalism maintain the open-ended society?

The legislator's awareness of the need to enforce routines and to prescribe order does not compel defense of any specific settlement he favors. To admit man's need for community is not to decide which community he requires. The practice of constitutionalism does no more than give point to the belief that the community which man does require is never obviously beyond challenge. If liberties must be curtailed when a substantive public interest defines itself under pressure, an operative constitutionalism will at least hold this to a minimum. It works so as to permit the ever-renewed redetermination of the area of freedom, asking for the credentials of forces which threaten to qualify freedom. By insisting on due and proper process, it allows hurt interest to be influential, and thus makes it possible to keep redrawing the boundaries of the private sectors invaded and occupied by public ones. While experience, as acted on by individuals, may seem to make it incessantly imperative to curb some human aspirations, to suspend some liberties, constitutionalism makes it possible to preserve a maximum of tolerance for them as the overriding public good. The problem of discovering the proper balance between private freedom and public power, the problem of ordering liberty, is thus to impose not abstract, final ends but rather an ever-changing practical one of means, one of determining just how the greatest diversity of interests may be preserved, by force if necessary, in specific situations and at particular times.

To preserve interests in their variety, to prevent the concerted imposition of any one to the exclusion of all others, we must remain intolerant of any full grants of substantive rights. The policies adopted by constitutional regimes must, in the absence of a pervasive consensus, consistently deny claims advanced in the absolute terms of natural law. The justification of public laws—whether these be executive orders, administrative rulings, legislative bills, or judicial decisions—cannot be natural law, the tortuous language of American constitutional interpretation to the contrary. The ground of an appeal to convert private insight into public law can only be that the tradition of constitutionalism itself will thereby be enhanced.

Those who espouse liberalism actually have no choice in the matter. They might let positive law reign, play pure power politics, appeal not to morality but to utility and expediency. Alternatively, to preserve the peace, they might appeal to an unstained revelation about the substance of the good society. But in either case, their liberalism is obviously compromised. If policy is to be rationally justified, the appeal can only be to constitutional tradition. All claims for a slice of the national budget or for a part of community resources must be made by referring to constitutional practice. They must be based on supposed procedural benefits, not on substantive rights. What may be ignored when claims are entered is the source of rights as Grotius had defined it, namely, as "that quality in a person which makes it just or right for him either to possess certain things or to do certain actions."[6] In a constitutional regime, all inviolable rights are procedural, and any conflict between them, even when substantive rights appear to be involved, should be seen and analyzed as a conflict between procedural ones.[7] Thus alternative policies presented by interested parties must be reviewed not as pleas for the enactment of alternative creeds (which they may well be) but instead as alternative interpretations of methods by which such special creeds can be kept from becoming common ones. About these interpretations men will differ, thereby justifying the elaborate machinery through which agreement and disagreement may find expression. These differences cannot, however, be seen as disagreements about ends, about the right to enjoy substantive goods, "to possess certain things or to do certain actions."

This view should make clear that all substantive rights—the right to work, to follow one's calling, to free speech, to voluntary association, to unfettered movement—are properly absorbed by procedural rights. One practical consequence should be manifest in the nature of the brief which would have to be offered in behalf of claimed rights. Petitions or bills couched in the absolutist language of the true believer must suffer translation into terms revealing how what is demanded is ultimately related to constitutionalism. This should open the opportunity for demonstration, observation, and testing. The argument in behalf of a claimed right—unsupported by a natural law which, if it testifies at all, can testify only about private goods—must indicate in what way a denied right will violate the integrity of the mechanisms, the processes, the institutions of constitutionalism. Even where the alleged imperatives of natural law or of empirical science are explicitly introduced to support the soundness of a public grant or deprivation, the only source of legitimacy must be constitutionalism itself. Thus the plea to furnish individuals with the benefits of an education, for example, cannot rest on the ground that schooling is their inalienable, substantive right, essential to their health and happiness, or that a healthy personality structure cannot, empirically, be achieved otherwise. Rather it must be shown that without a certain type of education the devices of constitutionalism are not likely to be widely used, that interest in employing them is likely to wane, and that unless such education is provided the settlement of controversies by force can reasonably be anticipated. Insofar as the test to be applied to policy is whether it tends to destroy the viability of constitutional procedures, we may reject as unjustified even thoroughly popular or tacitly accepted policies. If the decisions arrived at by the methods of constitutionalism threaten the continuous use of these methods, these decisions themselves become objectionable.

Because not all procedures are equally crucial to the continuance of constitutionalism, a hierarchy of procedural priorities may in practice be established, with the right to be free to register a meaningful vote necessarily topping all others. To abridge that right and all that it entails must require the ultimate argument that, unless it is abridged, the entire republic is certain to perish. To alter it in the absence of a total threat must therefore be made difficult in the extreme. Thus change of personnel or policy will require far less consent than proposals to affect the procedures by which public officials are selected and by which they legislate. To change such procedures is to amend the constitution itself, justifiable only by the need to keep alive the possibility of dissent, the likelihood of free consensus.

There may well be no other ultimate justification for the right to dissent than man's natural inclination to assert it—to assert it, indeed, even in the very effort of disavowing it. To keep men from acting on the basis of their conviction that dissent from their own view is intolerable, to keep the dissenter from subverting the civil order, they must be themselves persuaded that the reasons for their position do not go unconsidered.

Nothing less can actually satisfy those of us who recognize that something more than an uncomplicated individualism is necessary and who at the same time will not trust others to specify its ingredients. Those who cannot bring themselves to accept the visionary prepared to define social justice but who are nevertheless intent on considering his view (if for no other reason than to involve and discipline him in a functioning procedural system) have no choice but to value whatever institutions lead individuals to submit their visions for public consideration. What thus becomes legitimate, in sum, is not some substantive definition of either freedom or order, but a set of variable procedures. If these procedures are complicated, this is only because they are designed to invite men to offer their programs.

To make this invitation significant requires that public law be publicly enacted, that legislators and judges are compelled to make their laws and decisions explicit. The reason for this is not the pathetic hope that our rulers will hesitate to convert what is inhuman, evil, or cruel into law, not Lon L. Fuller's faith that "coherence and goodness have more affinity than coherence and evil."[8] It is rather the probability that legislators and judges, when forced to be coherent, reflective, and explicit, will actually consider the views of potential dissenters, partisans, and subversives. Thus the question is not whether a governor will be struck by his conscience when he must openly say what he means, but merely whether he will respond to all the various competing claims before him.

Because this is likely, specific procedures and institutions become instrumentally valuable to constitutionalism, and it becomes essential to stipulate that public decisions be responsible and representative ones in the sense that their enactment is preceded by a process which makes each person count for one politically, a process which compels consideration of interests because policy will affect them.

It is only by preserving the possibility of dissent—and thereby of social friction, of value alternatives, of individual freedom—that the norm of constitutionalism will implement the individualist impulse of liberalism. Since the opportunity to register dissent lies at the very center of the constitutional regime, constitutionalism must be identified with the institution of peaceful compromise by means of politics, by means of publicly adjusting antagonistic interests without forcefully suppressing them. It must value the limitation of conflict between interests, and as a corollary, the establishment of the one instrument through which conflict can be effectively maintained—an institutionalized opposition. The governmental machinery, in its actual design tolerating the greatest of variations, must direct the pressures of the opposition so that they will make themselves felt even when those who exercise public power are thereby made uncomfortable. The discomfort of not heeding opposing voices must simply be greater than that of heeding them. This places public officials not only into an office where they must listen to all comers but into one where they know they will be rewarded if they are consistently attentive.

It is easy to determine whether a system having such effects functions properly by noting whether officials are really forced to take the variety of existing interests into account. As long as all the various publics in question have the opportunity to express and register what is in their interest, officials will be sensitive to them, for their very offices depend on public favor. These publics, it is here assumed, need not be enlightened about anything but their own interests. And he who governs need not be enlightened about anything but his own interests. His task, however, is more demanding than theirs, for he must weigh his stake in his office against his own ideals. Thus an effort to achieve unity of policy, to make officials weigh private and public goods simultaneously, naturally assumes some degree of rationality in those who govern; it assumes they will be inclined to calculate their interests rationally. However dubious, this assumption is at least less implausible than the only alternative: that officials are not likely to confuse private desires and public interests. Taking account of human weaknesses, it makes for a government of modest, merely human aims. A government constructed in accordance with it, Jefferson wrote in 1798, "is founded in jealousy and not in confidence; it is jealousy and not confidence which prescribes limited constitutions to bind down those whom we are obliged to trust with power. . . ."[9] Hamilton said as much when he noted that writers on politics

have established it as a maxim that, in contriving any system of government, and fixing the several checks and controls of the constitution, every man ought to be supposed a knave; and to have no other end, in all his actions, but private interests. By this interest we must govern him; and, by means of it, make him co-operate to public good, notwithstanding his insatiable avarice and ambition. Without this, we shall in vain boast of the advantages of any constitution.[10]

The steady moderation of ideals this enforces was clearly seen by Tocqueville:

The principle of self-interest rightly understood is not a lofty one, but it is clear and sure. It does not aim at mighty objects, but it attains . . . all those at which it aims. By its admirable conformity to human weaknesses it easily obtains great dominion; nor is that dominion precarious, since the principle checks one personal interest by another, and uses, to direct the passions, the very same instrument that excites them.[11]

Such an institutionalized public attempt to check personal interests cannot make for a spirited and exhilarating political order. Neutralizing public vice, it dispenses with the need for public virtue. At the same time, it does respond to the warnings we find implicit in history. History, after all, has shown how all warring parties but one will be quieted when conflicts between interests are not restrained. It has shown that when minorities or majorities are free to operate without inhibition they will want and get their way; they will take full charge, become the infallible state, and standardize the ends of life by forcing all interests to blend in the name of that Platonic unity which Aristotle thought it necessary to criticize. Constitutionalism responds to the experience which indicates that force and violence, when permitted to run their course, settle matters with finality; it responds by making it possible to formulate public policy by peaceful bargaining, bargaining resting on political statesmanship which recognizes that what negotiation closes renegotiation may open. To foreclose the full institution of any particular interest, constitutionalism guarantees that in the fight for public policy no clear-cut victories can be won. It is this guarantee, and no other, which in a constitutional regime must be generally valued and accepted as the fundamental element of political life.

In practice, every power bloc, because it is potentially overbearing, must therefore be accessible to challenge by an opposition prepared to counter it on terms of equality. This, in turn, requires that particular single-interest minorities have the freedom to organize an opposition equipped with resources for making itself felt. They must have the opportunity to become temporary, revolving majorities. Such an opportunity, exercised through institutionalized coalitions, must always be present since individuals ought not to be compelled to exhaust themselves in public functions by being forced to participate in the leisure-killing task of organizing majorities *ad hoc,* again and again. The organizational bases for an opposition party system which gives an electorate the option of choice between alternative policies must therefore be stable and durable, protected from serious disorganization and humiliation, able to survive repeated defeats. When such publicly supported bases exist, majority decisions, even when engineered by minorities, tend to become acceptable to all, not because they have merit but because they are understood to be impermanent.

The institutions which secure the transitory character of decisions will protect the citizen's paramount public interest: his right to unsettle a majority settlement. As long as this public interest is not touched by majorities, the individual may, without blame, tend to his private interests. Concerned as he is, then, not with good government but with the frustration of misgovernment, he may remain politically apathetic, letting professionals fight it out until their fights affect him and stir him out of his apathy. While his moral sense must still oblige him to participate when what should be transitory becomes intransigent and hardened, the very basest of his inclinations will quite naturally oblige him to participate the moment he feels that his private economic, spiritual, and moral goods are somehow threatened.

Ideally, an arrangement which takes account of these premises, which checks unfettered individualism, immoderate partisanship, and monopolistic officialdom, is one for making public policy by forcing aspiring policy makers to acquire their power through an open competition for votes. Seeking to form a majority to gain the power to legislate—power which may be as sharply concentrated as it is in the American Presidency—candidates (and those who push them to become candidates) are compelled to moderate their opinions because every voter is seen as potentially in opposition. He is seen as potentially favoring opposed legislative programs. In such a system there is always the record made by those who have gained the majority's confidence; and there are the promises made by those who still seek to gain it. When effective, this system provides for rule by civil majorities genuinely free to vote. What makes the majorities civil is an opposition naturally inclined to insist that no one who informs the public may monopolize the channels of communication, that those who listen must have had an opportunity to make up minds which they can call their own because they are unintimidated, because they are economically and psychologically secure.

There is of course plentiful evidence showing that the revolving coalitions which seek to exercise governmental power will be run by oligarchies interested in advancing their own welfare. Michels, Mosca, and Pareto remain as right as ever: political parties tend to be complex, bureaucratic, and oligarchical. While an opposing oligarchy is certain to make the effort to expose the incompetence and injustices of the oligarchy in power, this may not be sufficient to keep constitutionalism alive. "The democratic currents of history resemble successive waves," Robert Michels had written in 1915. "They break ever on the same shoals. . . . It is probable that this cruel game will continue without end."[12] But these pessimistic conclusions should lose power when an additional social force—a complicated, multiform, open-ended society—is present and effective. Moreover, the very desire of every rational oligarchy to maintain itself in an environment it finds only partially manageable will tend to compel it to extend a helping hand to those who, within limits, represent different ideas and different interests. To conserve that range of economic and social values which its own position seeks to secure, to prevent itself from becoming detached from a restless, ever-reorganizing social base, an oligarchy itself is likely to provide regular procedures for criticism. Seen in this light, a constitutionalism which legalizes loyal oppositions becomes a function of the determination of an oligarchy to remain viable.[18] Thus the presence of oligarchical tendencies need spell no end to the kind of policy which gives all men the opportunity to familiarize themselves with parliamentarianism, that is, with the procedures and traditions of the kind of politics which frustrates efforts to give ideals some final institutional embodiment.

Although the large-scale, oligarchically governed organization is not inherently incompatible with constitutionalism, other forces may well be. To make a constitutional system workable, to operate its machinery once gifted statesmen have had the opportunity to design it, requires more than the kind of patriotism displayed during periods of national crisis. It requires public-spiritedness. There must be a concern—its extent depending on ever-varying circumstances—for the public good, a willingness to agree on public issues so that it may be possible to form a provisionally concurring majority from which no one, or practically no one, feels alienated. Temporarily agreeing on some policies, individuals need not, of course, feel impelled to agree on any in particular. The solidarity of the community will be sufficiently secure as long as individuals are not driven en masse to become enemies of those classes—the middle classes—who obviously and immediately benefit by the health of the system. Since the need is but for a partial consensus on social objectives, the political disinterestedness of even the most virtuous of citizens cannot be deemed reprehensible. Excused from taking part in every public contest, they may abstain from politics, guarding their capacity to understand and judge it. To the extent that they become interested, they are burdened with the freedom to examine, judge, and reverse those in power, but no more. While they must be assumed to have a decent respect for the public order, they are not expected to contribute a "rational" or "objective" view to politics. Their participation in specific political contests is not premised on their rationality, on their capacity for objectivity. All that is expected is that they respond when public policy happens to attract or repel them. Given the recurring opportunity to register dissatisfactions, they are not driven into the political wilderness, induced to become partisan fanatics and forced to involve their whole selves in the pursuit of any single good. Men of diverse parts, they can remain ambiguous and thus hard for politicians to commit, to activate, and to pin down. Their ultimate commitment will be not to the commands of the legislator but to the rules which, specifying basic lawmaking procedures, accredit the legislator's action.

If this is the sole definition of public morality—an allegiance to constitutionalism—it should not be surprising to find few members of society prepared to express an emotional commitment to it. During normal times, one should not expect its vigorous exaltation and defense. On the contrary, one should find it, if at all, well submerged, not an object of contention, not actually involved in any domestic political struggle. Thus the public good will remain undebated, unmobilized, something quite simply accepted.

And it is this implicit, ordinarily unconscious consensus which, if the mandate to act in the public interest is to be obeyed, must be explicitly weighed by those who have been elevated to administer the public domain. What the administrator must recognize is the interest of man as citizen, of man as needful not of this contract or that statute but of lawfulness and the conditions which ensure its perpetuity. Thus constitutionalism per se again emerges as the merely formal standard it is here postulated to be.

This, however, is not enough; constitutionalism is not self-sustaining. There must be the will to carry it out, the public spirit to make it work. Even the existence of mechanisms aiding the growth of countervailing power in society will not, in itself, guarantee that these mechanisms remain autonomous; they, too, depend on men and their ideas. There is no institutionalized check on power unless men agree to sustain the institutions which make the check effective. Hence there must be agreement on what is fundamental to the institutions, and this is the liberal ideal of settling power conflicts gently, without force. This agreement is likely to commend itself on utilitarian grounds. But even beyond all utility, it must remain, as an ideal, the crucial moral basis for the good society.

Beyond the general resolve to make it work, the institutionalization of civil politics requires a citizenry able to take for granted that due process of law is popularly respected. There must be a consensus on form, on the institutions which ensure disagreement with public enactments. To attain such respect and consensus, contemporary historical conditions impose an additional requirement. Even if social equality is as little intrinsic to constitutionalism as social inequality, there has emerged a connection between social equality (indeed, equality of social and economic opportunity) and constitutionalism. It is no longer likely that information about the material living standards of all social classes can be withheld and kept from creating resentments. After both literacy and a kind of means-ends rationality have become widespread through technology, all groups in society are bound to learn about the conditions of others. It therefore becomes questionable whether constitutionalism can today be maintained in the face of social inequality, whether an awareness of social inequality would not create the frustrations and discontents which doom constitutionalism. Those who lack what some define as intelligence may be ultimately beyond consolation unless they know they too have genuine authority. Thus the general knowledge, supported by experience, that no elite—not even a "natural" elite of the well educated, the talented, and the benevolent—has final authority to govern becomes a condition of constitutionalism. Constitutionalism today would seem to be incapable of dispensing with a democratic element, an equalitarian base.

That the necessary diffusion of authority due to the enlargement of the citizenry poses problems for the viability of constitutionalism is obvious enough. The citizenry, however extensive, must still possess that degree of civility, charity, and rationality

without which there can be no effective leadership, and no satisfaction in exercising it. In the absence of a public-spirited body
politic, the very best government will be government by a leadership consistently more attached to office than to principles. Such
a government—often the only possible government, and always
better than tyranny—can do no more than reflect and reinforce
the social and economic status quo. But if constitutionalism is
to be maintained under ever-changing historical conditions, conditions which even the most powerful of elites have so far found
it impossible to control, the officeholder must more than mirror
the public will. He must be imaginative and active, reflecting even
the submerged, imponderable, and remote concerns that find no
organized manifestation in the society he leads. These inchoate
concerns he must discover. A two-party system which compels
consideration of multitudinous interests will not spontaneously
incorporate those incipient, potential, or muted interests which
the political leader must take note of to preserve the constitutional
system in times of stress. In itself, a two-party system will not force
him to devise corrective programs, to transcend the common denominator of existing interests. Because it will not, it has been
tempting to speak of "the failure of representative democracy"
and "the need for government by aristocracy." This new conservatism, clarifying the limits of a party system, is not beside the
point. But it fails to address itself to the problem of institutionalizing the responsibility of governors whose horizon must be
broader than the combination of all entrenched and organized
interests. To meet this problem—and thus to make constitutionalism operative and durable—the education of leadership must
be conceived as not merely private business. The formation of
character, in the best constitutional order, must be a public concern. It cannot find its proper foundation in the tastes and inclinations of parochial minorities who employ servile or self-serving
superintendents of public instruction. The state, Jefferson wrote
in 1782, must be supplied with

those talents which nature has sown as liberally among the poor as the
rich, but which perish without use, if not sought for and cultivated. . . .
Every government degenerates when trusted to the rulers of the people

alone. The people themselves therefore are its only safe depositories. *And to render even them safe, their minds must be improved to a certain degree.* This indeed is not all that is necessary, though it be essentially necessary. An amendment of our constitution must here come in aid of the public education.[14]

A view which denies that constitutional democracy aims at instituting absolutes, which demands, as central to its creed, at least some separation of church and state, is an embarrassment to liberals who will not recognize that in the public arena no natural law is needed.[15] Constitutionalism, it is true, is feasible only as long as unspecified objectives are sought by society, when there is no need for the righteous pursuit of public causes. Constitutionalism impedes those intransigents who know right from wrong and are ready to impose their vision with enthusiasm. Such an impediment, it may be conceded, does not consistently work in behalf of the public good. Still, natural law may be enforced without reservations only when its meaning is *fully* revealed, when it is devoid of *all* ambiguity, and when, in fact, its enforcement has become quite indispensable because men have entered that absolutely best society in which public and private areas are indistinguishable and questions about the desirability of institutions need no longer be raised. What constitutionalism disallows, then, is precisely a public philosophy and a brotherhood of man—in the public sphere.

This formulation does not compel us to say that as nonpolitical beings men are unable to apprehend a transcendental good, that they cannot transcend self-interest. Indeed, the realization that they can, as the previous discussion showed, makes majority rule tolerable to the minority. There is in fact a normative public interest: the public interest in constitutional democracy, in a civil process of law. And this interest entails personal concern for whatever conditions make procedures effective and meaningful. Such a sentiment, properly seen, is patriotic. Thus constitutional democracy cannot wholly agree with Orestes Brownson's estimate: "Patriotism and philanthropy with the planter are in his cotton bags, with the farmer in his wheatfield, with the manufacturer in his spindle and loom, with the banker in his notes, with the merchant in his shops or counting room."[16] Man thus conceived is wholly the victim of his passions and unable to transcend them. He is wholly attached to his emotions, to his interests, to himself.

The theory of constitutional democracy, on the other hand, recognizes man's capacity to pursue specific goods with repeated references to the general good, to the rights of due process. As men engage in debate concerning their own goods, they bring about a confrontation of conflicting goods, broaden their perceptions, and enhance sensitivity to the justice in conflicting claims. That each of them in fact has such moral sensitivity cannot be shown empirically; indeed, there may be no persuasive refutation to the contention that nothing is above man's self-interest. Yet constitutional democrats can be comforted by the knowledge that a convincing case for determinism must rest on the assumption that at least some matters are indeterminate, exempt from the grasp of determinism. Of course, specific propositions advanced by particular individuals are rarely the embodiment of pure rationality; hence a constitutional regime may rightly frustrate one of its citizens as he presses his case. But at the same time, it should always be possible to make clear to him that he has, in Ralph Barton Perry's language, "also willed the system within which he has been outvoted, and with this will even his defeat is in agreement."[17] Therefore he supports not particular decisions but a political system in general, a universal process for political conciliation and compromise, a means for communication and negotiation between social interests, a method for hedging and qualifying, for making amendable decisions. Through this technique, it is assumed, the necessary common life of individuals is best ordered. Merely being instrumental, denouncing substantive goals provided by those who know good and evil conclusively, the system asks its supporters to share and, if necessary, to sacrifice their money, leisure, and lives to defend those principles which make compromises ever possible.

Constitutional democracy therefore does imply a theory of the general good of the whole community, a theory always referring to the specific goods of individuals but encompassing the interests of all classes. It is true, as Harold J. Laski argued all his life, that this theory had been the ideology of a class whose special interests it sought to justify. But it was never restrictive in its claims. No principle—only material conditions, only natural limitations—precludes the possibility that a liberal social order implemented by the devices of constitutionalism may be extended to permeate the entire community. All that is essential is to find the resources to inhibit those contingent forces which keep property, education, and leisure from being widely distributed. The universalistic affirmation of constitutional democracy—that all but the best things in life are definable social goods—rests on the nondeterminist, non-Marxian conviction that these social goods can be agreed upon by every class and faction. It suggests that some significant action is rational and disinterested, inspired by something other than innate drives, class instincts, culture patterns, or historical facts. It postulates a basic consensus, a shared loyalty to the governmental, constitutional mechanisms which secure for all equally the right to formulate a just organization of interests, the freedom for moral action. And although it can never respond conclusively to the articulated intuitions of the irreconcilable elements of society, its prejudice continually obligates it to come through with an answer, at least to react by a genuine consideration of the ground upon which the fanatic objector takes his stand. It must acknowledge the dissenter's rationality, for without assuming it, democracy is inconceivable. It is best to concede this—as well as to realize that nothing compels us to believe that democracy must prevail.

The individual's capability of freely exercising his right reason is ultimately a precondition of democracy. If the alternatives to democracy are undesirable, so is any alternative postulate about the nature of the individual. Although he must therefore be conceived of as rational (as long as democracy is to be conceived of as possible), we are not forced to conclude that democracy will at any one time be more widespread than individual rationality. If rationality cannot be forcefully instilled without upsetting the very institutions rationality supposedly supports, if at best it can be but cautiously cultivated, a good deal of luck is necessary to maintain democratic institutions. It is no longer fashionable to counsel reliance on the presence of hoped-for coincidences. But working actively to *produce* the necessary coincidences, as opposed to making the most of those which providentially occur, will help destroy the very regime we deem good. Without a bit of luck, then, democratic constitutionalism is undone. There is no harm in saying so.

Of course an acute problem is posed when we require that individuals commit themselves to preserve procedural freedom and when we insist, at the same time, that they develop no lasting affection for any incarnated community good. Should a galvanizing myth be needed to make men work together, constitutional democracy is dangerously exposed, for it is surely hard to fire people with faith in a procedural system. Nevertheless, the problem is not beyond reduction. Not all men need a myth of unifying symbols. Some might rationally perceive that their private goods are best realized in its absence, that men can be saved only when there is no public good. These will surely prize the interest politics engendered by the realization that virtue is not to be instituted. They will cherish a system which, as Fred W. Riggs has said, "grants to every interest a means of seeking relief, a safety valve whereby every minority may obtain a modicum of justice. Injustice cannot be eliminated, but at least it is not frozen into the political structure beyond any possibility of change."[18] There will be some who can appreciate, in reference to their own desires, that the price of not gaining virtue in society—for those who would make us virtuous could not avail themselves of the coercive power of the state—is that of not eliminating sin. They would understand that, if sin is to be eliminated, the purge must be a private one. And they would conceivably esteem a system which makes it impossible to define and establish what the words of the preamble of the United States Constitution so imperiously demand.

Of course nothing guarantees that those who have such modest expectations will be in the majority. But this is no cause for despair. Today, the needs of community-craving men may well be channeled; their excessive energies may perhaps be given the opportunity to become exhausted in private. It is not impossible to provide them with at least some of the ground for self-fulfillment within associations, to encourage the growth of limited states in which their ideal self and the general will are in fact one. When they are either too distracted or too committed to engage in the intellectual calculation which leads to an awareness of the value of separating public from private goods, they may be led to find their fulfillment in private, or else in single-purpose, limited-objective organizations—not in the nation as total community, not in the great society. True, this would hardly give full credit to their cosmological vision of the just society. After all, the all-comprehensive myth which activates them is for them not a hypothetical postulate but indubitable truth. Still, we need not deprive them of the very conviction which gives meaning to their lives. We need merely insist that such dedication and conviction—without which men and their societies admittedly fall apart—must be pushed toward the private arena, that justice for society can only be negatively defined, that the truly just society is the noninstituted, unrealized city of God. For that city alone, men may claim substantive due process. To the extent that they are prepared to communicate, to enter into human society, their own belief in the purity of their ideal may well be relied on to evoke their always qualified loyalty to the prevailing institutions of this world, to the formal procedures of constitutional regimes, to a civil polity. Thus while sustained by the faith which gives individuals their peculiar significance and destiny, they may yet be encouraged to make a free and rational commitment to a constitutional democracy, both as theory and as practice.

With Josiah Royce, they may be loyal to a system which recognizes man's communities as ever-unfinished processes, as always subject to human error. They may, in short, value a system which postulates a body politic acknowledging the loyalty and good will of the opposition because otherwise, as Santayana had noted (writing in 1920 on "English Liberty in America"), a majority decision "would be as alien a fatality to any minority as the decree of a foreign tyrant, and at every election the right of rebellion would come into play." It presupposes, as John Stuart Mill rightly stressed, a homogeneous society devoted to those constitutional bonds which are artfully contrived to leave some of the ends of life open, to provide the conditions for the good life. And it assumes what Mill would not formulate: the existence, beyond the world of positive power politics, of an order of truth and justice—one that man has sufficient reason to apprehend and approach, one that supports the institution of politics by challenging those participants who claim to know virtue and resolve to act morally in public.

14

The Regulation of Groups

Before proposing to reform a society which has mechanized human industry and restricted freedom under the aegis of governmental pluralism, we should clearly map out those tracts of American life in which the conflict between ideal and practice has slowly become glaring. Knowing just where our norms are relevant, we may then feel entitled to revamp the prevailing governmental order as well as the economy which modern technology is bringing into being.

In the course of this study, we have become well aware of the extent to which our lives today are in fact circumscribed both by our political heritage—with its eighteenth-century stress on rights against government, on federalism, and on a separation of powers—and by our unquestioning acceptance of the impact of the machine on the productive process. What has not yet been suggested is how our industrial technology, its attendant social organization, and public government might be transformed, how these, once brought into proper relation with one another, can help provide the conditions for the good life. It becomes essential, then, to ask how to implement our norms, how to bend, if need be, our governmental pluralism, our leviathan organizations, and perhaps even our technology so that they will square with democratic constitutionalism.

More specifically, what public policies should we support today to achieve constitutionalism and thereby to revitalize a dormant liberalism?

We surely cannot, at the outset, permit ourselves to treat our public government, our technology, and our private hierarchies simply as "givens"—implying that someone other than we ourselves fashioned the gift. They are not simply bestowed by God, by nature, or by manifest destiny. Those among us with authority have made them. Those among us with authority can unmake them. When we fail to control them, they do have an inner dynamism, obeying natural laws of development. But if it is possible to speak of the "natural behavior of organizations" or of the "imperatives of technology," this is not because political, technological, and social developments happen to move in a fixed direction but rather because men do not use their given rationality to decide the direction. If the movement of politics, technology, and society has obeyed seemingly inescapable natural laws, it is because men have permitted themselves to be captives of necessity. It is because men have abstained from providing the laws they are free to draft.

As we attempt to gear facts to norms, we should keep in mind that our very political foundation was the result of a convention—indeed, the result of innumerable subsequent conventions and usages, all intended to protect the rights of individual men. If those rights are to remain integral, or to be made so, our constitutional conventions will have to be considered not as finally posited but as open to adaptation, as amenable to deliberate reformulation.

The reformulation of our constitutional laws has been, of course, a continuing enterprise, and there is, in principle, little resistance to it. But the urge to tamper with technology—too often expressed by a nostalgic yearning for simplicity—is less readily respected. Nevertheless, such a concern is just as legitimate as the one which makes us question the splintered forms assumed by American constitutionalism. It may turn out that some of the supposed imperatives of technology are less imperative than they

seem, that we have false notions about the relation between efficiency and size, between economy and standardization, between
progress and conformity. Although we may want the products of
modern technology, the question remains whether we need the
kind and quantity of technology which is at present scheduled to
supply our wants. And even if it should turn out that our un-
checked desire for industrial products and services imposes the
prevailing definitions of efficiency, economy, and progress, we may
yet profit by insisting on a widening of these concepts. We may
yet need to acknowledge that industry's products are not merely
those goods which get the inspector's approving nod at the end of
the assembly line but also the emotional deprivations suffered and
the opportunities enjoyed by workers who contribute their intelligence, skill, and energy to the work process.

If the concepts of efficiency, economy, and progress are to be
stretched so as to include a whole new variety of social values, we
will have to gain the genuine opportunity as citizens both to reflect
and to make our reflections felt. The only way to force industrial
management to consider and accept a broadened concept of efficiency—one which incorporates nontechnological factors—is by
insisting on it through public instrumentalities. Should this not
require the adoption of democratic procedures within the plant,
as it surely need not in any wholesale fashion, it will demand public
direction from the outside. How penetrating such control must
be cannot be answered in abstract terms. It is always a practical
question, and there can be no final answer to it. Thus control
may well be minimal when industrial managers freely accept a
widened concept of efficiency. But when experience keeps us from
believing that voluntary benevolence persists automatically for
very long, there must be the willingness to exercise governmental
power so as to ensure it. Since constitutionalism will not spontaneously result from undirected social evolution, direction is essential. The pressing problem today is that of delimiting the area
properly subject to public control.

There should actually be no question at this point which sectors
of American public life *should* be publicly controlled. The arm
of public government must touch, as intimately and pervasively

as necessary to achieve public purposes, all private elites tending to incorporate society as well as all public agencies tending to collaborate with them. At the same time, public policy must leave alone what can be shown to be private. Once demarcation lines have been clearly drawn, we shall be free to act firmly, energetically, and consistently in the public sphere and, simultaneously, to respect the private sphere as utterly inviolable. While the public order is thereby recognized as one in which responsible conduct is expected, the private one might really be preserved as private— preserved, that is, as irresponsible, wild, disorganized, and nonpolitical. Thus an enlargement of the public sector should mean the simultaneous invigoration of the private one.

All this begs the central question: precisely what *is* public? What, during the second half of the twentieth century, may we consider the sector in which resolute state action is appropriate?

Insofar as an association pursues a single circumscribed, intelligible end, the standard of constitutionalism bars all state intervention in its affairs. There is no ground for interfering with the internal processes of the clearly voluntary single-interest group, however oligarchical, totalitarian, or exclusive its character. If organizations such as the American Legion, the Women's Christian Temperance Union, or the Tobacco Industry Research Council are not single-purpose organizations, it is after all within the power of their members to make them thus: they can leave. Where organizations concerned with the ends of life are separated from the state, where state-sanctioned action does not suffocate a genuine pluralism in the realm of ends, where the perversion of existing churches by an incumbent oligarchy is not fatal to the true believer, there can be no justification for state intervention.

It is imperative to preserve the integrity of whatever associations in society do not exercise the power of the state, for it is only within them, as was argued earlier, that men are able to fulfill themselves. Men must have the opportunity to join groups with which they are wholly in harmony, which do not invite conflict between ego and superego or force them to become hypocritical organization men. They require groups in which the price of membership is neither deception nor self-alienation, groups within which they can find themselves and relax. But there is an even more telling reason, labored to excess by European pluralists, for preserving associational integrity. Only associations can constitute a buffer between the individual and the state. The state is a far greater potential danger to the individual than his own intermediate groups, for the state's power is final. If all this be acknowledged as sound, under what conditions should the state exercise its power over associations?

When an association pursues more than a single objective and is at the same time clearly able to implement its range of objectives, its internal affairs cannot be considered its affairs alone. It is then not merely a coalition embracing numerous conflicting points of view. It is something far more significant: an organization able to immobilize and exploit its members because it can enforce its decisions. As long as the scale for industrial planning and production is large and as long as membership in the large-scale association is involuntary, the association is inevitably driven to establish patterns of work and leisure oligarchically. And the order it then establishes is a public order. Its law affects diversified publics. It confronts the individual directly and loses its role as a buffer. This is all the more true when it avails itself of the instrumentalities of public government to maintain itself, to decide between alternative policies, and to prevent individuals from finding vocational or spiritual fulfillment outside its boundaries.

It is the objective of the association that is relevant here, not its size. Liberalism requires that the norm of constitutionalism be operative in every public order, whatever its size. Of course, the fact that an association is large will increase its likelihood of being a public order, but it does not determine it. However unlikely, the small association may be public and the large one private. Thus the determination in specific cases cannot turn simply on size but rather on the extent of the association's internal consensus.

When a common purpose can be shown to pervade the group, when internal interests do not significantly diverge, the group, to repeat, is emphatically private, and the norm of constitutionalism is irrelevant. Indeed, to insist that constitutionalism be forced on private groups might well frustrate the realization of private goods without serving the fully legitimate public purpose of preserving constitutionalism by allowing for pressure politics, for petitioning and lobbying, in the public sphere. But when the association in fact constitutes the state, the norms which apply to the state must apply to the association as well. Because its constituents, involuntarily drawn together, are affected by its bargains, they must be given the opportunity to participate in its law-making process.

Government, then, should be expected to regulate those associations we can properly designate as public ones; it should force them to work for purposes defined by the processes of democratic constitutionalism. It may force them to admit to membership all *de facto* members, even those whose entry will challenge the prevailing hierarchy. It may force them to grant all rights attached to membership and to allow for review where an unjustified deprivation of rights is claimed. It may force them either to confine their purposes or to guarantee procedural rights to their own membership. The price they must pay for remaining internally unaffected by governmental action is either restricting their general purposes to specific ones or constitutionalizing the processes by which their general purposes and particular policies are determined.

Wherever some "private" group is public, it cannot be immune to the regulations which this analysis justifies. Thus as business corporations aim less at short-term profit and more at long-range welfare, they invite public control. They invite the replacement of consumer choice by citizen choice, of "economic" criteria by political ones. The test for judging corporate action must then be subjected to political judgments, judgments about alternative moral ends rather than economic means. As the ideal of the rational consumer is made irrelevant by the effectiveness of techniques which limit his alternatives and control his choices, the check on the corporation embodied in a free market fades out; it becomes impossible to assess the "efficiency" of the corporation by its capacity to satisfy consumer wants. Economic criteria become irrelevant when the corporation seeks to provide general or public benefits, when it encourages its budget to provide for the good life of all the interests it touches. When this is the case, the cost of its products becomes as incalculable as the diverse aspirations of its constituents. The check on its activity ceases to be an economic one. As economic criteria which assume given ends collapse, the channels must be cleared for the operation of political processes. The state must assert itself vis-à-vis the economy.

What applies to the business corporation applies no less to the labor union, especially as its initial aim—to enlarge its share of the profits, to shorten hours, to correct management abuses—is being realized. It too is open to public control when it ceases to be homogeneous and begins to multiply its goals. Of course, it is true that union leaders, aware of the state's indifference to worker welfare and set to treat their organizations as fighting units under siege, were entitled to discipline their army of workers. When rank-and-file consensus on the need to do battle could be assumed, there was no reason to check the coercive power of union government. The limits which American constitutional practice imposes on public government could have no place in a labor union, for the union could well be thought of as militant fighter for individual rights. But once such consensually defined rights are won, the demand for closing labor's ranks, the cry for unity under a union government whose power brooks only such limits as the outside world can impose, lacks justification. To the extent, then, that the union takes over and claims to represent more than the most specific of workers' interests, it must tolerate a check on its power to govern. And if corporations and unions are open to public control when they are apart, they are all the more so when they meet and collaborate.

Since the facts make clear that mass organizations—whether national corporations, national unions, or national professional associations—cannot be relied on to protect the individual against repression by his group, the state itself is his sole resort. True, the state may act unjustly. The threat to men is not only that the group may absorb and diminish them but also that the state can pierce the group and manage to manipulate them directly. Yet, when all this has been acknowledged, there remains the need to approximate the purposes for which men divide their labor, cooperate, and organize: not to achieve some abstract group goal but to sustain their separate selves, to achieve personal integrity. When the governments of groups eclipse this overriding purpose, the appeal of the affiliated—as Rousseau saw so sharply—can only be to the public law of the community at large, to the general government transcending that of any specific group. It can only be to the state whose source of power is independent of mass organizations, the state which is representative of nonincorporated, disassociated interests. Nothing else can be counted on to vindicate the rights of individuals. Against large-scale groups, only the state can maintain or create rights for the protection of the individual. Only the state can assure free passage between groups, compelling them to accept a theory of limits for the sake of their members, compelling those who wield power within groups to account for their conduct through institutionalized political processes.

Guaranteeing procedural rights for the affiliated becomes especially crucial in an industrial society in which man, to satisfy his wants, has no alternative but to join up or go under. In practice, it has become clear that the member of the leviathan organization can no more make his affiliation contingent on the voice of his conscience, as Harold Laski hoped, than the citizen of the liberal state of John Locke can count on his ability to secede, as Hume rightly pointed out. To the extent, then, that the individual is dependent on associations, he must rely on the state; to the extent that their power is public power, he must rely on state machinery ready to impose a constitutional order. The purpose of such reliance on the instruments of the general government is to keep the group's power in line with the possible interests of the individual, to shield him from the unjust exercise of group power.

Granting the validity of the conclusion that in accordance with our tradition and our principles public groups demand public control, what might be our alternative courses of action? By what means, specifically, might public control be best exercised in the public sector?

The range of possibilities is wide enough. At one extreme, we might respond to the suggestion for a new form of laissez-faire policy—new only because it is applied not to individuals but to corporations. Such a policy, however, can hardly satisfy us. Although the conscience of the corporation might possibly be left alone, although it might be trusted to be sensitive, in Adolf Berle's phrase, to the public consensus, we cannot assume that it will be sensitive to all that needs to be done when consensus is absent. What of the other extreme of public control, nationalization or socialization? It requires no stressing that planning under public auspices has not in itself proved to be better than planning under private ones.[1] Between these extremes—and that is where we must make our way—there are many possible courses for action. In reviewing them and in proposing new ones it will be doubly necessary to be on guard lest we reintroduce, under new names, the very institutions condemned by constitutionalism.

Provided that we take care to structure the economy so that any of its components find it too painful to become overbearing, we could certainly leave economic groups alone. Indeed, we then would be obliged to ignore the separate ends they pursue. Alternatively, we could be indifferent to the structure of the economy. But in that case we would be obliged to direct the whole of it toward publicly determined ends, however it may be structured.

These two courses, while not mutually exclusive, merit consideration in turn. Surely we could break into the various existing units of the economy and arrange them so that they would each comply with public objectives. Our major device for reconstructing the corporate order has of course been antitrust action. It would be naïve to assume, however, that this can significantly disperse and equalize economic power in the face of the goods and services which a hierarchical, large-scale industrial order manages to deliver. There is no doubt that an antitrust campaign can effectively unsettle the well-entrenched. When called on to do so, it can make inroads on industry-spanning firms like Du Pont; it can even help loosen the internal ties of groups like the American Medical Association.[2] But given the potent inhibitions under which antitrust policy operates in the United States—the nature of the judicial process for undoing wrongs as well as the realization that an unqualified adherence to the Sherman Act frustrates the attainment of other social objectives—there is little reason to hope for more than sporadic efforts to correct the less subtle forms of economic discrimination.

Is more dependable, more consistent, more penetrating action possible? Of course, we could really invade the corporate domain and seek to constitutionalize its political processes. We could insist, for example, on shareholder democracy—only to recognize that this constitutes a form of economic franchise which is indefensible when an absolute equality of economic opportunity does not obtain.[3] If, then, the state really is a corporate state, why not let each of its constituent members conduct itself in a constitutional manner? Just as the Constitution of 1787 guaranteed a republican form of government to each of the states, Earl Latham has suggested that it might well guarantee a republican form of government to each of the new public institutions—the new corporations.[4] Yet such a proposal, even if it were intended to enfranchise syndicalism and include labor organizations, does not touch the roots of the matter. It necessarily accepts the conventional, legal definition of the corporation. It deals precisely with that institution to which public law assigns the obligations and grants the privileges of "the corporation." Of course, the law may be changed. But to broaden the definition—to be utterly realistic and include all groups which are significantly affected by the corporation—would make any effort to control the resulting corporate order unwieldy; it would encourage a blending of politics and economics which would make it ultimately impossible to have the former control the latter.

Recognizing this should not, however, prevent the adoption of the devices associated with democratic constitutionalism in specific instances. It *is* possible to run a business corporation or a labor union along constitutional lines. The now classic and unique case in point would seem to be that of the International Typographical Union. But here it is worth noting that the typographers did not learn to esteem their two-party system as a result of farsighted governmental intervention. As the study by Lipset, Trow, and Coleman has pointed out, rival groups within the ITU compete for office on even terms because the most fortuitous of circumstances happen to have reinforced one another: informal groupings of typographers outside the ITU have fostered a sense of community; the printing industry is decentralized and allows for informal relations between workers whose skill and wages are fairly uniform; and union officers have not been separated from the rank and file by marked salary distinctions, making the defeated officer's move back to the shop relatively painless.[5] If these preconditions for union democracy are not easy to transfer to other groups, there is good reason for believing that large-scale associations will continue to be governed by oligarchies who have more affection for holding office than for a party system which encourages leadership rotation. Given the conditions under which Standard Oil of New Jersey or the American Medical Association operate, it would be absurd to expect that a governmentally imposed two-party system would be workable.

Although we cannot reasonably call for spreading a two-party system, it may still remain desirable to enforce an increased adherence to the political techniques institutionalized by constitutional regimes. It is surely possible to enlarge the opportunities of individual members of multipurpose associations. Thus they can be provided with the facilities for appealing corporate decisions affecting them to agencies whose source of power is independent of the association. Although this places the burden of taking the initiative on individual members, and consequently does not promise much, it is something—as might be apparent when considering its likely impact on the policies of the AMA. Those who govern organized medicine might find themselves unable to have the final word in the formation of medical policy—health insurance plans, the geographical distribution of medical services, the spread of medical education—when the individual physician can challenge AMA policy and can appeal to an independent tribunal from a judgment by competitors (who have a stake in his exclusion from the profession).

A similar approach should govern our policies in the field of labor. We should continue to go beyond the view of unions as autonomous private organizations entitled to equalize their bargaining strength and to protect the employment status of their members. To be sure, the Taft-Hartley Act attempted to make it possible for the worker to escape the power exercised by those engaged in collective bargaining. But it provided him with no rights against a leadership which in fact did sit down to bargain. The unrecognized worker, both in and out of the union, could still be safely discriminated against, especially when mutual convenience wedded labor and management. Today, in order to secure the rights of all whom organized labor is capable of embracing, we must give workers the opportunity to join, to make an impact on the leadership, and thereby to share equally in the benefits of membership. Making these opportunities genuine requires more than outlawing racketeering or directing the trustees of pension funds to become honorable men. The individual worker will have to be enabled to get his bearings by providing him, whether at union or government expense, with information relating to union policies. Should he be interested, he must be able to determine what policies are in fact being pursued, how his economic stake in welfare plans is being safeguarded, and by what procedures he can express his disapproval. And having such information, he must be granted the opportunity first to organize fellow members who share his interests and then to register his choices in periodic secret-ballot elections. He certainly cannot feel free to exercise his rights unless he knows that no arbitrary retaliatory action can be taken against him. Hence there must be tribunals whose source of authority lies outside the union, tribunals empowered to compel performance, to enjoin behavior denying due process of law, and to award damages.[6] Whatever enlarges the sphere of individual rights within unions must be seen as desirable. This very standard, the standard of constitutionalism, must also be the one to limit the rights of union members. When there is evidence that dissident factions disrupt the union's procedures for maintaining its internal constitutional order, these factions are justly checked. Even though dissidents have a perfect right to disagree with the policies of their unions, they cannot be permitted to disrupt a sound system of procedures. To encourage unrestrained faction-alism within unions cannot help but undermine their effective-ness vis-à-vis business corporations.

And it is precisely the opposition role of the union which it is essential to preserve. As long as unions are opposed to outside interests, they will not, of course, incorporate them. Their own interests will consequently remain limited—and so will state inter-vention in their internal affairs. What it is desirable to guard against, if state intervention is to be avoided, is an overlapping of business and union interests. Union participation in public government as well as in private management must be seen as impairing an association's independence, and hence its power. Unions are powerful because they are detached, free to disturb production, to pressure politicians and threaten industrial mana-gers. If it were their prime responsibility to secure industrial peace, they would no longer be able to develop the criticisms and the programs which, to get an effective hearing, depend on the availability of sanctions. Labor-management demarkation is thus to be welcomed consistently, especially since the equality of bar-gaining power provided by existing legislation gives both labor and management the opportunity to discriminate against those not partaking in "collective" bargaining—namely, repressed groups inside and inchoate publics outside.

When it is not socially desirable to insist on constitutionalizing large-scale, multipurpose collectivities of power by interfering with their internal affairs, there must be that minimal opportunity for insiders to appeal to an effective outside tribunal. Once again, this course of action does not promise much, though it can be ameliorative. The cost of initiating private litigation or public prosecution will not readily be borne by the individual union member. He cannot really feel or calculate the full impact of abused power. The costs of abused union power are, after all, small in specific cases; they are cumulative, diffuse, and social. The law of equity provides remedies, but none of great import.

Other ways of coping obliquely with the corporate order reveal further limitations. Should public bodies monitor corporations directly? There is little reason for confidence in consumer advisory councils or in consumer and worker representation on boards of directors. "Public" representatives on corporate boards not only learn to understand the problems of their companies all too well but also find themselves at a loss when seeking to discover precisely what standards might guide them. As for workers' efforts to share in policy-making, there is not merely a patent absence of desire on their part but also, once again, the danger of obscuring and eliminating their opposition role. Arguments for employee participation in the making of major corporate decisions—decisions above the level of the shop—rest on false notions about human nature and interests. To act on the assumption that workers really want to engage in politics is therefore to foster counterfeit participation. And this is worse than the real thing, for it exposes employees to manipulation.

These points all reveal an impatience with piecemeal social engineering. Yet they are not meant to condemn partial efforts to compel management—union, corporation, or professional group management—to become responsive to affected interests, including outside interests. A Fair Employment Practices Commission taking the initiative in behalf of dissidents and would-be members has its genuine place in a reform program. But such a commission, whatever one's hopes for it, remains in a weak position. Is it really distinguishable from the group of monitors appointed in January 1958 by a United States District Court to control the Teamsters or, indeed, from the independent regulatory commission? It simply cannot remain effective when at the mercy of a congressional committee which is in turn at the mercy of the very groups a commission would seek to regulate. To remain viable, it must respond slowly and legalistically, learning to live with those who exercise power.

What, then, might we do? Finding it impossible to favor the total socialization of nominally private enterprises, we may twist and turn to make do with lesser solutions. In fact, we should always make minimal attempts first. But as we see each of them through, we are again confronted by the practical problem posed when private groups exercise public power. We may implore large-scale associations to adopt devices for an organized opposition, for internal appeals and review procedures. We may demand that management decisions be subject to "codetermination" by workers, owners, or consumers. We may wish to enforce "workable" competition and facilitate technological advance by antitrust action. We may hope to use the courts to make the whole of the public sector conform to the dictates of liberal constitutionalism. We may have a measure of confidence in all of these devices for enforcing responsibility, knowing from experience that they all have their uses despite their flaws and limits. When they are skillfully mixed and jointly brought to bear on the economic sector, we may feel that our politicians are serving us well. And we may then praise the virtues of patience, underachievement, moderation, and consensus.

But when these devices fail to achieve public purposes, when they become a façade behind which private groups exercise public power, we are no longer justified in relying on a widely pluralized government—on that diversity of semiautonomous legislative, administrative, and judicial organs which somehow seek to get the sense of public wants, struggle to register the soft currents of public opinion, and then mediate, adjust, and appease in the hallowed name of piecemeal social engineering. Where private associations must be compelled to abandon their internally reached agreements because these conflict with public policy, where public action is mandatory because private checks can be shown to be spurious, we should confidently engage in direct, bold, affirmative, national, across-the-board regulation. The justification for this is to guarantee the rights of individual persons. It is not to politicize life. It is rather to prevent the politicizing of life by well-organized enterprise which calls itself private.

To keep such seemingly private enterprise in line with liberal constitutionalism, far more specific policy directives will have to be formulated. We may well note initially that whether an economic market is imperfect depends on the ends we seek. Thus when the results of large-scale production are believed to enhance the public welfare, when there is a broad consensus on the desirability of what technology produces in an unfree market, many of the so-called imperfections of the market will actually be perfections. And once we frankly commit ourselves to an unfree market, aware that a free one is incompatible with the scale demanded by the full use of our productive capacities and that an unfree one is simply not self-regulating, we find ourselves assenting to control of the market by public agencies. State action, then, would seem justified where competition is undesired (and possibly undesirable), where the price system does not act as a regulator, and where professional or private moral standards are too narrow. While this formal conclusion meets little opposition when stated as a general principle, efforts to give content to it are often opposed as if the principle itself were unsound; proposals to give it substance and meaning are not treated as practical or impractical but as right or wrong "in principle."

Elaboration in one area may help illustrate the point. There should be no objection "in principle" to the transfer of the power to make key price and wage decisions from management-union partnerships to public agencies. When labor and business find it in their joint interest to combine—agreeing, for example, to raise the level of wages along with the price of products—their action should invite governmental intervention. Either the new and probably inadvertent partnerships must be dissolved to clear the ground for renewed conflict and hard bargaining, or else the partnership must be publicly directed toward ends determined by a constituency wider than the corporate one. If the costs of wage settlements are passed on to the consumer, the consumer, acting as a citizen, has clear title to some form of representation. To discomfit those who make wage or price policies, the unrepresented public might insist on being heard before any settlement of wages or determination of prices is announced. Alternatively, it might insist on participating directly in the making of wage or price decisions.

These alternatives are nothing more than matters of practical policy, not of principle. The principle is the preservation of constitutionalism, procedurally defined, in the public realm. And to make such proceduralism effective demands that we be dissatisfied even with altruistic industrial regimes whose policies are substantively beneficent. Merely to preserve flexibility in our economic and technological order, it is imperative to keep the procedural checks on corporate power in good working order. The fact that business or union managements are wise and virtuous in governing society should not appease us; the question is whether the procedure exists for making them right should we chance to feel they are wrong.

What, finally, should guide the state in supervising the pace as well as the direction of human work and technological change? The state must recurrently assure itself that the scale of technology is never larger than is essential for maximum productivity and continued technological advancement. To exceed what is essential is to impose an industrial discipline, however mild and subtle, where none is needed. And such an excess is all the more deplorable where factory work remains degrading, stupefying, and exhausting. It may be true that venture capital must be concentrated, that industrial society must be bureaucratized, and that the market, too, must be rationalized. Yet with ingenuity, and under steady public pressure, the discipline of industrialism should always be cut to a minimum.

Just what constitutes this minimum is an empirical, testable question, which can be answered properly only by experts.* Nevertheless, after the experts of economics have had their say about the relation between size and efficiency, it remains the task of the state to intervene and force a widening of the prevailing concept of efficiency. Public instrumentalities will have to be available to

---

* The answer to the question should always be a variable one. One of the most persuasive attempts to show that *today* the multiplant operation by the single firm does not necessarily economize production is Ward S. Bowman, Jr., "Toward Less Monopoly," *University of Pennsylvania Law Review,* 101 (March 1953), 577–642, especially 600–11. Firms may well be broken up, he says, "without the slightest change in the actual patterns of production" (p. 611). Yet it has also been possible to end on a different note: "Examining the hypothesis of large-scale efficiency, the high proportion of large-scale firms and plants in many British and American manufactures, and the increase in the proportion of persons employed in large plants are quantitative indications, tested by survival and growth, of superior efficiency." (P. Sargant Florence, *The Logic of British and American Industry* [Chapel Hill: University of North Carolina Press, 1953], p. 337.)

define the concept of efficiency so that it can include the nontechnological factors about which the economist is properly silent. Individual and social goals may be gained by jettisoning some of the economies of large-scale production, or at least by exchanging them for other economies.

By becoming sensitive to latent interests, we may learn that there are alternative ways of organizing work and "consuming" leisure. It may be feasible to subsidize experiments which are unprofitable except in human terms, to provide, for example, for the decentralization of plant sites, for a radical extension of educational opportunities, or for an extension of the range of recreational facilities. When the basis for cost accounting is broadened by the state, we may find that in some cases it is more costly to transport workers rather than raw material to the plant. It may become possible to rearrange, variegate, and thereby humanize the work process itself, even if this proves to be uneconomical to private operators. Should bringing such changes about not require democracy within the industrial plant, as it clearly need not, it will require governmental subsidy and control from outside the plant.

If what is defined as economical is thus deliberately enlarged so as to include matters not susceptible to monetary calculation—namely, the subjective satisfaction of workers and consumers—the ultimate test for the legitimacy of the economic order cannot be simply its relative "capacity to perform." To be sure, "performance" is one relevant consideration in determining what constitutes the public good. Unwilling to embrace an ethics of asceticism, we certainly want what is called, without further definition, industrial progress. Moreover, we realize that oligopoly is its price. At the same time, however, mass production at lower costs per unit in ever greater volumes should not be assumed to be our only goal. Consequently "performance" cannot be our exclusive standard. We may justly make industrial organization "inefficient" and ask ourselves whether to restructure it so as to achieve public objectives. A "structure" test will then be seen as a real option.

But when we do desire to test the legitimacy of the economic and technological order pre-eminently in reference to its capacity to perform, governmental regulation must be expected. The reasons are evident enough. A performance test, it has often been pointed out, has built-in values. It encourages business to increase in size in relation to the market. When this test alone is applied, it favors output and growth, rise in per capita income, capacity to improve techniques, products, and services, and an ever-renewed acceptance of products by consumers who help pay the costs of having their wants duly stimulated. It thereby enhances the discretionary power of those who make business decisions—and invites pervasive state regulation lest corporate enterprises gain the upper hand in dealing with "independent" public agencies. To use a performance test, then, is to make way for public control. Those who counsel its use should recognize as much. Where we want and look for performance we must expect to see the effective arm of the public. And where we believe we can afford something other than purely economic performance, something other than the full exploitation of material resources, we may well insist on no more governmental action than would effectively fragment and structure the economy. We must then merely demand that no monopolistic *private* control of the economy be considered reasonable either by judges or by lawmakers.

Because casual and intermittent efforts to deal with the economic order cannot be effective today, the state must be in constant readiness to exercise control. Of course, where industrial managers accept a broadened, more inclusive, and never finally defined concept of efficiency, freely or prudently choosing it themselves, there is no need for public action. Experience suggests, however, that voluntary benevolence is short lived. Hence there must be, at a minimum, continuous governmental surveillance of corporate affairs, and vigorous publicity about its ramifications. There must be the governmental power, even though delicately held in suspense, to discriminate against self-regarding industrial leadership.

Because the individual is encroached upon by large-scale organizations, an administered market, and the increased opportunity to manipulate a newly consuming and a newly leisured public, it remains necessary to keep him, by state action if need be, as unattached to the economic and technological order as possible. If his autonomy and essential equality are to be respected, he must be made as free as possible from the hierarchy imposed by modern industrialism. The state, in his behalf, must fight all efforts to attach him to giant-size groups; it must act directly to support workers, consumers, and citizens.[7] It must especially check those who are primed to coerce and attach the newly leisured individual. It must do this especially because the creation of leisure has not meant, Marx to the contrary, a jump into freedom but the emergence of new types of social coercion.

It remains on the state's agenda to trim those power blocs which threaten to become all-pervasive, to keep in check whatever forces subvert the aesthetic, intellectual, moral, or spiritual goods of the individual. In practice, therefore, governments will have to enable him to leave one group and join another. They will have to steel him to dissent within groups. Governmental budgets will have to cover the risks and losses which result from the encouragement of self-development; they will have to subsidize an arena in which individual impulses can run spontaneously, a private field allowing for expression (even organized expression) of that excess of ideals which, in human society, cannot be safely translated into action. Thus governmental officials must see themselves as authorized to liberate human energies by reducing man's preoccupation with the means to life, with the innumerable distractions from the ends.

Unquestionably, the belief that the state should check the enervating routines which tend to standardize life is as generally accepted as the one that it should provide the basic material necessities for existence. But what requires continuous emphasis is the need for the state to frustrate those private arrangements which, masquerading as healthy pluralism, tend to stratify and congeal society, to freeze markets, and to control individuals. A "pluralistic" economy made rigid by guaranteed annual wages, pension plans, price and profit guarantees, patent pools, licensing boards, building codes, and the multitude of devices which underwrite monopoly must be consistently challenged in behalf of a theory which defines the just state as intolerant of all fixed deals, as equipped to keep all markets open.

Thus it is imperative, among other things, that the state keep old-age, unemployment, and sickness benefits from being localized.* What is more, it must detach educational, recreational, and cultural opportunities from both parochial organizations and the industrial order lest the educational curriculum as well as leisure-time activities respond to overspecialized demands. In sum, the state must support any and all institutions which keep society pluralistic in the realm of human ends. Such institutions hold no profit for any single enterprise other than the state. Thus the state must enter what, under modern conditions, is the realm of the public, the realm of means. It must maintain and enlarge the framework for making private life not merely more bearable and comfortable but also more various and dramatic, for making it genuinely pluralistic.

If governments are to be encouraged to sponsor alternative ways of organizing the economic and technological order, they must be made aware not only of the obvious blessings of technology but also of its costs. To heighten the awareness of policy-makers, competing publics must have access to them. Those interested in making political what is falsely advertised as being above politics must be in a position to widen the range of policy options. In practice, this can mean nothing short of introducing under-represented majorities into the policy-making process. Whether this objective can be realized today without the deliberate redistribution of social power is an open question. But it is clearly our task to reform government so that all members of society can enter the political arena on equal terms in fact as well as in theory.

* One newspaperman's reflections on the difficulty of quitting employers who compel their reporters to slant the news may be to the point: "The trap has been strengthened in recent years, I believe, by the retirement-pay and severance-pay agreements the Newspaper Guild has forced on publishers. These make it harder for a man to quit a job he has held for any number of years, because in doing so he must forfeit months' worth of pay that has been set aside for him in benefits. The benefits are a carrot the reporter can see but cannot touch unless he finishes his life stretch without causing trouble. However noble in purpose, the agreements tend to make peons of us." (Christopher Rand, "Reporting in China," *Harper's Magazine*, 207 [September 1953], 82–89, 84.)

15

The Reform of Government

What kind of governmental reorganization is necessary to equip ourselves to act both effectively and responsibly in the public arena? How can we do what we must because of the kind of world in which we live and what we should because of our commitment to liberal constitutionalism?

That these are relevant questions has been far from evident to Americans, for in the past they have not struck us as posing dilemmas. In the past, effective action was, after all, responsible action; environmental demands readily coincided with our moral commitments. It is becoming apparent, however, that the need to survive in the present-day world makes us submit to technological and organizational forces which threaten the very possibility of a republic whose members are equal, not because they have equal merit but because they are equally incommensurable.

How then can we respond to the enormous contemporary pressure to make our industrial society even more hierarchical and imposing? If we lack the moral passion to paralyze the ascending technological and economic hierarchies of power, we should at least seek to assure ourselves that individuals are consistently respected as equals within the public realm, even if this should entail radically redesigning it. It is true that essential reforms may irritate firmly vested interests, whether these interests be sectional or economic, agricultural or commercial, technological or bureaucratic. But it is worth noting at the same time that the individuals aligned with these interests also have an irrepressible attachment to liberal constitutionalism. Their interests are dual, and over the last 150 years, whenever their divided interests have come into conflict their concern for liberal constitutionalism has been the abiding one. Thus it may not be naïve to make a case for "unrealistic" or "politically impossible" reforms. In specific conflicts between a political order and the norms of liberal constitutionalism it is really possible for liberal constitutionalism to emerge victorious. A theory of the open frontier, an economic interpretation, or a retelling of American history in terms of a massive Lockean consensus will not wholly explain the capacity of reason to transcend special interests. And so long as it remains plausible to hold that we can escape the reach of the prevailing ideology, why trim our demands? We should be especially hesitant to do so when they rest on a belief in rationality which is shared by those who argue, quite reasonably, in opposition to the very governmental reforms which will be proposed here.

To make public action effective, reserving for the moment the equally demanding problem of making it responsible as well, we should make every effort to unify a geographically pluralized government. To put it bluntly, government must be centralized to carry out the tasks of public regulation. Virtually all our public problems today are national problems, and they must be dealt with nationally. The administration of education, welfare, housing, building, recreation, health, transportation, and defense must become subject to national standards.

This imperative seems least evident in the field of education, where our localist tradition is at its most extreme. Yet here, too, integration must be achieved. Initially, this will require joining educational government and general government at the local level.[1]

But as we recognize that no relation obtains between the mélange of school districts and the demands of our contemporary political life, more becomes essential. We must regulate the framework of the curriculum, the subsidization of students, the salaries of teachers and administrators, and the construction of plants in accordance with national needs and national standards arrived at publicly.[2]

Similarly, we cannot relegate the power to define the conditions for the fruitful use of leisure to local bodies, leaving it up to a plethora of local governments to promote the facilities which enable us to lead rewarding lives: medical clinics, asylums, hospitals, museums, libraries, research centers, forests, beaches, refuges, playgrounds, and amusement parks. We know that in the long run, which is rapidly becoming shorter, local bodies active in these areas cannot help but succumb to private interests which are neither locally nor nationally accountable. The point of national coordination of governmental instrumentalities is to prevent the standardization of American life, to prevent its socialization under private auspices, to extend the range of individual opportunities available in local communities.

This goal cannot be achieved by devices which have the effect of condoning the prevailing practices of local governments. Thus the kind of conditions we now attach to federal grants-in-aid require basic rethinking. The critics of federal grants to local bodies have been right for the wrong reasons. They have feared the subversion of the states by the national government. The states, as responsible organs of government, are indeed being subverted, but not by national agencies. What the grants have generally done is simply to sustain a host of local but insulated principalities.[3] Effective administration has been interpreted to mean deference to the state government and, ultimately, deference to the dominant private interest affected. The pattern has clearly been one of passive collaboration by the states, not firm direction by the national government. The entire federal grants-in-aid program rests on the false assumption that the discretion of the state administrator is duly limited, that action by the state highway department, the state health department, the public health commission, or the social welfare administration is duly circumscribed and that these agencies are prevented from making their peace with the strongest of the conflicting interests they serve. Yet since the execution of grant-in-aid progams is designed to allow for a wide margin of compromise and accommodation to local pressures, the programs necessarily reinforce irresponsibility. The system of federal grants to the states, according to Rowland Eggers's study, has "underwritten the continuance of archaic local governmental jurisdictions and irresponsible local administrative structures and procedures."[4] And just as federal grants are excessively permissive in the conditions attached to them, so are state grants which subsidize unrepresentative cliques at the county and village level.

What is being reinforced—not so much by grants-in-aid as by an inability to transcend an anachronistic way of thinking about governmental problems—bears more detailed description at the level of the metropolitan area. Robert C. Wood has given us a picture which we still find charming to the extent that we fail to envisage it concretely. Within the metropolitan area, Wood has written,

hundreds and hundreds of local governments jostle one another about. Counties overlie school districts, which overlie municipalities, which overlie sanitary and water districts, which sometimes overlie townships and villages. Except for the special-purpose "districts," each suburban government maintains its own police force, its fire station, its health department, its library, its welfare service. Each retains its authority to enact ordinances, hold elections, zone land, raise taxes, grant building licenses, borrow money, and fix speed limits.

The existence of ancient jurisdictions in perpetual conflict is grossly wasteful:

Across a typical suburban terrain, twenty or thirty or fifty volunteer fire departments buy equipment and, with varying degrees of efficiency, put out fires. A welter of semi-professional police forces, usually poorly equipped and inadequately staffed, jealously compete or lackadaisically cooperate, uncertain of the limits of their jurisdiction. Independent school systems build costly plants, some crammed to capacity, others with excess space. In one municipality the water table dips perilously low; in another, foresighted or fortunate enough to have access to a reservoir, sprinklers turn all summer long. And, always, for suburban governments taken together, there is the . . . cost of doing individually what might be done collectively: the additional expense of making separate purchases without benefit of quantity discounts, of administrative and political overhead, of holding local elections and hiring city managers, of reporting, accounting, and auditing these separate activities.[5]

What is wasted here in resources is in no way recouped to help approximate the norms of liberal constitutionalism. The evidence is clear that behind a fence of honorific terms—local nonpartisan government, fraternal decision-making, a politics of personality, informality in administration, grass-roots democracy—exist practices that make responsibility in the execution of public policy largely accidental.

There would be nothing wrong with such homely, face-to-face government if our interests were singular, if everyone really saw eye to eye on the objectives of policy, if the only problems were those of finding the efficient means to achieve common ends. Government then could be engaged in pure administration, in helping the community attain its common objective economically simply by eliminating waste and regulating the traffic. But paradoxical as it may yet seem to us, we must repress so-called grass-roots democracy if we really want to maintain a genuinely pluralistic society. We must decline every invitation to delegate public power to private groups, guard against clientele participation in the making of public policy, and keep multi-interest groups from becoming involved in the formulation of "administrative" regulation—doing all this whether it lies in the fields of education, health, housing, recreation, transportation, communication, building construction, fiscal policy, land management, defense contracting, or tax law enforcement. It is necessary to cut into the indiscriminate tangle of governments poised between the citizen and his state, for these governments have been shown to be anything but buffers protecting him from the irresponsible use of state power. Instead, they deliver him to the group, to the unrepresentative and far from local association which is prepared to tax, educate, entertain, cajole, and energize him. If such national associations are to be checked, only a central government is in position to do so.

To provide the ground for positive, purposeful action, a new division of governmental power along functional lines (as substitute for a geographical federalism) may seem appealing. But this could hardly be expected to solve the problems confronting us. Where the effort has been made—as it has in the establishment of national economic councils in Europe—none of the questions we have had to face were solved. On the contrary, they were simply advanced to a level at which they proved even more difficult to answer within a context of constitutionalism. But we do have a clear alternative: the resolute unification of the national government. We can bring executive power, which is in fact legislative power, into sharp focus.

To do so, it will have to be greatest at the top. The locus of power, given the fact that governmental power is widely dispersed today, must be moved up the administrative hierarchy.[6] It might be best to begin by acknowledging that today's Cabinet is no more an integral part of the administrative hierarchy than the innumerable agencies, councils, and committees now clustered around the President. The attachments of its members are necessarily various. Richard F. Fenno, Jr., has characterized a Cabinet member as

a man with a particular departmental viewpoint, responsive to particular clientele interests and pursuing a particular program. His political behavior is shaped to a large degree by the kinds of extra-presidential relationships he establishes as he seeks solutions to his particular problems— the support of his policies, the survival of his organization, the control of his environment. Where extra-presidential relationships exist, then extra-presidential—perhaps, anti-presidential—actions are not far behind.[7]

Reform proposals which have the effect of throwing the Cabinet even further from the President—proposals to select Cabinet members from Congress, to give them seats in Congress, to make them answerable to Congress—are surely misguided. They all suffer from a failure to conceive of the possibility of making the President responsible by means other than tying him to the only legislature to which our tradition has accustomed us, the one located on Capitol Hill. How many of the staff aides, the study and coordinating committees, the advisory conferences, and the policy planning councils do less to help the President personally than to make him seem safe in the eyes of Congress? To what extent do they really facilitate the formulation, execution, and surveillance of presidential policy? Today it would make sense if the President could invite the members of his Cabinet first to develop national policies within the framework of his views and then to assume responsibility for executing them (as the plethora of policy and advisory committees of the 1950's never could). It must be added immediately that the President can feel encouraged to do what "would make sense" only if he knows he really has the leverage for upholding his basic position in the states, in Congress, and throughout his own branch of government. To give him such leverage requires fundamental shifts in political power, and not mere academic exhortations to Presidents busy maintaining a nonpartisan calm.

The more thoroughgoing the integration of the executive branch, provided always that its legitimacy is preserved because of the quality of the men whom the excellence of the system induces to lead, the more likely will national policies be firm and consistent. To achieve the clear articulation of policy, as a score of students of American government have urged for decades, regulatory agencies must operate within departments which deal with broad sectors of the economy and not merely with single industries. Transportation policy, for example, cannot be left to the myriad of governmental bodies now claiming jurisdiction. The Federal Trade Commission, the Food and Drug Administration, and the Antitrust Division cannot be allowed to find their own interpretations of a reasonable trade practice. Nor can the Federal Communications Commission be left at the mercy of its clientele. These and other such commissions must be absorbed by the various Executive departments; only in this way can they be protected against both direct clientele pressure and the indirect influence their clienteles exercise by pressuring Congress.* Administrators with a wide range of discretion will have to be able to depend on firm presidential leadership if they are to succeed in disentangling them-

* Clifford J. Durr, a former member of the FCC, has rightly asked, "How do you regulate a medium which is itself a molder of public opinion and which can mold the opinion of Congress as well?" He remembers a Congressman inquiring about a constituent's pending license application. A half an hour after the inquiry, the Congressman called back to say that he didn't actually want any special favors, "but you know how hard it is when your constituent is sitting just across the desk." (Quoted in *Broadcasting and Government Regulation in a Free Society* [Santa Barbara: Fund for the Republic, 1959], pp. 12, 14.)

selves from alliances with regulated groups. And where it is the function of the lower echelon of administrators merely to police or to engineer programs, they must be made all the more subordinate to publicly accountable policy-makers rather than to private interests.

That it is in fact possible for an administrative agency to vindicate the integrity of the political process, to work with steadfastness, single-mindedness, and a marked immunity to dominant clientele pressures may be illustrated by considering the experience of the Office of Price Administration during the Second World War. Victor A. Thompson's extensive study of the OPA describes an agency which did have the strong support of the incumbent President as well as the benefit of a well-integrated organization—a field service almost wholly dependent on a centralized staff given support by the common language and background of attorneys. Of course, the pressure of a fighting war facilitated the acceptance of an administrative program. But not even during war do all interests coalesce, as shown by the innumerable petitioners asking for increased gasoline allotments in the name of the public interest.* It is also true that the OPA was short lived and was not given the ample time the ICC has had to accommodate itself to an economic status quo. Yet the fact remains that even despite the OPA's reliance on industry advisory committees, the OPA again and again got its way, inducing the members of affected industries, in Thompson's words, to "feel a joint responsibility" for policy and, what is more, "to defend it when it is criticized within the

---

* The Brewing Industry Foundation requested preferred gasoline allotments from the Gasoline Eligibility Committee so that its field investigators might inspect "the sanitary and moral conditions of saloons," especially those near military installations. The Michigan Music Company sought additional gasoline to install a device piping mood music into war plants. Mississippi asked for a larger gasoline quota after organizing salesmen in the state into an "Auxiliary Highway Patrol"—a presumably essential wartime service. The National Retail Furniture Association petitioned for preferred eligibility for installment collectors because, it contended, installment buying encourages a mass market and thus lowers prices. All claims were made "in the national interest." (See Victor A. Thompson, *The Regulatory Process in OPA Rationing* [New York: King's Crown Press, 1950], pp. 87, 445, 93, 239.)

industry." Nor did it make any difference when Leon Henderson, who had taken a tough line, was replaced as chief administrator by Chester Bowles, who was appointed to mollify business and the supply agencies. What happened to Mr. Bowles? At the end of his tenure, Thompson reports, "he was Mr. Henderson reincarnated."[8]

Once the power to govern is hierarchically organized it becomes reasonable to take politics out of the base of the organization. The further one goes down the hierarchy, the less discretion should be permissible. The Hoover Commission was emphatically right in its 1955 recommendation: while the Executive departments should carry the major decision-making burden—formulating, advocating, defending, and assessing policies—those below the departmental level should act as technicians.[9] Congress, of course, seeks to maintain its relations with lower-level agencies and private groups try to deal with "technicians" who can let their superiors know what is "really feasible." But in a context of more thoroughgoing reforms, a proportionate removal from politics of part of the government can become a real possibility. The opportunity of technicians to deflate policies from within the government would thereby be minimized. At the same time the pervasively political nature of the upper echelon can be faced. Frank political staffing for offices at the top must be expected. There, the only expertise is and should be political, properly beyond certification by the Civil Service Commission.

More generally, the problem is to make the administrative arm of the President (in more accurate terms, the legislative establishment over which a President presides) represent dormant, inchoate, and inarticulate interests in addition to well expressed ones. To create and maintain a vigorously representative government, competing views must be represented within it.* They must

---

* That they do already, to an extent not generally recognized, is shown in Norton E. Long, "Bureaucracy and Constitutionalism," *American Political Science Review*, 46 (September 1952), 808–18. If administrative agencies have been dominated by single private interests, Long holds, so have Congressional committees. He affirms (p. 814) that "the rich diversity that makes up the United States is better represented in its civil service than anywhere else."

be given audience within the administration so that the President is able to choose between positions sharpened by argument. When the structure of an administration fails to encourage such argument, the President himself is compelled, as Franklin D. Roosevelt was, to generate internal opposition, to set personality against personality and agency against agency. Such continuous debate and conflict within the administrative branch of the government is eminently desirable. Without it, a President is given a vast edifice of affirmation. And this, as the Hoover and Eisenhower administrations revealed, makes for rigidity, for an inability to respond to new technological, social, and moral forces welling up outside the walls of the bureaucracy. But the question is whether we can rely on a Roosevelt to generate discontent and argument or whether we should institutionalize such politics.

It should be evident that the institutionalization of politics is especially imperative when the executive establishment is integrated and coordinated. If integration and coordination reduce the possibility of democratic constitutionalism imposed by a traditional separation of powers, the techniques for securing the consideration of alternatives within the administration must be cultivated all the more. When it is possible for alternatives to be compromised, the compromised interest should be able to find continued representation. To provide such representation, senior officials must be encouraged to display programmatic interests; they must feel free to work with a sense of dedication, purpose, and commitment. They should not be disinterested "generalists" above programmatic battles and kept harmless by a political quarantine. To galvanize interest conflicts within the administration, we must somehow secure administrators who have deep concerns, and who are therefore likely to be inventive, likely to take the initiative, to stand by their decisions, and to follow them through. To improve the tone and ultimately the representative nature of the bureaucracy, proper recruiting, staffing, and salaries must be relied on. Moreover, the bureaucracy must be enabled to conceive of itself as more than a passive instrument for producing decisions which will minimize deprivations and penalties, which will merely achieve what hurts all groups least. It must see its task as more than offering plans which no group is likely to veto. What is essential is that it actively ferret out interests so diffuse, disorganized, and inarticulate, (and nonetheless real for being so) that they cannot constitute a semiautonomous pressure group. The fact that such interests are not neatly spelled out, that they are unrealized ideals, should not exclude them from consideration in the bureaucracy's effort to maintain a genuinely pluralist society.

It is easy, of course, to prevail on administrators to consider values which transcend those of any concurrent majority, which are more profound than those approved by any prevailing consensus. The difficulty lies in applying the prescription. What is necessary, at a minimum, is to provide some institutional means for the consideration of a group-transcending public interest; to provide, quite literally, the time and the room for research and reflection; to allow administrators to consider general public objectives; and to facilitate the selection of public servants who are predisposed by education and outlook to take advantage of the opportunity. This means, at a minimum, reducing the work load of some and letting the budget underwrite the risk that they will be fruitlessly idle. Ultimately, we must make government service attractive to those intellectually able and temperamentally inclined to move beyond the lowest common denominator of interests.

And then we must tenaciously protect them. This means abandoning the search for the careerist civil servant who, if he is dedicated, is dedicated to an ineffable, spiritualized Public Interest. It means cherishing a Billy Mitchell, a Gifford Pinchot, or a General Maxwell D. Taylor, recognizing that they are at once relentlessly interested and deeply loyal. It means doing what is far more difficult: safeguarding the legions of less spectacular public officials who decide to take embarrassing stands. Thus we should not invite or expect them to resign if they dissent. We should check them within the administration, not push them out. By this approach, we would be building constitutionalism into the upper stratum of the bureaucracy. Where policy and administration fuse, the decision-making process would become truly political.

To achieve the unification and coordination of policies, it is essential to place the President in a political environment which constrains him to do more than drift and amiably reflect the current set of victorious interests. He must be given the conditions conducive to the exercise of leadership. He must be not merely enabled but also encouraged to define his goals clearly. Today, he is handicapped by constitutional forms rigged to prevent the integration of executive-congressional relations. Federalism, the localism of Congress, and, above all, a decentralized party system allow nongovernmental interests to exercise their veto. These interests thereby subvert the only public government which can be effective. Maneuvering themselves into positions of dominance behind an eighteenth-century façade, they themselves exercise the power to govern. They act as affirmative policy-makers in fields they righteously define as private. And they act as negative dissenters in fields which are public by default.

Yet the power to dissent must be lodged somewhere if effective action is also to be responsible action. Should we dismantle one set of restraints on the exercise of arbitrary power because they are dated, it is imperative that we erect another. When we streamline government we have not, after all, determined the direction in which it will move. How, then, can we force effective government, government we have duly centralized and integrated, to move so as to serve the public interest?

As observers have agreed again and again since the days when Woodrow Wilson and Henry Jones Ford first speculated about American politics, forces that already exist in the character of our party system would seem to present the best chance for effecting reform. In the last analysis, the range of fundamental alternatives is limited. We may, it is true, perpetuate the institutions which have served us well, or at least enabled us to survive so far. John Fischer, Peter Drucker, and Max Lerner, to name but three notable publicists, have eloquently opted for the political status quo. But it should be noted that, although none of these writers has as yet issued a clear call for a political aristocracy because the status quo exasperates them, the tendency on the part of reflective intellectuals in America has always been precisely that. Beholding the status quo, and made vaguely uneasy by it, they succumb to visions of an elite-governed state. But even where there is no breakthrough to advocacy of an elite, there is a recognition of the shortcomings of the present party system. Those who defend it do not deny that it keeps the branches of government separate, that it reinforces centrifugal tendencies, that it permits the overrepresentation of minority interests, that it prevents the definition of public issues, and that, as a consequence, it enables politics to become quite literally a kind of sideshow for Americans. They recognize these traits and affirm, with Herbert Agar, that this is the price we must pay for union.

Significantly, one of the most convincing cases for the party system, Agar's *Price of Union* (1950), is not at all an ideological defense; it is an engaging narrative of American political history. Yet the question which confronts us is precisely whether we can escape the hold of history, whether we can now perceive as deficient a political arrangement which an anachronous point of view makes us vindicate, whether we can recognize as dysfunctional what a generation of theorists has characterized as functional. If we can—and this is far from easy, for it requires that we deliberate and change our minds—we will be free to face what has become a political truism: parties claimed by theory and ideology to be responsive to local interests are in fact so responsive to national ones that the seeming triumph of the locality is the actual triumph of nationally organized, large-scale, well-incorporated private groups. When we finally come to see this, we will know the real price of salvation from what is still solemnly alleged to be nothing less than anarchy. Then we will recognize the terms of our bargain; we will know that the prevailing political machinery cannot enhance local autonomy and self-reliance but can only give private groups power to impose an inequality of conditions. Once this becomes apparent and frankly disturbing to us, perhaps we can feel more justified in devoting ourselves to the task of transforming the party system, of making it the paramount instrument for popular control of the national leadership, of making it provide for majority representation.

If we want to prevent incumbent administrations from relying on quasi-sovereign private groups for their power (or worse, from relying on the people en masse) we must, for lack of feasible alternatives, compel them to rely on political parties. It is not hard to see why. When a government in power fails to find the source of its strength in the parties, it is impelled to turn to the most potent groups in the community. In that case, it has always been justly castigated. Alternatively, an administration may of course seek to balance and counterbalance existing groups, on the assumption that this somehow protects the individuals within them. In that case, when it has acted as a balancer of group interests, it has been generally applauded. But the applause is dying out, or should be. Finally, a President may respond directly to his unmediated sense of the needs of the time. In a position of enormous power, he may then seek to get his program across by whipping up sentiment in its behalf. Divining "America's purpose," he may employ the techniques of public relations to communicate and merchandise his insight. To be sure, this will be a matter of temperament and style. A weak President will find such activity exhausting. A politically unskilled one will not be able to fathom the depth of his reservoir of power. And a strong one will constitute an incalculable danger.

If therefore the present system makes the President troublesome whether he be weak, strong, or simply awkward—and if, with Tocqueville, we shudder at the thought of his emerging as a charismatic popular sovereign—we must tie him to his party far more firmly than we have ventured to do so far. And believing in a competitive party system, we must do the same to the leader of the opposition.

What would seem initially important is to concede the basic soundness of this approach so that the debate about reforms can be practical in orientation, so that reform proposals cannot be attacked as "idolatry of the British system" or failure to appreciate "the genius of American politics." Whether or not we should strengthen the party bureaucracies, aid them financially out of public funds, establish party bodies (such as the Democratic Advisory Council) to consider national policy, and support party government by modifying the system of staggered presidential and congressional elections—whether or not we should do some or all of these things must become an altogether empirical question. Thus the proposals which were made by Woodrow Wilson in 1885, by William Y. Elliott in 1935, by an American Political Science Association committee in 1950, and by Stephen K. Bailey in 1959 must be viewed in the light of a new consensus: the consensus on the importance of making the party system an instrumentality through which the will of the majority finds expression.[10]

A reformed party system, while surely raising new problems of responsibility and accountability, will alleviate at least one condition we have come to see as pathological—the friction between President and Congress. This friction would be all to the good if it provided no opportunity to evade responsibility, if it really contributed to the maintenance of a tension-beset and hence flexible society, if it did not enable private groups to eradicate conflict and impose order. If, moreover, this were friction between a legislative organ of government obliged to make the laws and magisterial one obliged merely to execute the laws faithfully there would be further reason for preserving the relative independence and separation of the executive. Whatever irritation would result from this would be compensated for by the likelihood that an independent executive—like an independent judiciary—would not protect any group in society from the impact of public laws.

But the friction which the present system generates is demonstrably not the kind which enhances the sensitivity of our policy-making organs. These public organs are confronted by privately agreed on possibilities. While large-scale private groups do not generally make the law, they do prevent it from being made. Limiting the range of alternatives, they restrict the maneuverability of public government. They restrain not Congress but that *de facto* legislative chamber which includes the executive establishment. Thus, realistically speaking, the friction generated by the present system is friction within the legislature. Notwithstanding Section 1, Article I, of the United States Constitution, "all legislative powers herein granted" are no longer vested in the Congress. Congress's willingness to delegate legislative power throughout American history is evidence enough. The complete otherworldliness of the argument that whatever has been delegated, "essential" legislative power "cannot" be delegated and therefore "is" retained, should always have condemned it. When Congress gives regulatory commissions the authority to act in behalf of the public interest, convenience, and necessity, it surrenders legislative authority. In much-repeated theory, the surrender is strictly conditional. But in fact, there is no recall, for the conditions which impel Congress to delegate power remain unmodified. Congress itself knows that it is unable to regulate modern technological society. Is it not naïve, therefore, to hanker for a reinvigoration of Congress by returning delegated powers to it, by hoping to equip it with the machinery for increasing its practical knowledge of technology, economics, and warfare? If Congress is to be a significant part of a constitutional democracy, its reform must be consistently in the direction of enabling it to criticize and publicize the work carried on under the great authority of the President. Although the specifics for this have been the subject of countless reform proposals, the ultimate objectives of the proposals have frequently remained cloudy. What we might keep clearly in mind is that their desirability should be measured by their ability to contribute to coordinated program planning, by their ability to allow the members of Congress to deal with general policy and to escape the choking hold of local constituents.

If the power to legislate must devolve jointly on the President and the Congress, and if it is to be systematically coordinated, the problem of responsibility becomes more acute than ever, for the check on government inherent in a basic separation of powers is seriously weakened. Once governmental power is sharply concentrated to ensure its effectiveness, it must be all the more firmly checked, and the only political institutions available for the purpose are the parties. Whoever gives form to policies, Congress no less than the President, must consequently be geared to the party system.

A deliberate, calculated shift of power toward the President and the political parties—a shift away from associations operating either directly or through congressional and federal agencies—must be seen as a necessary but insufficient condition for responsible government. For there remains the specter of party tyranny.

If we continue to recall, however, that the public control of public bodies is always essential, we will have no reason to shield the parties from public action. Their legal status—and hence their amenability to formal, legal, and enforceable control—has been difficult to define.[11] But the basic function of a sound party system may be stated easily enough: it is to ensure the permanent presence of opposition. Thus public regulation of the parties need have no more ambitious objective than making them perform this function. We need not regulate parties to make them less bureaucratic and less oligarchical but merely to ensure continuous, sustained competition between them.

Such competition demands no more ideological distinction between parties than exists between the major parties of Great Britain. An accurate picture of the British party system should remind us that party government need not be government by ideological parties. Whatever the myth, the fact is that Britain does not have government by parties advancing distinct and coherent programs. "Two monolithic structures now face each other and conduct furious arguments about the comparatively minor issues that separate them," R. T. McKenzie concluded in 1955.[12] True, British parties do impose policies. Furthermore, like the Republicans and the Democrats, broad tendencies and economic interests unite each of them. Yet, as Samuel H. Beer has noted,

each party is a coalition of groups with interests and values which compel recognition in program-making. And similarly when a party is in power, its ministers and Cabinet, concerned with successful administration, party unity and victory at the next election, adjust and shape policy in response to the claims of interest groups.[13]

Favoring parties able to keep officials in line need not, therefore, commit us to programmatic parties. All that must be expected of an adequate party system is that the party out of office formulate just enough of a program to embarrass and hence challenge the party in office. The incumbent party's platform is likely to be at once conservative, defensive, and general; the challenger's is likely to be reformist, aggressive, and specific. Parties clashing on this basis will neither formulate ambitious social plans nor activate the citizenry. But this is not to be regretted, for the norms of constitutional liberalism do not demand it. On the contrary, they positively require that architectonic programs affecting the ends of life be formulated outside the public arena by individuals or their voluntary associations. Within the public arena, parties must be held to do no more than to provide recurrent threats of a change of key personnel, making for the personal insecurity of those who exercise the power to govern. The point of such a system is not to guarantee the emergence of public virtue or of truth but to assure the responsiveness and responsibility of those in power. It is to compel those in power to remain constantly interested in the publicly unattached and privately virtuous voter. A political system which allows a plurality of groups to give meaning to what their members deem moral need not be excellent in any substantive sense. Excellence relates to individuals and their private associations. In public life, we should expect only the negative virtue of moderation and the procedures which assure its perpetuity.[14]

If these imperatives be accepted, we need not concern ourselves with the autocratic character of our parties. We must focus instead on the political environment within which they operate. And here we must enable each adult to whom we extend the suffrage to remain alert to every possible deprivation of his ultimate right: the opportunity of leading the good life. Because we require a citizenry which is meaningfully free to influence government, every monopolization of the channels of public information and public debate must be frustrated. Our aim must be to provide a profusion of media to report and interpret public affairs. These must constitute the ground on which individuals who choose to share in the legislative process can rest their case for the extension or restriction of governmental power. What is demanded—not for its own sake but to provide the context for responsible parties and, consequently, for a nontyrannical government—is, in the very broadest sense, a system of universal adult education. Such a system is not to indoctrinate, not to attach individuals to official doctrine or incumbent governments, but to furnish suitable conditions for the detached search for virtue and truth.

On a far more pedestrian, more easily realized level, we must make aspirants to public office less sensitive to the unequal private power of their potential constituents. That is to say, we will have to make them far less dependent on the most powerful element of their electorate than they are now. To sever the link between the government and the economy, between public officials and organizational giants, the power base of elected public officials must be widened. And this requires giving the candidates for public office state support, perhaps in the form of graduated tax concessions to his supporters. As he is made less responsive to private groups, he may feel free to become responsive to a public of political equals, to work within a realm of means for the sake of a society that is pluralistic in the realm of ends.

The political reforms needed today are neither theoretically abstract nor divorced from historical tendencies. On the one hand, they are demanded by our principled belief in political equality and government by consent of the governed. On the other, they give explicit recognition to already existing institutional forces. We should note and welcome the emergence of the National Democratic Advisory Council as well as the rising importance of the chairmen of the two parties and their committees.[15] These tendencies, if that is what they are, may well be attributed to the fact that politics is in fact being nationalized. It is becoming increasingly difficult for the Democratic Party to hold its Southern wing, and no less difficult for the Republican Party to put up with its progressive wing. For good or ill, the parties are becoming increasingly homogeneous. If we are committed to a theory of government responsible to national popular majorities, we might unashamedly acknowledge these tendencies and the force behind them. Our problem may not be so much to think or to do something radically new as to give added weight to what exists, permitting it to move in the right direction. To see this clearly should enable us to act with less doubt and more composure.

16

An Orientation for Research

It is not easy to arrest, disturb, and transcend an approach to American politics which uncritically accepts the status quo as functional and, confident in the knowledge that all will turn out for the best, becomes cheerfully analytical. Yet it does remain possible to appeal to the ideals of liberalism and constitutionalism, for social scientists themselves profess their dedication to them. Insofar as they can be persuaded to see these ideals not as goals which they should diligently implement or which their labor will fortunately vindicate but instead as directives analogous to the ideals of social science, then an argument for reorienting part of current research, for making it more generous and inclusive, may have a chance of taking hold.

It will bear reiterating that liberalism unequivocally demands that room be always left for the unique and the incommensurable in human affairs. Because our knowledge is necessarily finite, a commitment to liberalism implies recognizing the impossibility of avoiding ambiguity not only in all human action but also in all human discourse. Constitutionalism, in turn, insists on procedures which preserve the variety of possible opinions. It insists that the requirements of due process be satisfied before we arrive at moral judgments. As one eminent student of jurisprudence has suggested, it is not only our public action which must meet the test of due process but also our philosophical methods. Edmond Cahn's carefully measured restatement of the main requirements of due process captures its relevant ingredients:

We must not accuse anyone of an act violating some standard of behavior unless he could have ascertained the existence and meaning of the standard before he committed the act. We must let him know what he is accused of doing and must give him a fair opportunity to collect his evidence and then to present it. The judge and jury who hear his case must be unbiased and attentive; and, especially where the accusation is a grave one, the accused is entitled to the assistance of a counsel and advocate. Moreover, even after an accused has been found guilty, due process of law requires that we provide some sort of remedial procedure to uncover and correct any serious error that may have been committed in the trial of his case.[1]

Constitutionalism, seen in these terms, compels perpetual review. It will thereby impede those who, having defined the ideal once and for all, would righteously have us make it synonymous with the real; it will frustrate those who would have us eliminate the tension between value and fact. There are lessons here for the practitioners of modern social science.

The vision of social science should properly span patterned, uniform, and recurrent as well as unique phenomena. Our need for the former requires no stressing today. Descriptions of behavior substantiated by a method of formal deduction and empirical fact-finding must be welcomed to make the business of living as practical as possible, to establish the correlations which enable us to come to terms with our world, to reduce private searches for meaning, and to make life less perplexing and unnerving. There is every need to check the trustworthiness of subjective insights empirically. Without such verifications, men cannot master even the meanest of chores, not to mention the running of an industrial society. To succeed without being exhausted, they may rightly demand generalizations from all scientists who are working to discover the causes, conditions, and results of behavior, to refine a social technology, and to sharpen the tools for gathering and relating facts. Unless such work is encouraged, society is deprived of the practical knowledge by which it may efficiently approximate a just regime. Only a science concerned with contingencies is able to help adjust the various ends of individuals to larger purposes.

To be sure, what society considers urgent at the moment cannot dictate the aim of a science committed to gain purely hypothetical knowledge. But it can dictate the aim of a science whose practitioners are intent on supplying practical knowledge for the solution of social problems. To the extent that science leaves its theoretical quest and turns to problem-solving, it loses its claim to independence. As long as it is content to veto, qualify, and refute hypotheses, its claim to autonomy remains unchallengeable. But when social science is engaged in creating balance, in acting on the phenomena under investigation, it cannot validly consider itself immune to public control. The reasons for this have only recently been driven home by history: the material on which a problem-solving social science operates is all too human and pliable. The nature known to the physicist or biologist will not bend when technicians put hypotheses to the test; it remains intractable. But our ideas of what is valuable are far from firm. In fact, for the duration of an experiment, whether with cooperative students in psychology courses or the inmates of concentration camps, they can be made to shrivel and vanish altogether.

Yet that we ought to employ scientific knowledge to solve problems and resolve conflicts should go without saying. No testing of variables, within ethical limits, is inherently undesirable; nothing that adds to the knowledge of tangible reality is intrinsically noxious. An applied social science, however much it will have the effect of denying some human interests in favor of others, should certainly help to make the ideal state a real one by planning and regulating for it, by searching for the most efficient means to civilize our lives. Especially when survival itself is in doubt and conflicting interests beg to be neutralized the social sciences must be enlisted. They can serve, we know, to maintain morale by "clarifying" national objectives, thus helping to control the garrison—whether it be an infantry platoon, an internment camp, an industrial plant, or an entire nation.

Making full room for this instrumental role of the social sciences, we should remain wary of the potent reconciliations they are capable of bringing about. The desire for balance and peace is frequently less unanimous than claimed, reflecting the uneasiness of well-settled groups which prefer a tranquil state marked by a minimum of friction. Hence we cannot simply accept every or-else-we-perish case for employing the armory of techniques of the social sciences. Survival at any price may be agreed on. But it would be difficult indeed to determine how genuine an agreement is when men, now "understood" with ever-increasing accuracy, are adjusted and satisfied simply by being kept busy and productive. When the social sciences are engaged to achieve some specific balance, the balance toward which they work cannot be assumed to be grounded in "the nature of things" or in "the logic of the situation." True, there is so much consensus in Western society about what is warranted by "nature" or "logic" that it would be unobjectionable in a great many fields—notably, racial conflict, labor-management violence, or the mental battleground of schizophrenics—to view the desirability of social and personal peace as axiomatic. But we have no reason for universalizing what is axiomatic only in some areas. In a liberal society, consensus will always be limited by the variety of man's visions and consequent loyalties. Furthermore, there are some things which cannot be conclusively settled without compromising the very basis of a liberal society. These have always been worth fighting about, worth trading for part or for all of one's life —even when such an exchange shocks and irritates an economic system, a social structure, or an international order.

Thus we cannot in all cases simply take it for granted that the end of life is to keep it going or that the whole purpose of the social sciences is to create public consensus by a science of means. We cannot assume that it is proper for a social technology to practice unrestricted therapy. The healthy state toward which it would benevolently lead us is a debatable good.[2] Consequently all offered justifications for a new allocation of men and their goods must remain suspect.* When we permit social science to act on society, we must make certain that what is defined as an emergency, a disease, an anomie, or a dysfunctional arrangement is in fact experienced as such by the people affected. The definition of order is the business not of social engineers but of the citizenry. We cannot let expert technicians point to the so-called facts and then allow them to settle what the institution of civil politics will leave up in the air. All men potentially moved by a promised new equilibrium have the right to be represented in the debate. Unless their various interests are considered, we permit the knowledge of how to run society to be used only for society's endless and inhuman perpetuation.

What is intolerable, in short, is any final definition of an ideal state and any experimentation which tends to drive men into it by means of the "scientific method" rather than the "unscientific" processes of politics. To the extent, then, that social science is problem-oriented, it must be thoroughly subordinated to the ever-retractable, always ambiguous, and never wholly persuasive conclusions reached by political processes.

But even a combination of (1) a politically harnessed social science specifying the means to achieve socially desired ends and (2) an unharnessed theory-oriented social science which remains consistently tentative, relativistic, and hypothetical should not be permitted to exhaust the proper task of the social sciences. A science concerned with man's natural, determinate behavior is insufficient: for us, the limits of a behavioral approach which tells us how things keep happening, in the nexus of cause and effect, cannot define the limits of reality. We should like to know not only what men and social organisms are likely to do but also what

---

* Of course there are always practical difficulties. It may be imprudent to publicize facts relevant to the formulation of public policy. And it may be necessary to act dictatorially to maintain the conditions for individualism, politics, and conflict. Still, the areas for secrecy or for bipartisan action are not as self-evident as we permit ourselves to think. The systematic consideration of limits, as for example in Clinton Rossiter's *Constitutional Dictatorship: Crisis Government in the Modern Democracies* (1948), remains an ever-relevant task.

their actions mean. Automatic and unconscious behavior can be made understandable by the methods of empirical science, but purposive, goal-oriented action requires explanations facing up to norms as ends in themselves. Because these norms are never wholly definable, they cannot be eased into the deductive framework erected by a positive science of behavior. Such a science takes note only of unequivocal relationships, signifying these by quantitative, functional symbols. It is not able to come to grips with human action unless it assumes that all values are mere functions of a "real" substructure, of an underlying order that is empirically definable.

But such an assumption is no more than a methodological necessity essential to get results in science. Because every effort to prove its validity generates contradictions, we have warrant to base some of our research on the postulate that at least part of man is indeterminate. If there is always more to be discovered about man—and if we do not wish to leave the articulation of whatever additional elements there may be to the journalist, the novelist, the poet, the theologian, or the mystic with the itch to talk—then social science should be prepared to come to terms with purposive, value-oriented action. It is this which demands that we support a humanistic perspective.

To enlarge the range of our perceptions, we require approaches which will do justice to the richness, the color, the tang of man's political life. We must seek to apprehend and give expression to the qualities of man and his society in ways that nonhumanistic disciplines do not pretend to offer. Whereas science deliberately restricts and abstracts, what we need—not in its place but in addition—are formulas which express man in his fullness, articulating potentialities but rarely displayed. Thus it is not things as they are that require our discipline to be generous and humanistic: it is our need to disclose how they might be.

What this stress entails, more specifically, is an appreciation of formulations that serve to explicate, enlarge, and complicate our affairs. When the prevailing tendency is to reduce our world in theory and unify it in practice, the need is all the greater for the kind of presentations which dislodge the status quo simply by representing it in concentrated form, as all irony does. Keeping contradictions in suspense, such a discipline enables its adherents to project possibilities which it is unconventional to consider. Taking stock for individuals too absorbed by their environment, too captivated by present urgencies, it can expose our usual business and politics as incomplete ventures, as meager preoccupations, as flat and stale and unpromising. Recalling historical complications and reconstructing lost causes, it may free us from the dismal view that things had to turn out as they did. By developing new analogies and utopias, by extending the context in which we make specific decisions, it may help us detect riches we have failed to discern. By indicating that the future holds more possibilities than we like to think, it may enable us to break with the past. And by pointing to the concrete sources of impotence and vitality which tend to escape extremists—activists too much in touch and quietists too much out of touch—it may not only release us from the dictates of the past but also provide a new basis for mediation and reconciliation. Sensitive to continuities, it may chasten those who are merely expansive and fitful. It may thereby make it possible for us to stabilize our existence.

To enrich ourselves and our social environment in this way, to magnify our behavior by disclosing how magnificently noble and miserably base it can be, is to show a willingness to comprehend the unique, to approach it sympathetically despite the risk of losing a degree of social cohesion in celebrating the exceptional instance and tolerating idiosyncracy. But we cannot begin to care about political matters as they uniquely confront us unless we believe that our political order is not wholly explicable in quantitative or clearly operational terms. These terms, the only ones accommodated by empirical science, sacrifice part of conceivable reality, achieving reconciliation by elimination. What we have always required is an articulate appreciation for the political, for the clash of public opinions and ideals. We now require a tolerance, *within* the discipline of the social sciences, for that far from simple realm in which we exist as unfulfilled and disquieted, as unredeemed by our groups, institutions, and laws. Such tolerance, which is tolerance for the possibility of rational discourse about the partially inexplicable, requires the postulation of an order which lets men live precariously and which accepts the capricious, the accidental, and the miraculous.

Properly oriented, then, social science will not only be a naturalistic, behavioral science in quest of generalizations which explain and ultimately control reality but also a humanistic discipline in quest of knowledge about, and love for, the specific moment. Only by stressing the complementary nature of both can it successfully maintain that tension between the abstract and the specific which is always in danger of being resolved. It will consequently value the institutions and habits of scholarship which keep us restless, nervous, and argumentative. It will keep us from reveling in the particular and from impatiently embracing the general. It will, in a word, prevent us from coming to substantive conclusions.

What should these general requirements imply for American research today? If we are opposed to the conversion of methodological assumptions into absolute dogmas, we must subvert every tendency to make a mere approach to understanding into something absolute, autonomous, and objective. The current approach, which soothingly defines our existing political structure as pervasively pluralistic, hypostatizes pluralism. It uses this definition as its point of departure and uncritically treats public and "private" politics as functional (or dysfunctional) manifestations of a naturally laudable pluralistic social order. Failing to introduce distinctions, it confines the political imagination; artificially limiting the realm of meaningful action, it discourages the projection of alternative possibilities.

If we are still interested in expanding our knowledge, we must push beyond the emphasis on homogeneous interest groups as the ultimate determinant of public action. We must free ourselves to speculate about problems beyond those posed only by the assumption of pluralism. Thus the values of any social structure and political equilibrium should be seen as continuously debatable. They should be discussed in terms of mobility, conflict, and competition—even though this requires less reliance on the current structure-function approach and renewed trust in the historical sense.

The American political scene, moreover, might well be approached with more affection and wonder, with less of that methodological sophistication which makes so much of the "literature" of political science unreadable. Only a genuine sense of puzzlement over specific problems can lead to studies that reveal with precision and concrete exactness just how we live our lives politically. Research, after all, should enlist some human interest, and the attempt to make it do so should not be inimical to scholarship. Our writing should incorporate our perceptions of unfelt purposes, unexpressed interests, and unregistered aspirations, of only barely sensed trials, defeats, and resentments; our prose should reflect existing tensions, should make the most and not the least of ambiguities, willingly supplying the adjectives which add resonance to nouns. Our research should lead us to more acute knowledge of the peculiarities, incongruities, and eccentricities of the American political tradition. It should aspire to make the whole of our past (and thus the whole of our present) intelligible to us. Such research cannot help but expose the human complexity of seemingly natural, inexorable social phenomena, whether these be the division of labor, the structure of bureaucracy, or the character of our economic and industrial order. Analysis should reveal to what extent the attributing of iron imperatives to human organizations constitutes what Alvin W. Gouldner has called a metaphysical pathos.[3]

That men are not autonomous, that societies develop along predetermined lines, that governments reflect the unfree will of individuals—these are propositions we have been conditioned to accept as true. But we must remain alert to that perverse but honorable quality in man and his organizations which, at least so far, has always cheated a naturalistic social science of its success, just as it has challenged every totalitarian autocracy. We can sharpen our perception of this quality by attempting more historical studies which cherish, without apology, the unique event, the peculiar institution, or the exceptional case. These should reveal our possibilities as well as our limits. Such studies are needed not simply because they can be useful to the preservation of a body politic or essential for the cohesion of society. More significantly, they are needed because we expect science to show us truth in its largest dimensions.

Notes

NOTES TO CHAPTER 1

1. *The Organizational Revolution* (New York: Harper, 1953), pp. 3–4.

2. *The Unadjusted Man* (Boston: Beacon, 1956), pp. 330–31.

3. This theme, with a somewhat different accent, is brilliantly elaborated in Louis Hartz, *The Liberal Tradition in America* (New York: Harcourt, Brace, 1955).

NOTES TO CHAPTER 2

1. Dwight Waldo, "The Relationship of Democracy to Administration," unpublished paper, 1956, p. 5.

2. U.S. National Resources Committee, *The Structure of the American Economy*, Part I, 1939, p. 96; quoted in David Truman, *The Governmental Process* (New York: Knopf, 1951), pp. 53–54.

3. These historical consequences have been the subject of an extensive literature morally burdened by the phenomena of mass culture. See, for examples, Hannah Arendt's *Origins of Totalitarianism* (1951), Erich Fromm's *The Sane Society* (1955), Sigmund Freud's *Group Psychology and Analysis of the Ego* (1922), José Ortega y Gasset, *The Revolt of the Masses* (1950), and, of course, much contemporary science fiction.

4. "Notes on Work," *Encounter*, 8 (April 1957), 3–15, 11–12.

5. *Capitalism, Socialism, and Democracy* (New York: Harper, 1942),

pp. 132–33. The question here is not whether inventions originate in the big laboratory (probably they do not) but whether an industrial system absorbs those originating elsewhere (probably it does).

6. *Principles of Political Economy* (London: Longmans, Green, 1926), p. 111.

7. This has been persuasively argued with reference to the steel industry in Ward S. Bowman, "Toward Less Monopoly," *University of Pennsylvania Law Review*, 101 (March 1953), 566–642, 600–611. See also Joe S. Bain, "Economies of Scale, Concentration, and the Condition of Entry in Twenty Manufacturing Industries," *American Economic Review*, 44 (March 1954), 15–39.

8. See P. Sargant Florence, *The Logic of British and American Industry* (Chapel Hill: University of North Carolina Press, 1953), p. 354.

9. See Edward S. Mason, *Economic Concentration and the Monopoly Problem* (Cambridge: Harvard University Press, 1957), p. 39.

10. Dr. J. J. Brown of Aluminium, Ltd.; quoted in *Fortune* round table, "The Automatic Factory," *Fortune*, 48 (October 1953), 168 ff.

11. *The Power Elite* (New York: Oxford University Press, 1956), p. 123.

12. *America's Next Twenty Years* (New York: Harper, 1958), p. 34.

NOTES TO CHAPTER 3

1. See A. A. Berle, Jr., and Gardiner C. Means, *The Modern Corporation and Private Property* (New York: Commerce Clearing House, 1932), Book 1, chap. 2, and Book 2, chap. 1; Walton Hamilton, "The Genius of the Radical," in John W. Chase, ed., *Years of the Modern* (New York: Longmans, Green, 1949), and *The Politics of Industry* (New York: Knopf, 1957), chaps. 1–3; C. Wright Mills, *White Collar* (New York: Oxford University Press, 1951), chaps. 1–2.

2. *The Modern Corporation and Private Property*, p. 18.

3. See M. A. Adelman, "The Measurement of Industrial Concentration," *Review of Economics and Statistics*, 32 (November 1951), 269–96; for critiques, see the same journal, 34 (May 1952), 156–78.

4. *Economic Concentration and the Monopoly Problem* (Cambridge: Harvard University Press, 1957), p. 39.

5. See G. Warren Nutter, *The Extent of Enterprise Monopoly in the United States—1899–1939* (Chicago: University of Chicago Press, 1951).

6. See Senate Committee on the Judiciary, Subcommittee on Antitrust and Monopoly, *Concentration in American Industry*, 85th Congress, 1st Session, 1957.

7. These illustrations are supplied by Morton S. Baratz, "Corporate

Giants and the Power Structure," *Western Political Quarterly,* 9 (June 1956), 406–15.

8. *Maintaining Competition* (New York: McGraw-Hill, 1949), p. 117.

9. See Carl Kaysen, "The Corporation: How Much Power? What Scope?" in Edward S. Mason, ed., *The Corporation in Modern Society* (Cambridge: Harvard University Press, 1959), pp. 85–105, 86, and the references cited by Kaysen. See also Adelman, "The Measurement of Industrial Concentration," *loc. cit.,* pp. 269–96.

10. See Robert Tilove, *Pension Funds and Economic Freedom* (New York: Fund for the Republic, 1959); Adolf A. Berle, Jr., *Power without Property* (New York: Harcourt, Brace, 1959); Paul P. Harbrecht, *Pension Funds and Economic Power* (New York: Twentieth Century Fund, 1959).

11. "Corporate Giants and the Power Structure," *loc. cit.,* p. 412.

12. See *The Power Elite* (New York: Oxford University Press, 1956), p. 122.

13. The classic study is E. E. Schattschneider, *Politics, Pressure and the Tariff* (New York: Prentice-Hall, 1935). See also A. S. Cleveland, "NAM: Spokesman for Industry?" *Harvard Business Review,* 26 (May 1948), 353–71; "Renovation in N.A.M.," *Fortune,* 38 (July 1948), 72 ff.; and, on trade associations more generally, David Truman, *The Governmental Process* (New York: Knopf, 1951), pp. 74–86.

14. See especially Seymour Melman, "The Rise of Administrative Overhead in the Manufacturing Industries of the United States, 1899–1947," *Oxford Economic Papers,* 3 (January 1951), 66.

15. *Work and Authority in Industry* (New York: Wiley, 1956), p. 221.

16. J. M. Keynes, "The End of Laissez-Faire," in *Essays in Persuasion* (New York: Harcourt, Brace, 1932), pp. 314–15.

17. *Adventures of a White-Collar Man* (New York: Doubleday, 1941), p. 145; quoted in Reinhard Bendix, "Bureaucratization in Industry," in Arthur Kornhauser *et al.,* eds., *Industrial Conflict* (New York: Mc-Graw-Hill, 1954), pp. 164–75, 171.

18. "New Dimensions in Business Leadership," *Saturday Review,* January 18, 1958, 29–32.

19. *USA—The Permanent Revolution* (New York: Prentice-Hall, 1951), p. 88.

20. "Industrial Relations—1975," address, Michigan State University, April 24, 1957, published by Ford Motor Co., 1957. See also the testimony by businessmen before the Flanders Committee hearings on profits. (Senate Subcommittee of the Joint Committee on the Economic Report, *Hearings,* 80th Congress, 2nd Session, 1948, especially at pp. 212, 475).

21. "Management's Responsibilities in a Complex World," *Harvard Business Review,* 29 (May 1951), 29–30.

22. "The Danger of Drifting," *Harvard Business Review,* 28 (January 1950), 25–32. See also Bernard W. Dempsey, "The Roots of Business Responsibility," *Harvard Business Review,* 27 (July 1949), 393–404.

23. "What Is Right in Business," an address delivered at the Park Avenue Baptist Church, New York; quoted in John A. Sears, *The New Place of the Stockholder* (New York: Harper, 1929), p. 209.

24. For evidence of how elaborately this theme is developed in American business ideology, see Francis X. Sutton *et al., The American Business Creed* (Cambridge: Harvard University Press, 1956), pp. 155–60.

25. Quoted in *Time,* November 26, 1956, p. 98.

26. *Ibid.* For a report on the increasing pressure by business corporations to enact public policies not related to their immediate interests, see Peter Bart, "Big Corporations Mount Soapboxes: 'Political Awareness' Drive Enters the Stage of Espousing Causes," *The New York Times,* May 29, 1960, Sec. 3, pp. 1 ff.

27. *Time,* November 26, 1956, p. 98.

28. Roger M. Blough, "Great Expectations," address before the Economic Club of Chicago, March 13, 1957, published by the United States Steel Corporation, 1957.

29. *The Power Elite,* p. 145; Mills's quotations are from Ida M. Tarbell, *Owen D. Young* (New York: Macmillan, 1932), pp. 232, 113, 229–30, 121.

30. *Work and Authority in Industry,* p. 335.

31. *White Collar,* pp. 100, 234–35. See also Loren Baritz, *The Servants of Power: A History of the Use of Social Science in American Industry* (Middletown, Conn.: Wesleyan University Press, 1960).

32. *The Modern Corporation and Private Property,* p. 9.

33. Less familiar is owner control by the use of foundations: "It is this peculiar circumstance—*retention of control*—which largely explains the emergence of family foundations as the dominant feature on the foundation scene today. Men who have built successful enterprises and seen the value of their equity swell have sought, naturally, to keep control within the family. They have accordingly established charitable family foundations, minimized their tax, enjoyed the satisfaction of promoting good works, and retained practically all but the dividend benefits of ownership. Such persons, it has been said, actually do not give away their property at all, but only the income thereon—though this is perhaps an overstatement." (Note, *Virginia Law Review,* 34 [February 1948], 182–201, 188.)

34. *Business Leadership in the Large Corporation* (Washington, D.C.: Brookings Institution, 1945), pp. 160–61. See also Joseph A. Livingston, *The American Stockholder* (Philadelphia: Lippincott, 1958).

35. *The 20th Century Capitalist Revolution* (New York: Harcourt, Brace, 1954), p. 30.

36. Thus in the ten years preceding 1954, retained earnings averaged 54 per cent of corporate profits after taxes. See Report of the President's Council of Economic Advisors, January 1955, Table D-49; see also S. P. Dobrovolsky, *Corporate Income Retention, 1915–1943* (New York: National Bureau of Economic Research, 1951).

37. *The 20th Century Capitalist Revolution*, p. 41.

38. There is more specific material on membership in primitive folk societies, Greek city-states, medieval universities, or religious communities than there is on the relations between individuals and the modern corporation. See, however, Mills's *White Collar* (1951) and *The Power Elite* (1956), Whyte's *Is Anybody Listening?* (1952) and *The Organization Man* (1956), and the work of such novelists as John P. Marquand. No less revealing are the occasional autobiographical works of apostates, such as T. K. Quinn's *Giant Business* (1954) and Alan Harrington's *Life in the Crystal Palace* (1959).

39. Quoted in *Time,* November 26, 1956, p. 98.

40. See Senate Committee on Interstate and Foreign Commerce, *Hearings on S. 3865,* June 23 and 24, 1958.

41. "The Crown Princes of Business," *Fortune,* 48 (October 1953), 152 ff. See also "The Nine Hundred," *Fortune,* 46 (November 1952), 132 ff.

42. Mordecai Ezekiel, "Distribution of Gains from Rising Technical Efficiency in Progressing Economies," *American Economic Review, Papers and Proceedings,* 47 (May 1957), 361–73, 372.

43. See *A Creed for Free Enterprise* (Boston: Little, Brown, 1952), p. 83. See also "Corporations Make Politics Their Business," *Fortune,* 60 (December 1959), 100 ff.

44. Stuart Chase, *A Generation of Industrial Peace: Thirty Years of Labor Relations at Standard Oil Company (N.J.)* (New Jersey: Standard Oil Co., N.J., 1946), pp. 51–52.

45. "The New Conservatism: A Bold Creed for Modern Capitalism," *Time,* November 26, 1956, p. 98.

46. Berle has pointed out that in 1954 General Motors committed over a billion dollars in new capital development allegedly to counter the possibility of a nationwide depression. (See Berle, *The 20th Century Capitalist Revolution*, p. 34.)

47. See especially Ralph S. Brown, Jr., *Loyalty and Security* (New Haven: Yale University Press, 1958).

48. The prerogatives of management may "include power to determine that certain towns or areas shall be developed and shall become industrialized, and heretofore has included (the power is now in dispute) capacity to leave a community, taking its operations elsewhere, possibly leaving a broken city behind." (Berle, *The 20th Century Capitalist Revolution*, p. 33.)

NOTES TO CHAPTER 4

1. See especially Lloyd Ulman, *The Rise of the National Trade Union* (Cambridge: Harvard University Press, 1956).

2. House Committee on Education and Labor, 80th Congress, 2d Session, *Hearings on Restrictive Union Practices of the American Federation of Musicians,* 1948, Part 1, p. 343.

3. See especially House Committee on Education and Labor, *Hearings on Union Democracy,* 81st Congress, 1st and 2d Session, 1950; Senate Committee on Labor and Public Welfare, *Welfare and Pension Plan Investigation, Final Report,* 84th Congress, 2d Session, 1956; Select Senate Committee on Improper Activities in the Labor Management Field, *Hearings,* Part 8, 85th Congress, 1st Session, 1957, especially pp. 2800–2801, 2805, 3084–87; A. L. Gitlow, "Machine Politics in American Trade Unions," *Journal of Politics,* 14 (August 1952), 370–85.

4. Quoted in Grant McConnell, "The Spirit of Private Government," *American Political Science Review,* 52 (September 1958), 754–70, 760. For an explicit prohibition of factionalism, see the constitution of the International Brotherhood of Electrical Workers, Article 27.

5. I.L.W.U. *Proceedings of the Seventh Biennial Convention,* San Francisco, 1947, p. 178.

6. See *The New York Times,* September 16, 1958, p. 1. On conventions generally, see especially William M. Leiserson, *American Trade Union Democracy* (New York: Columbia University Press, 1959).

7. "The World of Jimmy Hoffa—II," *The Reporter,* February 7, 1957, pp. 10–17, 17.

8. In 1955, the National Industrial Conference, having examined the disciplinary provision of 194 national unions, found that in 44 of them a local union executive board was empowered to investigate charges and to impose penalties. In 72 of them, the national president or the executive board had the power to assume original jurisdiction to discipline members—with appeal always possible to the convention. See National Industrial Conference Board, *Handbook of Union Government and Procedures,* 1955, as cited in Sar A. Levitan, *Government Regulation of Internal Union Affairs Affecting the Rights of Members* (Washington, D.C.: Government Printing Office, 1958). See also Philip Taft, *The Structure and Government of Labor Unions* (Cambridge: Harvard University Press, 1954); Leo Bromwich, *Union Constitutions* (New York: Fund for the Republic, 1959); Clyde Summers, "Disciplinary Powers of Unions," *Industrial and Labor Relations Review,* 3 (July 1950), 483–513; and "Disciplinary Procedures of Unions," *Industrial and Labor Relations Review,* 4 (October 1950), 15–31; H. W. Benson, "Labor's Uncertain Trumpet," *The Progressive,* 23 (June 1959), 41–44.

9. Select Senate Committee on Improper Activities in the Labor or Management Field, *Hearings,* 85th Congress, 1st Session, 1957.

10. *Ibid.,* Part 5.

11. *Ibid.,* Part 5, p. 1611.

12. *New Men of Power* (New York: Harcourt, Brace, 1948), p. 160.

13. Select Senate Committee on Improper Activities in the Labor or Management Field, *Hearings,* Part 13, pp. 5107–5109.

14. Quoted by Jacobs, "The World of Jimmy Hoffa—II," *loc. cit.,* p. 11.

15. Jacobs, "The World of Jimmy Hoffa—I," *loc cit.,* p. 18. Perhaps more in line with traditional objectives of American unions was Beck's voting newly purchased stock in favor of an incumbent group of Montgomery Ward managers. Though successfully fighting off unionization until then, Montgomery Ward abruptly agreed to sign a contract with Beck.

16. Jacobs, "The World of Jimmy Hoffa—II," *loc cit.,* p. 16.

17. "The Unfinished Task," *The Progressive,* 23 (January 1959), 20–23, 22.

18. Excerpts from an address by Edward G. Fox before the Coal Mining Institute of America, quoted in Richard A. Lester, *As Unions Mature: An Analysis of the Evolution of American Unionism* (Princeton: Princeton University Press, 1958), p. 70.

19. *The New York Times,* November 9, 1958, p. 1.

20. United Automobile, Aircraft and Agricultural Implement Workers of America, C.I.O., *Proceedings,* Fifteenth Convention, 1955, pp. 9–10. See also Morris Marget Goldings, *Labor Philosophy in American Industrialism,* Harvard College Senior Honors Thesis, 1957.

21. Arthur J. Goldberg, *AFL-CIO: Labor United* (New York: McGraw-Hill, 1956), pp. 223, 225.

22. See "Your Community—Labor's New Frontier," *Nation's Business,* 44 (October 1956), 29–31, 84–85.

23. Quoted in Goldberg, *AFL-CIO,* p. 224.

24. Goldberg, *AFL-CIO,* p. 224.

25. International Ladies' Garment Workers' Union, *Report of the General Executive Board to the 30th Convention,* New York, 1959, p. 224.

26. See Irving Howe and B. J. Widdick, *The UAW and Walter Reuther* (New York: Random House, 1949), pp. 134–36.

27. See especially Senate Committee on Labor and Public Welfare, *Hearings,* 81st Congress, 1st Session, 1950, Parts 1–3. Note statements by William Green, pp. 992–94, and Philip Murray, p. 1089. Clyde E. Dankert was perhaps the first to observe that "there appears to be a trend in the direction of a broader point of view among those who hold leadership positions in the unions—a trend in the direction of genuine social-consciousness." Such consciousness, he significantly added, is not necessarily radical or socialist; it may find expression in an interest "in preserving the present system." Clyde E. Dankert, *Contemporary Unionism in the United States* (New York: Prentice-Hall, 1948), p. 426.

28. Quoted in Goldberg, *AFL-CIO*, p. 5.
29. Gus Tyler, *A New Philosophy for Labor* (New York: Fund for the Republic, 1959), pp. 7, 10, 12.

NOTES TO CHAPTER 5

1. *America as a Civilization* (New York: Simon & Schuster, 1957), p. 289. See also p. 340.
2. L. S. Lyon, M. W. Watkins, and V. Abramson, *Government and Economic Life* (Washington: Brookings Institution, 1939), I, 486.
3. *The Politics of Industry* (New York: Knopf, 1957), pp. 94–95.
4. Sidney Fine, "President Roosevelt and the Automobile Code," *Mississippi Valley Historical Review*, 45 (June 1958), 23–50, 50.
5. Lloyd H. Fisher, *The Harvest Labor Market in California* (Cambridge: Harvard University Press, 1953), p. 126. This view was far from unique. See also some of the accounts of other war-time programs operating on pluralistic premises: A. R. Richards, "Tripartitism and Regional War Labor Boards," *Journal of Politics*, 14 (February 1952), 72–103; Murray Edelman, "Governmental Organization and Public Policy," *Public Administration Review*, 12 (Autumn 1952), 276–83; Fred Witney, *War-time Experience of the National Labor Relations Board: 1941–1945* (Urbana: University of Illinois Press, 1949); Dorothea de Schweinitz, *Labor and Management in a Common Enterprise* (Cambridge: Harvard University Press, 1949).
6. Fisher, *The Harvest Labor Market in California*, p. 136.
7. Special Senate Committee Investigating the National Defense Program, *Report No. 480*, 77th Congress, 2nd Session, January 15, 1942, Part 5, pp. 11 ff.

NOTES TO CHAPTER 6

1. One of the new unsentimental cases for planting democracy in the soil is Yves R. Simon, *Philosophy of Democratic Government* (Chicago: University of Chicago Press, 1951), chap. 5.
2. Isaac Weld, Jr., *Travels through the States of North America . . . during the Years 1795, 1796, and 1797* (London, 1807), I, 124–25.
3. See L. Grant McConnell, *The Decline of Agrarian Democracy* (Berkeley: University of California Press, 1953).
4. Earl Latham, "The Group Basis of Politics," *American Political Science Review*, 46 (June 1952), 376–97, 388.
5. One of the best sources is M. R. Benedict, *Farm Policies of the United States, 1790–1950* (New York: Twentieth Century Fund, 1953).
6. "Agricultural Policy and Administration in the American Federal

System," in Arthur W. MacMahon, ed., *Federalism: Mature and Emergent* (New York: Doubleday, 1955), pp. 281–304.

7. *The Public Papers and Addresses of Franklin D. Roosevelt* (New York: Random House, 1938), I, 693.

8. For a description of the system, subsequent to its 1946 reorganization, see A. Whitney Griswold, *Farming and Democracy* (New Haven: Yale University Press, 1952), p. 184.

9. It is reprinted in Appendix B in John M. Gaus and Leon O. Wolcott, *Public Administration and the United States Department of Agriculture* (Chicago: Public Administration Service, 1940), pp. 463–65.

10. McConnell, *The Decline of Agrarian Democracy*, p. 125.

11. "Democratization of Administration," *American Political Science Review*, 47 (September 1953), 704–727.

12. "Reflections on Agricultural Policy Formation in the United States," *American Political Science Review*, 42 (October 1948), 881–905.

13. Quoted in Griswold, *Farming and Democracy*, p. 186.

14. *Wallaces' Farmer*, December 17, 1949, p. 1441, as quoted in McConnell, *The Decline of Agrarian Democracy*, p. 214.

15. See McConnell, *The Decline of Agrarian Democracy*, pp. 168 ff.

16. *Ibid.*, p. 169.

17. *TVA and the Grass Roots* (Berkeley: University of California Press, 1949), pp. 209–10, 72.

18. William Fellner, *Competition Among the Few* (New York: Knopf, 1949), p. 325.

NOTES TO CHAPTER 7

1. See especially Pendleton Herring, *Public Administration and the Public Interest* (New York: McGraw-Hill, 1936); Avery Leisersen, *Administrative Regulation: A Study in Representation of Interests* (Chicago: University of Chicago Press, 1942); Samuel P. Huntington, *Clientalism: A Study in Administrative Politics* (Ph.D. dissertation, Harvard University, 1950); Marver H. Bernstein, *Regulating Business by Independent Commission* (Princeton: Princeton University Press, 1955).

2. See Robert Bendiner, "The FCC—Who Will Regulate the Regulators?" *The Reporter*, September 19, 1957, pp. 26–30, 26. See also Senate Antitrust Subcommittee, *Report*, March 1957.

3. Referring to the hostilities generated by the ICC, Samuel P. Huntington has noted that this agency "is undoubtedly unique among governmental agencies in the extent to which it has been involved in legal controversies with other agencies." ("The Marasmus of the ICC: The Commission, the Railroads, and the Public Interest," *Yale Law Journal*, 61 [April 1952], 447–509, 506n.)

4. House Subcommittee on Study of Monopoly Power of the Commit-

tee on the Judiciary, *Hearings*, 1950, 81st Congress, 1st Session, No. 14, Part 2-A, pp. 468–69. Similarly, some of the personnel of the Food and Drug Administration, as one critic has pointed out, "enter the agency as a stepping stone to a more lucrative career with the drug industry and indeed there is a disquieting movement of top officials back and forth between the industry and the FDA." (Alek A. Rozental, "The Strange Ethics of the Ethical Drug Industry," *Harper's Magazine*, 220 [May 1960], 73–84, 81.)

5. "The Marasmus of the ICC," *loc. cit.*, p. 480.

6. Walter Adams, "The Role of Competition in the Regulated Industries," *American Economic Review, Papers and Proceedings*, 48 (May 1948), 527–543, 537.

7. Bernstein, *Regulating Business by Independent Commission*, p. 90.

8. Note to what extent the railroads have actually dictated ICC regulation of their financial structure; see Kent T. Healy, *The Economics of Transportation in America* (New York: Ronald Press, 1940), p. 533.

9. This summary follows Herbert R. Northrup, *Organized Labor and the Negro* (New York: Harper, 1944); Benjamin Aaron and Michael I. Komaroff, "Statutory Regulation of Internal Union Affairs—I," *Illinois Law Review*, 44 (September-October 1949), 425–466.

10. National Mediation Board, *The Railway Labor Act and the National Mediation Board* (1940), p. 17; quoted by Aaron and Komaroff, *loc. cit.*, p. 430.

11. *Ibid.*, p. 431.

12. National Mediation Board, *Annual Report*, I (1935), 21; quoted *ibid.*, p. 431.

13. Northrup, *Organized Labor and the Negro*, pp. 61–62. Discriminatory policy seems to apply also to Mexicans and Orientals; see p. 261, and Special House Subcommittee of the Committee on Education and Labor, *Hearings on H.R. 4453 and Companion Bills*, 81st Congress, 1st Session, 1949, pp. 127, 143, 177.

14. Cramp Shipbuilding Corp., 52 N.L.R.B. 309 (1943). See also Shell Petroleum Corp., 52 N.L.R.B. 313 (1943), partially revoking certification to exclude certain employees from a bargaining unit.

15. U.S. Bedding Company, 52 N.L.R.B. 382, 388 (1943).

16. Atlanta Oak Flooring Company, 62 N.L.R.B. 973, 975 (1945). *Cf.* Northrup, *Organized Labor and the Negro*, pp. 26–34, and Leiserson, *American Trade Union Democracy*, pp. 117–19. See also Larus and Brother Company, 62 N.L.R.B. 1075 (1945).

17. Aaron and Komaroff, *loc. cit.*, pp. 442–45, 446. For more about the relations between labor and government, see D. O. Bowman, *Public Control of Labor Relations: A Study of the NLRB* (New York: Macmillan, 1942); Sanford Cohen, "The NLRB and Its Customers," *Labor Law Journal*, 6 (February 1955), 109–14; F. E. Rourke, "The Department of

Labor and Trade Unions," *Western Political Quarterly*, 7 (December 1954), 656–72.

18. "The Marasmus of the ICC," *loc. cit.*, p. 472.

19. Of course railroad management does not represent a monolithic interest either. For the views of one maverick, see Robert R. Young, "A Strange Alliance for Monopoly," *Atlantic Monthly*, 178 (December 1946), 43–50.

20. *The Interstate Commerce Commission* (New York: Commonwealth Fund, 1931–37), I, 284–85.

21. See House Subcommittee on the Study of Monopoly Power, *Hearings, loc. cit.*, pp. 469–70.

22. *Loc. cit.*

23. For material further amplifying these points, see Federal Power Commission, "In the Matter of the Phillips Petroleum Company," Opinion No. 217, Docket No. G–1148, August 16, 1951; Robert D. Baum, *The Federal Power Commission and State Utility Regulation* (Washington, D.C.: Public Affairs Press, 1942); Symposium on the Federal Power Commission, *George Washington Law Review*, 14 (December 1945), 1–135; Ralph K. Huit, "Federal Regulation of the Uses of Natural Gas," *American Political Science Review*, 46 (June 1952), 455–69.

24. Charles McKinley, "The Impact of American Federalism Upon the Management of Land Resources," in Arthur W. Macmahon, ed., *Federalism: Mature and Emergent* (New York: Doubleday, 1955), pp. 305–327, 323.

25. *Ibid.*, p. 309.

26. "Home Rule on the Federal Range," unpublished paper presented at the Western Political Science Association meeting, Los Angeles, February 23, 1957. The material is scheduled for inclusion in two studies of the Inter-University Case Program: "The McCarran Purge" and "The Battle of Soldier Creek." See also: Marion Clawson and Burnell Held, *The Federal Lands: Their Use and Management* (Baltimore: Johns Hopkins University Press, 1957); Norman Wengert, *National Resources and the Political Struggle* (New York: Random House, 1955); Note, "The Management of Public Land Resources," *Yale Law Journal*, 60 (March 1951), 455–82.

27. *Loc. cit.*, pp. 7–8.

28. Senate Committee on Public Lands and Surveys, *Administration and Use of Public Lands, Hearings*, 1941, 77th Congress, 1st Session, Part 1, pp. 187, 190; Part 2, p. 375; quoted by Foss, *loc. cit.*, pp. 7, 9.

29. Foss, *loc. cit.*, p. 13.

30. Antitrust Subcommittee of the House Committee on the Judiciary, *Interim Report on the Business Advisory Council for the Department of Commerce*, 84th Congress, 1st Session, 1955, p. 1.

31. See *ibid.* and Antitrust Subcommittee of the House Committee on

the Judiciary, *WOC's and Government Advisory Groups, Hearings,* Part 2, 84th Congress, 1st Session, 1955, and subsequent *Interim Report,* 2nd Session, April 24, 1956; Norman F. Keiser, "Public Responsibility and Federal Advisory Groups: A Case Study," *Western Political Quarterly,* 11 (June 1958), 251–64. See also David S. Brown, "The Public Advisory Board as an Instrument of Government," *Public Administration Review,* 15 (Summer 1955), 196–204; Lewis C. Mainzer, "Science Democratized: Advisory Committees on Research," *Public Administration Review,* 18 (Autumn 1958), 314–23.

32. Secretary of Commerce Sinclair Weeks, quoted by Keiser, "Public Responsibility and Federal Advisory Groups," *loc. cit.,* p. 256

33. Antitrust Subcommittee, *Interim Report, loc. cit.,* p. 28; Keiser, *loc. cit.,* pp. 254, 257.

34. Letter dated February 16, 1951, cited in *Congressional Record, House,* July 10, 1957, p. 10141.

35. See especially John Kenneth Galbraith, "Market Structure and Stabilization Policy," *Review of Economics and Statistics,* 39 (May 1957), 124–33; George L. Bach, *Federal Reserve Policy-Making: A Study in Government Economic Policy Formation* (New York: Knopf, 1950); George Soule, "The Price of Money: The Federal Reserve vs. the Treasury," *Yale Review,* 41 (Summer 1952), 594–608; Bertram M. Gross and Wilfred Lumer, *The Hard Money Crusade* (Washington: Public Affairs Institute, 1954).

36. "Corporate Giants and the Power Structure," *loc. cit.,* pp. 411–12.

37. *Ibid.,* p. 414.

38. See Walter Adams and Horace M. Gray, *Monopoly in America* (New York: Macmillan, 1955), ch. 5.

39. There are many areas in which these points might be easily illustrated. Two may be of special interest. For material on the Atomic Energy Commission, see James R. Newman and Byron S. Miller, *The Control of Atomic Energy* (New York: McGraw-Hill, 1949); James R. Newman, "The Atomic Energy Industry: An Experiment in Hybridization," *Yale Law Journal,* 60 (December 1951), 1263–1394; Robert A. Dahl and Ralph S. Brown, *Domestic Control of Atomic Energy,* Social Science Research Council Pamphlet No. 8 (1951); Adams and Gray, *Monopoly in America,* ch. 7. For material on the Civil Aeronautics Board, see "CAB Policy: An Evaluation," *Yale Law Journal,* 58 (April 1948), 1053–84; Basil J. F. Mott, "The Effect of Political Interest Groups on CAB Policies," *Journal of Air Law and Commerce,* 19 (Autumn 1952), 379–410; Arne C. Wiprud, *Justice in Transportation: An Exposé of Monopoly Control* (Chicago: Ziff-Davis Co., 1945); and U.S. Senate, Small Business Committee, *Report on the Role of Irregular Airlines in the United States Air Transportation Industry,* 82nd Congress, 1st Session, Senate Report No. 540, 1951.

40. *White Collar,* p. 79.

41. Consider the negotiations arising out of the administration of section 102 of the Internal Revenue Code which taxes unreasonable surplus accumulations.

NOTES TO CHAPTER 8

1. York Y. Willbern, "Administrative Control of Petroleum Production in Texas," in Emmette S. Redford, ed., *Public Administration and Policy Formation* (Austin: University of Texas Press, 1956), pp. 3–50, 46, 50. The emphasis is supplied. See also James W. Fesler, *The Independence of State Regulatory Agencies* (Chicago: Public Administration Service, 1942).

2. Code of Alabama, 1940, Title 22, Sec. 1, as quoted in Robert T. Daland, *Government and Health: The Alabama Experience* (University of Alabama, 1955), p. 1.

3. *Ibid.,* pp. 117–20, 2, 115, 197.

4. See the letters to the editor of *The Reporter,* March 21, 1957, p. 6.

5. Approximately 85 per cent of the school districts in the United States are fiscally independent. This means, according to one observer, that "school boards are free to determine their own expenditures and set their own tax rates, without supervision or review by other agencies of local government." (Jesse V. Burkhead, "Financing Education," *American Economic Review, Papers and Proceedings,* 47 [May 1957], 198–208, 202. See also Thomas H. Eliot, "On Understanding Public School Politics," *American Political Science Review,* 53 [December 1959], 1032–51.)

6. For studies of the exercise of public authority by private associations at the State level, see especially Louis L. Jaffe, "Law Making by Private Groups," *Harvard Law Review,* 51 (December 1937), 201–53; Francis P. DeLancey, *The Licensing of Professions in West Virginia* (Chicago: Foundation Press, 1938); J. A. C. Grant, "The Gild Returns to America," *Journal of Politics,* 4 (August-November 1942), 303–35, 458–77; Note, "The State Courts and Delegation of Public Authority to Private Groups," *Harvard Law Review,* 67 (June 1954), 1398–1408; M. L. Rutherford, *The Influence of the American Bar Association on Public Opinion and Legislation* (Philadelphia: Foundation Press, 1937); Stanley Kelley, Jr., *Professional Public Relations and Political Power* (Baltimore: Johns Hopkins Press, 1956), ch. 3. See also *Kotch v. Pilot Commissioners,* 330 U.S. 552 (1947), and *Fink v. Cole,* 302 N.Y. 216, 97 N.E.2d 873 (1951), for two interesting cases of the delegation of legislative authority.

7. Conn. Gen. Stats., par. 4365 (1949). In Massachusetts, the governor appoints members only with the consent of the state medical association (Mass. Laws Ann. c. 13, par. 10 [1952]).

8. *A Philosophy of Labor,* pp. 141–42.

9. There is admittedly a further reason: the excellence of David R. Hyde's and Payson Wolff's detailed Note, "The American Medical Association: Power, Purpose and Politics in Organized Medicine," *Yale Law Journal,* 63 (May 1954), 938–1022. See also Oliver Garceau, *The Political Life of the American Medical Association* (Cambridge: Harvard University Press, 1941).

10. Hyde and Wolff, "The American Medical Association," *loc. cit.,* p. 953.

11. See House Committee on Education and Labor, *Hearings* on S. 1606, 79th Congress, 2d Session, 1946, p. 2642.

12. Hyde and Wolff, "The American Medical Association," *loc. cit.,* pp. 951–52; the quotations are from *Group Health Cooperative of Puget Sound v. King County Medical Society,* 39 Wash. 2d 586; 237 P.2d 737 (1951).

13. Bauer, "The Importance of the County Medical Society in the State and National Programs," an address given January 27, 1947, cited in Hyde and Wolff, "The American Medical Association," *loc. cit.,* p. 944.

14. Hyde and Wolff, "The American Medical Association," *loc. cit.,* p. 945.

15. *Ibid.,* p. 946.

16. See Garceau, *The Political Life of the American Medical Association,* p. 103; Hyde and Wolff, "The American Medical Association," *loc. cit.,* pp. 949–50.

17. See Hyde and Wolff, "The American Medical Association," *loc. cit.,* pp. 988–96, for an account of AMA opposition to various cooperatives. For a rigorous explanation of the structure and practices of organized medicine as a discriminating monopoly, see Reuben A. Kessel, "Price Discrimination in Medicine," *Journal of Law and Economics,* 1 (October 1958), 20–53. According to Kessel, the organization of medicine can be understood as a function of the medical profession's interest in maintaining a system of price discrimination, i.e., of scaling fees to the income of patients.

NOTES TO CHAPTER 9

1. Harvard University Commission to Advise on the Future of Psychology at Harvard, Alan Gregg, chairman, *The Place of Psychology in an Ideal University* (Cambridge: Harvard University Press, 1947), p. 2.

2. Dwight Waldo, *Political Science in the United States: A Trend Report* (Paris: UNESCO, 1956), p. 17. He also noted that "however great the heat engendered by professional disputes, the range of opinion has on the whole and in the larger perspective of all political thought been

remarkably small. The very fact that there could be widespread agree-ment on the possibility and desirability of reducing the study of politics to the single level of a 'science' signifies a large amount of basic agreement as to political ends." See also C. Wright Mills, *The Sociological Imagina-tion* (New York: Oxford, 1959) and Bernard Crick, *The American Sci-ence of Politics* (Berkeley: University of California Press, 1959).

3. "The Policy Orientation," in Daniel Lerner and Harold D. Lass-well, eds., *The Policy Sciences: Recent Developments in Science and Method* (Stanford: Stanford University Press, 1951), pp. 3–15, 3.

4. *Quest for Community* (New York: Oxford, 1953), pp. 28–29.

5. *Psychopathology and Politics* (Chicago: University of Chicago Press, 1930), pp. 203, 196–97.

6. The phrase is Conrad Arensberg's ("Behavior and Organization," in John H. Rohrer and Muzafer Sherif, eds., *Social Psychology at the Crossroads* [New York: Harper, 1951], pp. 324–52, 352).

7. Edward C. Tolman, "Kurt Lewin—1890–1947," *Journal of Social Issues*, VI, Suppl. ser. No. 1 (Fall 1948), 22–26, 23. "In short," Tolman adds, "it was his humanity, I believe, which would not allow him to dwell for long on any considerations other than those of the manipulable pres-ent." Thus Lewin's interest in manipulation would seem to have grown out of his desire to do good; and in America, at least, the nature of the good appeared sufficiently obvious to "all persons of good will."

8. F. J. Roethlisberger, *Management and Morale* (Cambridge: Har-vard University Press, 1950), pp. 192–93, 63; see also p. 111. While man-agement, having "economic objectives," communicates with the managed "in terms of the logical jargon and cold discriminations of the technical specialist . . . the bottom . . . is trying to communicate with the top through its own peculiar language of social sentiments and feelings."

9. See T. N. Whitehead, *The Industrial Worker*, 2 vols. (Cambridge: Harvard University Press, 1938), I, 248.

10. Alfred Marrow, "Conflict and Cooperation in Industry," in Schuy-ler Dean Hoslett, ed., *Human Factors in Management* (New York: Har-per, 1946), pp. 172–208, 204.

11. William Foote Whyte, ed., *Industry and Society* (New York: McGraw-Hill, 1946), p. 192.

12. Roethlisberger, *Management and Morale*, p. 193.

13. Burleigh B. Gardner, *Human Relations in Industry* (Chicago: Irwin, 1945), p. 292; the emphasis is Gardner's.

14. Ordway Tead, *New Adventures in Democracy* (New York: McGraw-Hill, 1939), p. 137.

15. Marshall Edward Dimock and Gladys Ogden Dimock, *Public Ad-ministration* (New York: Rinehart, 1953), p. 237.

16. Gardner, *Human Relations in Industry*, p. 216.

17. Otto Klineberg, *Social Psychology* (New York: Holt, 1954), p. 462.

There is no reason to doubt the words of Herbert A. Simon: "We now have a considerable body of evidence on the participation hypothesis— the hypothesis that significant changes in human behavior can be brought about rapidly only if the persons *who are expected to change* participate in deciding what the change shall be and how it shall be made." (In Stephen K. Bailey *et al., Research Frontiers in Politics and Government* [Washington, D.C.: The Brookings Institution, 1955], pp. 28–29; the emphasis is supplied.) Perhaps Stuart Chase's *Roads to Agreement: Successful Methods in the Science of Human Relations* (1951) is the most readable exposition, almost wholly sympathetic, of semantic reconciliations, group dynamics, Quaker meetings, group writing, role playing, and gripe weeks as techniques for overcoming intragroup hostility.

18. Lester Coch and John R. P. French, Jr., "Overcoming Resistance to Change," in Hoslett, ed., *Human Factors in Management*, pp. 242–68, 268.

19. Morris S. Viteles, *Motivation and Morale in Industry* (New York: Norton, 1953), pp. 436, 118.

20. See Kurt Lewin, *Resolving Social Conflicts* (New York: Harper, 1948), pp. 80, 82; Lewin, "Forces behind Food Habits and Methods of Change," in National Research Council, Committee on Food Habits, *The Problem of Changing Food Habits* (Washington, D.C.: National Research Council, 1943), pp. 35–65.

21. Kurt Lewin, "Time Perspective and Morale," in Goodwin Watson, ed., *Civilian Morale* (New York: Houghton Mifflin, 1942), pp. 48–70, 51–52.

22. Gardner Murphy, "The Role of Psychologists in the Establishment of Better Human Relations," in Lyman Bryson *et al.,* eds., *Perspectives on a Troubled Decade* (New York: Harper, 1950), pp. 1–11, 2–3.

23. T. N. Whitehead, *Leadership in a Free Society* (Cambridge: Harvard University Press, 1936), p. 255.

24. Hoslett, *Human Factors in Management*, p. 105.

25. Gardner Murphy, in Murphy, *Human Nature and Enduring Peace* (Boston: Houghton Mifflin, 1945), pp. 298–99; Jerome S. Bruner, pp. 372–84; Ronald Lippitt and Charles Henry, pp. 313, 315–18. See also the discussion in "Citizen Participation in World Affairs: Problems and Possibilities," *Journal of Social Issues,* 4 (Winter 1948), 21–61.

26. Lasswell, "The Policy Orientation," *loc. cit.,* p. 10.

27. Note Leo Strauss's analysis of Machiavelli's method (*Natural Right and History* [Chicago: University of Chicago Press, 1953], pp. 177–80).

28. See Bernard Barber, "Structural-Functional Analysis," *American Sociological Review,* 21 (April 1956), 129–35.

29. The work of Karl Mannheim testifies, of course, that this type of propaganda analysis does not merely arise in an American context. But

it should be noted that only Mannheim's faith in the benign working out of historical forces, only his ultimately conservative assumption that all is right in the world, could sustain his analytical activity. Systematic debunking, it must have seemed to him, would surely not despoil a reality worthy of vindication. Not until the rise of Hitler, not until a substantive transformation in a political regime had taken place, did Mannheim have those misgivings about inevitable progress which Americans could escape experiencing at home.

30. *The Process of Government: A Study of Social Pressures* (Chicago: University of Chicago Press, 1908); the volume has been twice republished, most recently by Principia Press (Bloomington, Indiana) in 1949.

31. *The Group Basis of Politics: A Study in Basing-Point Legislation* (Ithaca, N.Y.: Cornell University Press, 1952), p. 10.

32. See especially the writings of Muzafer Sherif, Kurt Lewin, Nelson N. Foote, Jerome S. Bruner, Hadley Cantril, Gardner Murphy, Dorwin Cartwright, and Theodore M. Newcomb.

33. *The Governmental Process* (New York: Knopf, 1951), p. 21.

34. See especially the work of Arthur F. Bentley (*The Process of Government*, p. 269, and his *Behavior, Knowledge, Fact* [Bloomington, Indiana: Principia Press, 1935], p. 29) and David B. Truman (*The Governmental Process*, p. 31). The limitations of Truman's approach are fully discussed in Stanley Rothman, "Systematic Political Theory: Observations on the Group Approach," *American Political Science Review*, 54 (March 1960), 15–33.

35. See especially the descriptive and critical accounts of William G. Carleton, "Political Science and the Group Process," *South Atlantic Quarterly*, 54 (July 1955), 340–50; W. J. M. Mackenzie, "Pressure Groups: The 'Conceptual Framework,'" *Political Studies*, 3 (October 1955), 247–55; Bernard Crick, *The American Science of Politics*, ch. 7.

36. See C. B. MacPherson, "World Trends in Political Science Research," *American Political Science Review*, 48 (June 1954), 427–49, 430–37; Bernard Barber, *Science and the Social Order* (Glencoe, Illinois: The Free Press, 1952), p. 244; Stephen K. Bailey *et al.*, *Research Frontiers in Politics and Government* (Washington, D.C.: The Brookings Institution, 1955); Harold D. Lasswell and Abraham Kaplan, *Power and Society: A Framework for Political Inquiry* (New Haven: Yale University Press, 1950); Roy R. Grinker, ed., *Toward a Unified Theory of Human Behavior* (New York: Basic Books, 1956); John Gillin, ed., *For a Science of Social Man: Convergences in Anthropology, Psychology and Sociology* (New York: Macmillan, 1954); James G. Miller, "Toward a General Theory for the Behavioral Sciences," in Leonard D. White, ed., *The State of the Social Sciences* (Chicago: University of Chicago Press, 1956), pp. 29–65; and Roland Young, ed., *Approaches to the Study of Politics* (Evanston, Illinois: Northwestern University Press, 1958), *passim*. For some attempts

to put new models to work, see Stuart C. Dodd, *Dimensions of Society: Quantitative Systematics for the Social Sciences* (New York: Macmillan, 1942); Nicolas Rashevsky, *Mathematical Biology of Social Behavior* (Chicago: University of Chicago Press, 1951); Marion J. Levy, *The Structure of Society* (Princeton: Princeton University Press, 1952); Morton A. Kaplan, *System and Process in International Politics* (New York: Wiley, 1957).

37. *Power and Society*, p. xxiv.

38. See, for examples, Pitirim Sorokin, *Fads and Foibles in Modern Sociology and Related Sciences* (Chicago: Regnery, 1956); Mills, *The Sociological Imagination*; Crick, *The American Science of Politics*.

NOTES TO CHAPTER 10

1. Excellent secondary sources, all of which have been relied on in the following review of European pluralism, are Latham, *The Group Basis of Politics*, ch. 1; Walter Milne-Bailey, *Trade Unions and the State* (London: G. Allen, 1934); Adam B. Ulam, *Philosophical Foundations of English Socialism* (Cambridge: Harvard University Press, 1951); and William Y. Elliott, *The Pragmatic Revolt in Politics* (New York: Macmillan, 1928), parts 1–3.

2. In *The Federalist*, No. 9, Hamilton relied on Montesquieu to maintain that the states in a confederate republic would be immune to contagious political diseases. Much later, dissenting in *Truax v. Corrigan*, Justice Holmes was to speak of the "insulated chambers afforded by the several States."

3. For an admirable account of French pluralism, though not including Duguit, see Stanley Hoffmann, "The Areal Division of Powers in the Writings of French Political Thinkers," in Arthur Maass, ed., *Area and Power: A Theory of Local Government* (Glencoe, Illinois: The Free Press, 1959), pp. 113–49.

4. *The Life and Work of John Adams*, 10 vols., Charles Francis Adams, ed. (Boston: Little, Brown, 1851), IV, 427.

5. "Notes on Virginia," in *The Works of Thomas Jefferson*, 12 vols. (New York: Federal Edition, 1904–5), VI, 85–86. Jefferson was not alone. St. George Tucker, Spencer Roane, and John Taylor, all Virginians, had similar sentiments. In 1803, Taylor revealed: "At the awful day of judgment, the discrimination of the good from the wicked is not made by the criterion of sects or of dogmas, but by one which constitutes the daily employment and great end of agriculture. The judge upon this occasion has by anticipation pronounced that to feed the hungry, clothe the naked, and give drink to the thirsty are the passports to future happiness; and the divine intelligence which selected an agricultural state as a paradise for its first favorites, has here again prescribed the agricultural virtues

as the means for admission of their posterity into heaven." (*Arator* [Petersburg: 1818], 5th ed., pp. 188–89.)

6. Jefferson to Madison, December 20, 1787, in *Writings,* 20 vols. (Washington, D.C.: Thomas Jefferson Memorial Association, 1903–5), VI, 392–93; Jefferson to Rush, September 23, 1800, X, 173.

7. "The Internal State of America," in *The Writings of Benjamin Franklin,* 10 vols., Albert H. Smyth, ed. (New York: Macmillan, 1905–7), X, 117.

8. This point was first stressed by Samuel P. Huntington, "The Founding Fathers and the Division of Powers," in Maass, ed., *Area and Power,* pp. 150–205. Huntington has also observed that Jefferson's assumption of an underlying harmony of interests allowed him to consider each of the branches, including the judiciary, as "co-equal and co-sovereign." Each was to tend its own business. Such jurisdictional conflicts as might arise—between Supreme Court and Congress or between the Executive and the states—the people would resolve.

9. Jefferson, *Writings,* 1892–99, VII, 289–301.

10. *An Inquiry into the Principles and Policy of the Government of the United States* (1814) (New Haven: Yale University Press, 1950), pp. 362, 412.

11. See Jefferson's letter to Benjamin Austin, January 9, 1816, in *Works,* XI, 504.

12. John C. Calhoun, *A Disquisition on Government and a Discourse on the Constitution of the United States,* Richard K. Crallé, ed. (Columbia, S.C.: 1852), pp. 48–49.

13. Quoted in Hartz, *The Liberal Tradition in America,* pp. 156–57.

14. "An Erie Raid," *North American Review,* 112 (April 1871), 241–91.

15. See Paul K. Conkin, *Tomorrow a New World: The New Deal Community Program* (Ithaca, N.Y.: Cornell University Press, 1959).

16. See Senate Committee on Education and Labor, *Investigation of the Relation between Labor and Capital,* 48th Congress, 1885.

17. Belloc, *The Servile State* (1911) (New York: Holt, 1946).

18. John Crowe Ransom *et al., I'll Take My Stand* (New York: Harper, 1930). Interestingly enough, Henry Ford had advocated both decentralization and industrialization; see his *Today and Tomorrow* (New York: Doubleday, 1926).

19. See especially Erich Fromm, *Escape from Freedom* (New York: Rinehart, 1941). For a critique, see Henry S. Kariel, "Erich Fromm's Escape from Freedom," *Journal of Politics,* 19 (November 1957), 640–54.

20. Fromm, *op. cit.,* pp. 41, 62–63.

21. *Ibid.,* pp. 123–32, 272.

22. Erich Fromm, *The Sane Society* (New York: Rinehart, 1955), pp. 327, 340–43.

23. Fromm, *Escape from Freedom,* pp. 273, 129, 126, 271.

24. See Mumford's works, *passim*; Borsodi, *This Ugly Civilization* (New York: Simon & Schuster, 1929); Brownell, *The Human Community* (New York: Harper, 1950). See also Milburn Lincoln Wilson, *Democracy Has Roots* (New York: Carrick and Evans, 1939) and "Agricultural Adjustment," *Harvard Business Review*, 13 (Summer 1935), 405–16; Arthur E. Morgan, *The Small Community: The Foundation of Democratic Life* (New York: Harper, 1942); and O. E. Baker, Ralph Borsodi, and M. L. Wilson, *Agriculture in Modern Life* (New York: Harper, 1939).

25. *The Public and Its Problems* (New York: Holt, 1927), p. 215.

26. Samuel Seabury, *The New Federalism* (New York: Dutton, 1950), pp. 21, 302, 6. See also Donald Davidson, *The Attack on Leviathan: Regionalism and Nationalism in the United States* (Chapel Hill, N.C.: University of North Carolina Press, 1938); James Jackson Kilpatrick, *The Sovereign States* (Chicago: Regnery, 1957); Felix Morley, *Freedom and Federalism* (Chicago: Regnery, 1959).

27. For a detailed analysis, see Henry S. Kariel, "The New Order of Mary Parker Follett," *Western Political Quarterly*, 8 (September 1955), 425–40.

28. Henry C. Metcalf and L. Urwick, eds. (New York: Harper, 1942).

29. Follett, *The New State* (New York: Longman's, Green, 1918), pp. 3, 19.

30. Follett, *Creative Experience* (New York: Longman's, Green, 1924), pp. 41, xiii, 47.

31. Follett, *Dynamic Administration*, p. 58.

32. Follett, *The New State*, pp. 111–13; *Dynamic Administration*, p. 138.

33. Follett, *The New State*, pp. 114, 117, 4, 160, 12.

34. *Ibid.*, pp. 237n., 339–40. Follett's professed antifeudalism should be noted: "The medieval church broke up," she says in one place, "and this was a wholly liberating phenomenon" (*Creative Experience*, p. 178).

35. Follett, *The New State*, pp. 258–82, 284. This belief in dialectically progressive motion distinguished Follett from the political pluralists. She condemned them for not going far enough. They start, properly, with groups, but stop short of demanding their progressive unification.

36. Follett, *Creative Experience*, pp. 224–25.

37. Follett, *Dynamic Administration*, pp. 30, 43, 44, 51, 248, 284, 18.

38. *Ibid.*, pp. 207–8.

39. Follett, *Creative Experience*, p. ix; *Dynamic Administration*, p. 18.

40. Follett, *Creative Experience*, pp. xi, xii.

41. *Big Business: A New Era* (New York: Harper, 1952). See also Donald Richberg, *Tents of the Mighty* (New York: Willett, 1930) and *Government and Business Tomorrow* (New York: Harper, 1943); Robert Wood Johnson, *Or Forfeit Freedom* (New York: Doubleday, 1947);

Harrymon Maurer, *Great Enterprise* (New York: Macmillan, 1955); Peter F. Drucker, *The New Society* (New York: Harper, 1950) and *Concept of the Corporation* (New York: John Day, 1946); Russell Davenport, "The Greatest Opportunity on Earth," *Fortune*, 40 (October 1949), 65 ff.

42. *TVA: Democracy on the March* (New York: Harper, 1944); see especially p. 125.

43. *American Capitalism: The Concept of Countervailing Power* (Cambridge: Houghton Mifflin, 1952).

44. *The 20th Century Capitalist Revolution* (New York: Harcourt, Brace, 1954).

45. *Ibid.*, pp. 105, 179, 63.

46. See *ibid.*, pp. 166–67

47. *Ibid.*, p. 169.

48. *Ibid.*, pp. 66, 69, 180, 181, 175.

49. See *Power without Property* (New York: Harcourt, Brace, 1959), pp. 136, 113, 111, 135, 97.

50. Lilienthal, *Big Business*, p. 30.

51. See especially J. M. Clark, "Toward a Concept of Workable Competition," *American Economic Review*, 30 (June 1940), 241–56; A. D. H. Kaplan, *Big Enterprise in a Competitive System* (Washington, D.C.: The Brookings Institution, 1954). The work which has been most influential is Joseph A. Schumpeter, *Communism, Socialism and Democracy* (New York: Harper, 1942).

52. At least some modern biographers have embraced the pragmatism offered by economics; see Allan Nevins's *John D. Rockefeller* (2nd ed., 1959) and Frederick Lewis Allen's *The Great Pierpont Morgan* (1949). Like presidential candidate Franklin D. Roosevelt, they have come to realize that "the financiers who pushed the railroads to the Pacific were always ruthless, often wasteful and frequently corrupt, but they did build the railroads and we have them today." (Franklin D. Roosevelt at the Commonwealth Club, San Francisco, September 23, 1932, in *Public Papers and Addresses* [New York: Random House, 1938], I, 742. In *The Democratic Roosevelt*, Rexford Guy Tugwell recalled that he and Adolf Berle wrote the speech, and that Roosevelt did not see it until he opened it on the lectern.)

53. *American Capitalism*, p. 98.

54. For public endorsements of this view by leaders of business, see House Subcommittee on the Study of Monopoly Power of the Committee on the Judiciary, *Hearings*, 1949, 81st Congress, 1st Session, Part 2A, pp. 543–92 (testimony of Crawford H. Greenewald, president of Du Pont; Part 2B, pp. 1158–66, 1208–39 (testimony of Charles E. Wilson, president of General Electric); Part 4A, pp. 465–71 (testimony of Benjamin F. Fairless, president of United States Steel). For a judicial vindication of the

new competition see *United States v. E. I. du Pont de Nemours and Co.,* 351 U.S. 377 (1956).

55. *Looking Forward* (New York: John Day, 1933), p. 243.

56. John Knox Jessup, "A Political Role for the Corporation," *Fortune,* 44 (August 1952), 113 ff. See also Editors of *Fortune, USA: The Permanent Revolution* (New York: Prentice-Hall, 1951).

57. Stuart Chase, *A Generation of Industrial Peace: Thirty Years of Labor Relations at Standard Oil Company (N.J)* (New Jersey: Standard Oil Co., 1946), p. 53.

58. Frank Tannenbaum, *A Philosophy of Labor* (New York: Knopf, 1951), pp. 11, 12, 71, 168–69, 183, 143.

59. Frank Tannenbaum, "The Balance of Power in Society," *Political Science Quarterly,* 61 (December 1945), 481–504, 491, 501; see also "On Political Stability," *Political Science Quarterly,* 75 (June 1960), 161–80.

60. See Elton Mayo, *Democracy and Freedom* (Melbourne: Macmillan, 1919), pp. 13, 12, 44; *The Human Problems of an Industrial Civilization* (New York: Macmillan, 1933), p. 126.

61. Mayo, *Democracy and Freedom,* pp. 6, 73, 48.

62. *Ibid.,* pp. 42, 38, 27, 20–25, 30–32.

63. *Ibid.,* pp. 42–43, 48–49.

64. *Ibid.,* pp. 32–34.

65. Mayo, *The Social Problems of an Industrial Civilization* (Cambridge: Harvard University Press, 1945), pp. 122, 13; *Human Problems,* pp. 177, 145.

66. Mayo, *Social Problems,* pp. 20–21, 32–33. Needless to say, Mayo himself is not one of the new men; he freely quotes classical authority.

67. *Ibid.,* pp. 10, xv–xvi; *Democracy and Freedom,* p. 44; *The Political Problems of an Industrial Civilization* (Cambridge: Harvard University Press, 1947), pp. 22, 12.

68. See Mayo, *Social Problems,* pp. 20–23.

69. *Ibid.,* pp. xv–xvi; *Human Problems,* pp. 183, 177; *Democracy and Freedom,* pp. 54–55, 49.

70. Mayo, *Human Problems,* p. 172.

71. Mayo, *Social Problems,* p. 119; *Human Problems,* pp. 119, 28. "Studies on the performances of men or of the laboratory dogs while in this 'steady state' give no present support to the business-economic theory of fatigue, gradual in onset, which is related to the depletion of fuel reserves." (*Human Problems,* p. 169.)

72. See Stuart Chase, "What Makes the Worker Like to Work," *Reader's Digest,* 38 (February 1941), 15–20.

73. Mayo, *Human Problems,* pp. 126–27; *Social Problems,* p. 5.

74. Mayo, *Social Problems,* pp. xv–xvi.

75. Mayo, *Democracy and Freedom,* pp. 37, 64.

76. Mayo, *Social Problems,* p. 123.

NOTES TO CHAPTER 11

1. Fisher, *The Farm Harvest Labor Market in California*, pp. 137, 142.

2. An interesting but seldom-explored area in which coercive economic power has been transferred to private groups is the termination of federal authority over Indian tribes. A case in point is the federal government's "liberation" of the Klamath Indians. (See especially U.S. Congress, Senate Committee on Interior and Insular Affairs, *Joint Hearings on Termination of Federal Supervision over Certain Tribes of Indians*, Joint Hearings, 83d Congress, 2d Session, 1954, Part 4.)

3. David Hume, "Idea of a Perfect Commonwealth," *Essays, Literary, Moral, and Political* (London: Ward, Lock & Tyler, n.d.), p. 308.

4. Note, in this connection, how poorly the states have protected civil liberties. (See Walter Gellhorn, ed., *The States and Subversion* [Ithaca, N.Y.: Cornell University Press, 1952]. For an even broader critique of the states as obstructions to national legislation aimed at furthering the welfare of individuals, see George C. S. Benson, *The New Centralization* [New York: Farrar and Rinehart, 1941], pp. 23–24, 30, 38, 40.)

5. *Politics, Parties, and Pressure Groups*, 3d edition (New York: Crowell, 1956), p. 102.

NOTES TO CHAPTER 12

1. See his *Reflections on the French Revolution* (London: Everyman's Library, 1910), p. 226.

2. "Individual Liberty Today: Challenge and Prospect," in Morroe Berger *et al.*, eds., *Freedom and Control in Modern Society* (New York: Van Nostrand, 1954), pp. 177–91.

3. Zoltán Haraszti, *John Adams and the Prophets of Progress* (Cambridge: Harvard University Press, 1952), pp. 203, 219. (For this unusual source, thanks are due to John P. Roche.)

4. Opinion as to the Constitutionality of the Bank of the United States, as quoted in Frederick C. Prescott, ed., *Alexander Hamilton and Thomas Jefferson* (New York: American Book Co., 1934), p. 104.

5. Jefferson, who had also been asked to advise Washington, wrote that "the very power now proposed *as a means* was rejected as *an end* by the Convention. . . ." Opinion against the Constitutionality of a National Bank, *ibid.*, p. 308.

6. *The Federalist*, No. 23.

7. See *Penhallow v. Doane*, 3 Dall. 54 (1795); *United States v. Curtiss-Wright Export Corp.*, 299 U.S. 304 (1936). Inescapably, executive power exercised in the field of foreign relations will encroach on domestic affairs; see *United States v. Belmont*, 301 U.S. 324 (1937) and the first of the Tidelands Cases, *United States v. California*, 332 U.S. 19 (1947).

8. *Missouri v. Holland*, 252 U.S. 416, 433 (1920), quoting *Andrews v. Andrews*, 188 U.S. 14, 33 (1903).

9. See Joseph Dorfman, "The Role of the German Historical School in American Economic Thought," *American Economic Review, Papers and Proceedings*, 45 (May 1955), 17–28.

10. See Sidney Fine, *Laissez Faire and the General-Welfare State* (Ann Arbor: University of Michigan Press, 1956), pp. 169–351.

11. *A Cycle of Adams Letters: 1861–1865*, 2 vols., Worthington Chauncey Ford, ed. (Boston: Houghton Mifflin, 1920), I, 196.

12. *Drift and Mastery* (New York: Mitchell Kennerly, 1914), p. 46.

13. *Progressive Democracy* (New York: Macmillan, 1914), p. 365; "Surely Good Americanism," *New Republic*, 32 (November 15, 1922), 294–96.

14. Herbert Croly, *The Promise of American Life* (New York: Macmillan, 1909) and *Progressive Democracy*. For a discussion of the role of the West as political myth, see Henry Nash Smith, *Virgin Land* (Cambridge: Harvard University Press, 1950); for a discussion of the way a number of thinkers at the turn of the century, including Croly, accepted the end of an era but nonetheless clung to the myth of innocence, see David W. Noble, *The Paradox of Progressive Thought* (Minneapolis: University of Minnesota Press, 1958).

15. See Croly, *The Promise of American Life*, pp. 207–14, 281. In his *Progressive Democracy*, Croly simply *postulated* the politicized individual; there was no change in orientation.

16. On this point, see especially Walter Gellhorn, *Federal Administration Proceedings* (Baltimore: The Johns Hopkins Press, 1941); J. Roland Pennock, *Administration and the Rule of Law* (New York: Rinehart, 1941); Charles M. Wiltse, "The Representative Function of Bureaucracy," *American Political Science Review*, 35 (April 1941), 510–16; Herman Miles Somers, "The Federal Bureaucracy and the Change of Administration," *American Political Science Review*, 48 (March 1954), 131–51; Norton E. Long, "Bureaucracy and Constitutionalism," *American Political Science Review*, 46 (September 1952), 808–18.

17. Dissenting in *Myers v. United States*, 272 U.S. 52, 293 (1926).

18. "American Political Thought and the Study of Politics," *American Political Science Review*, 51 (March 1957), 115–29, 125.

19. Dissenting in *Shaughnessy v. United States ex rel. Mezei*, 345 U.S. 206, 244 (1953).

20. See *United States v. Carolene Products Co.*, 304 U.S. 144, 152–53n (1938); *Beauharnais v. Illinois*, 343 U.S. 250 (1952); *Brown v. Board of Education of Topeka*, 347 U.S. 483 (1954).

21. "From Lochner to Brown v. Topeka: The Court and Conflicting Concepts of the Political Process," *American Political Science Review*, 52 (September 1958), 641–64, 642.

22. See Henry W. Farnam, *Chapters in the History of Social Legislation in the United States to 1860* (1938); R. B. Morris, *Government and Labor in Early America* (1946); Oscar and Mary Flug Handlin, *Commonwealth: A Study of the Role of Government in the American Economy* (1947); Louis Hartz, *Economic Policy and Democratic Thought* (1948); Carter Goodrich, "The Virginia System of Mixed Enterprise: A Study of State Planning of Internal Improvements," *Political Science Quarterly*, 64 (September 1949), 355–87; James Neal Primm, *Economic Policy in the Development of a Western State* (1954); E. M. Dodd, *American Business Corporations until 1860* (1954); Henry Carter Adams, *Relation of the State to Industrial Action and Economics and Jurisprudence* (1954); Milton Sydney Heath, *Constructive Liberalism: The Role of the State in the Economic Development in Georgia to 1860* (1954); Sidney Fine, *Laissez Faire and the General-Welfare State* (1956); George J. Kuehnl, *The Wisconsin Business Corporation* (1959); Forest G. Hill, "Formative Relations of American Enterprise, Government and Science," *Political Science Quarterly*, 75 (September 1960), 400–418; Carter Goodrich, *Government Promotion of American Canals and Railroads: 1800–1890* (1960).

23. See the excellent summary in Fine's *Laissez Faire and the General-Welfare State*; see also James Willard Hurst, *Law and the Conditions of Freedom in the Nineteenth-Century United States* (Madison: University of Wisconsin Press, 1956).

24. See *Hague v. C.I.O.*, 307 U.S. 496 (1939); *Marsh v. Alabama*, 326 U.S. 501 (1946).

25. See *Terry v. Adams*, 345 U.S. 461 (1953); *Steele v. Louisville and Nashville Railroad Co.*, 323 U.S. 192 (1944); *Railway Mail Association v. Corsi*, 326 U.S. 88 (1945).

26. *The 20th Century Capitalist Revolution*, p. 135.

27. Probably the most comprehensive survey of efforts to achieve freedom through positive governmental action in the United States is Robert L. Hale, *Freedom through Law: Public Control of Private Governing Power* (New York: Columbia University Press, 1952), especially Part III.

The following are of general relevance: Thomas I. Cook, "The Functions of Modern Government," *Western Political Quarterly* 1 (March 1948), 16–28; Alexander Pekelis, *Law and Social Action* (1950); M. Anshen and F. D. Wormuth, *Private Enterprise and Public Policy* (1954); Robert A. Horn, *Groups and the Constitution* (1956); J. W. Hurst, *Law and the Conditions of Freedom* (1956); Milton R. Konvitz, *Fundamental Liberties of a Free People* (1957); Merle Fainsod and Lincoln Gordon, *Government and the American Economy* (1959); Cornelius P. Cutter, *Government and Private Enterprise* (1960).

The following deal more specifically with the control of business:

Harry L. Purdy *et al.*, *Corporation Concentration and Public Policy* (1950); George W. Stocking and Myron W. Watkins, *Monopoly and Free Enterprise* (1951); A. B. Levy, *Private Corporations and Their Control* (1953); Harold Koontz and Richard W. Gable, *Public Control of Economic Enterprise* (1956).

The following deal more specifically with the control of labor: H. A. Millis and Emily C. Brown, *From the Wagner Act to Taft-Hartley* (1950); Richard A. Lester, *Labor and Industrial Relations* (1954), chs. 15–16. A comment on the use of antitrust statutes to regulate medical associations is in *University of Chicago Law Review*, 22 (Spring 1955), 694.

The following deal more specifically with the control of the political market and the vindication of civil rights: Milton R. Konvitz, *The Constitution and Civil Rights* (1947); Robert K. Carr, *Federal Protection of Civil Rights* (1947); Malcolm Ross, *All Manner of Men* (1948); Thomas I. Emerson and David M. Haber, *Political and Civil Rights in the United States: A Collection of Legal and Related Materials* (1952); Morroe Berger, *Equality by Statute* (1952); Will Maslow and Joseph B. Robinson, "Civil Rights Legislation and the Fight for Equality, 1862–1952," *University of Chicago Law Review* 20 (Spring 1953), 363–413; Stanley H. Smith, *Freedom to Work* (1955); Robert E. Cushman, *Civil Liberties in the United States: A Guide to Current Problems and Experience* (1956).

28. See Zechariah Chafee, Jr., "The Internal Affairs of Associations Not for Profit," *Harvard Law Review*, 43 (May 1930), 993–1029. For examples, see *Obergfell v. Green*, 29 Fed. Supp. 589 (1940); *Randolph v. First Baptist Church*, 120 N.E.2d 485 (Ohio Com. Pl. 1954); *Orloff v. Los Angeles Turf Club*, 30 Cal.2d 110, 180 P.2d 321 (1947); *Ross v. Ebert*, 275 Wis. 523, 82 N.W.2d 315 (1957). Also see John P. Troxell, "Protecting Members' Rights Within the Union," *American Economic Review*, 32 (March 1942), 460–75; H. Helmut Loring, "The Power of Courts over the Internal Affairs of Religious Groups," *California Law Review*, 43 (May 1955), 322–34.

29. See *Smith v. Kern County Medical Association*, 19 Cal.2d 263, 120 P.2d 874 (1942).

30. *Home Telegraph and Telephone Co. v. Los Angeles*, 227 U.S. 278 (1913).

31. That the decisions imposing constitutional restrictions on private groups are *ad hoc* and do not rest on "reasons that in their generality and their neutrality transcend any immediate result" has been persuasively argued by Herbert Wechsler, "Toward Neutral Principles of Constitutional Law," *Harvard Law Review*, 73 (November 1959), 1–35, 19, 26–30. Compare, for example, *Shelley v. Kraemer*, 334 U.S. 1 (1948) with *Black v. Cutter Labs.*, 351 U.S. 292 (1956) or with the denial of *certiorari* (339 U.S. 981 [1950]) for *Dorsey v. Stuyvesant Town Corp.*, 299 N.Y. 512, 87 N.E.2d 541 (1949). Not even in the segregation cases has the Supreme

Court articulated a broadly applicable rationale transcending immediate results. A selective review of judicial decisions can therefore do little more than suggest that whatever is, is surely possible.

32. *James v. Marinship Corporation,* 25 Cal.2d 721, 155 P.2d 329 (1944).

33. *People v. Brown,* 407 Ill. 565, 95 N.E.2d 888 (1951).

34. See *Steele v. Louisville and Nashville Railroad Co.,* 323 U.S. 192 (1944); *Tunstall v. Locomotive Firemen and Enginemen,* 323 U.S. 210 (1944); *Graham v. Southern Railway Co.,* 338 U.S. 232 (1949); *Brotherhood of Railroad Trainmen v. Howard,* 343 U.S. 768 (1952); *Syres v. Oil Workers, Local 23,* 350 U.S. 892 (1955); *Conley v. Gibson,* 355 U.S. 41 (1957). In 1946, the Supreme Court of Kansas went further, affirming that equal representation demands integrated membership (*Betts v. Easley,* 161 Kan. 459, 169 P.2d 831 [1946]).

35. See *Konigsberg v. State Bar of California,* 353 U.S. 252 (1957); *Schware v. Board of Bar Examiners of the State of New Mexico,* 353 U.S. 232 (1957).

36. For a full discussion, see Benjamin Aaron and Michael I. Komaroff, "Statutory Regulation of Internal Union Affairs—I," *Illinois Law Review,* 44 (September–October 1949), 425–66; and Sar A. Levitan, *Government Regulation of Internal Union Affairs Affecting the Rights of Members* (Washington, D.C.: Legislative Reference Service, Library of Congress, May 1, 1958), pp. 26–33.

37. For a more extensive discussion of the regulation by the national government of the internal affairs of associations, see Levitan, *op. cit.*; Aaron and Komaroff, *loc. cit.*; Robert J. Rosenthal, "Taft-Hartley Limits on Union Security," *Labor Law Journal,* 4 (October 1953), 663–76; Clyde Summers, "Union Powers and Workers' Rights," *Michigan Law Review,* 49 (April 1951), 805–38, and "Legislative Limits on Union Discipline," *Harvard Law Review,* 64 (May 1951), 1049–1102; Paul V. Johnson, "Government Regulation of Internal Union Affairs," *Labor Law Journal,* 5 (December 1954), 807–18; L. Kearns, "Non-Communist Affidavits under the Taft-Hartley Act," *Georgetown Law Journal,* 37 (March 1949), 297–318; Joseph Kovner, "The Legal Protection of Civil Liberties within Unions," *Wisconsin Law Review,* 1948 (January 1948), 18–27.

38. See *Howell Chevrolet Co. v. National Labor Relations Board,* 346 U.S. 482 (1953).

39. See Walston S. Brown and Allan F. Conwill, "Automobile Manufacturer-Dealer Legislation," *Columbia Law Review,* 57 (February 1957), 219–38.

40. See especially two instances of procedural injustice so far not overruled: *Hirabayashi v. United States,* 320 U.S. 81 (1943) and *Shaughnessy v. United States ex rel. Mezei,* 345 U.S. 206 (1953).

NOTES TO CHAPTER 13

1. Thomas Jefferson to Spencer Roane, September 6, 1819, *The Works of Thomas Jefferson*, 12 vols. (New York: Federal Edition, 1904–5, XII, 137.

2. *Individualism Old and New* (New York: Putnam, 1930), pp. 81–82.

3. Reinhold Niebuhr, *The Nature and Destiny of Man*, 2 vols. (London: Nisbet and Co., 1943), II, 276.

4. *Philosophy of Democratic Government* (Chicago: University of Chicago Press, 1956), p. 304.

5. *Essays on Freedom and Power* (Boston: Beacon Press, 1948), p. 199.

6. Quoted by Roscoe Pound, *The Spirit of the Common Law* (Boston: Marshall Jones Co., 1921), p. 90.

7. For a jurisprudential system which rests wholly on such proceduralism, see the work of Rudolph Stammler, especially his "Fundamental Tendencies in Modern Jurisprudence," *Michigan Law Review*, 21 (June 1923), 862–903. For a criticism, see W. E. Hocking, *Present Status of the Philosophy of Law and of Rights* (New Haven: Yale University Press, 1926). Hocking argues what is here implicitly denied, that Stammler's system is so formal as to justify any content of law whatsoever.

8. Lon L. Fuller, "Positivism and Fidelity to Law—A Reply to Professor Hart," *Harvard Law Review*, 71 (February 1958), 630–72, 636.

9. Kentucky Resolutions, November 16, 1798; quoted in Henry Steele Commager, ed., *Documents in American History*, 5th ed. (New York: Appleton-Century-Crofts, 1949), p. 181.

10. Quoted by Saul K. Padover, "The 'Singular' Mr. Hamilton," *Social Research*, 24 (Summer 1957), 157–90, 174.

11. *Democracy in America* (New York: Knopf, 1951), II, 122–23.

12. *Political Parties*, p. 408.

13. This point is brilliantly illustrated in Harvey Wheeler, "Problems of Stalinism," *Western Political Quarterly*, 10 (September 1957), 634–75.

14. Quoted in Saul K. Padover, ed., *The Complete Jefferson* (New York: Duell, Sloan & Pearce, 1943), p. 668. The emphasis is supplied.

15. See, for example, John H. Hollowell, *The Moral Foundation of Democracy* (Chicago: University of Chicago Press, 1954), especially p. 35.

16. O. A. Brownson, *Works*, H. F. Brownson, ed., 20 vols. (Detroit: 1882–1907), XV, 238.

17. *Realms of Value* (Cambridge: Harvard University Press, 1954), p. 205.

18. *Pressures on Congress: A Study of the Repeal of Chinese Exclusion* (New York: King's Crown Press, 1950), p. 199.

NOTES TO CHAPTER 14

1. For a cogent statement by a British socialist—one who has conceded that "for the first time for a century there is equivocation of the Left about

the future of nationalization"—see C. A. R. Crosland, *The Future of Socialism* (London: Jonathan Cape, 1956), pp. 466–74. See also his "The Future of the Left," *Encounter,* 14 (March 1960), 3–12.

2. See Reuben A. Kessel, "Price Discrimination in Medicine," *Journal of Law and Economics,* 1 (October 1958), 20–53. For the more general promise of antitrust action, see Carl Kaysen and Donald F. Turner, *Antitrust Policy: An Economic and Legal Analysis* (Cambridge: Harvard University Press, 1959).

3. There are other criticisms of what seems like an attractive solution; see Abram Chayes in Edward S. Mason, ed., *The Corporation in Modern Society* (Cambridge: Harvard University Press, 1959), pp. 40–41.

4. See Earl Latham, "Anthropomorphic Corporations, Elites and Monopoly Power," *American Economic Review, Papers and Proceedings,* 47 (May 1957), 303–10.

5. *Union Democracy* (Glencoe: The Free Press, 1956), especially p. 394.

6. For helpful discussions, see especially Benjamin Aaron and Michael I. Komaroff, "Statutory Regulation of Internal Union Affairs—II," *Illinois Law Review,* 44 (November–December 1949), 631–74; Sar A. Levitan, *Government Regulation of Internal Union Affairs Affecting the Rights of Members* (Washington, D.C.: Government Printing Office, 1958), ch. 6; Archibald Cox, "The Role of Law in Preserving Union Democracy," *Harvard Law Review,* 72 (February 1959), 609–44; Clyde W. Summers, "The Public Interest in Union Democracy," *Northwestern University Law Review,* 53 (November-December, 1958), 610–25, and "The Role of Legislation in Internal Union Affairs," *Labor Law Journal,* 10 (March 1959), 155–64 ff.; Benjamin Aaron, "The Labor-Management Reporting and Disclosure Act of 1959," *Harvard Law Review,* 73 (March 1960), 851–907.

7. The inconstancy and diffidence of present governmental action in behalf of consumers is fully reviewed in Warren J. Bilkey, "Government and the Consumer Interest," *American Economic Review, Papers and Proceedings,* 47 (May 1957), 556–68.

NOTES TO CHAPTER 15

1. See Eldon L. Johnson, "Coordination: The Viewpoint of a Political Scientist," *Annals,* 302 (November 1955), 136–42; Ernest A. Engelbert, "Educational Administration and Responsible Government," *School and Society,* 75 (January 19, 1952), 33–36, and the subsequent discussion in the issues of April 5 and August 2, 1952; John C. Bollens, *Special District Governments in the United States* (Berkeley: University of California Press, 1957), ch. 6; and "Special Survey of Metropolitan Areas," *The New York Times,* January 27 through February 3, 1957.

2. In this connection, see Dawson Hales, *Federal Control of Public Education* (New York: Columbia University, 1954).

3. See V. O. Key, Jr., *An Introduction to State Politics* (New York: Knopf, 1956), p. 7; "The Battle of Blue Earth County," and "The Natural Cement Issue," in Harold Stein, ed., *Public Administration and Policy Development* (New York: Harcourt, Brace, 1952), pp. 89–141.

4. "Nature Over Art: No More Local Finance," *American Political Science Review*, 47 (June 1953), 461–77.

5. *Suburbia: Its People and Their Politics* (Boston: Houghton Mifflin, 1959), pp. 9–10. See also Roscoe C. Martin, *Grass Roots* (University, Ala.: University of Alabama Press, 1957).

6. This view reaffirms the often-mocked premises, and some of the proposals, embodied in the *Report of the President's Committee on Administrative Management* (1937), especially its Introduction and the section by Robert E. Cushman; and in the first Hoover Commission's *General Management of the Executive Branch,* especially its two Task Force Reports on *Department Management* and *Regulatory Commissions* (1949).

7. "President-Cabinet Relations: A Pattern and a Case Study," *American Political Science Review*, 52 (June 1958), 388–405, 390–91. See also his exemplary study, *The President's Cabinet* (Cambridge: Harvard University Press, 1959). Warning reformers, he concludes by stressing, in italics, *"the relative difficulty of promoting unity in the face of the basic pluralism of the American political system"* (p. 271).

8. Victor A. Thompson, *The Regulatory Process in OPA Rationing* (New York: King's Crown Press, 1950), pp. 151, 238.

9. See its Task Force Report on *Personnel and Civil Service* (Washington, D.C.: Government Printing Office, 1955).

10. Wilson, *Congressional Government* (Boston: Houghton Mifflin, 1885); Elliott, *The Need for Constitutional Reform* (New York: McGraw-Hill, 1935); American Political Science Association Committee on Political Parties, *Toward a More Responsible Two-Party System* (New York: Rinehart, 1950); Bailey, *The Condition of Our National Political Parties* (New York: Fund for the Republic, 1959). See also Alexander Heard, *The Costs of Democracy* (Chapel Hill: University of North Carolina Press, 1960).

11. But see Joseph R. Starr, "The Legal Status of American Political Parties," *American Political Science Review*, 34 (June, August, 1940), 439–55, 685–99; and Horn, *Groups and the Constitution*, ch. 5.

12. *British Political Parties* (New York: St. Martin's Press, 1955), p. 586.

13. "The Representation of Interests in British Government," *American Political Science Review*, 51 (September 1957), 613–50, 650.

14. This view takes issue with, and has been given an edge by, a most provocative article: Harvey Wheeler, "Constitutional Obsolescence in a Duocratic Party System" *Ethics*, 67 (January 1957), 79–88.

15. See especially David S. Broder, "The Changing Face of the Party Chairman," *New York Times Magazine,* October 18, 1959, pp. 16 ff.; Sydney Hyman, "Can a Democrat Win in '60?" *The Reporter,* March 5, 1959, pp. 11–15; and Hugh A. Bone, *Party Committees and National Politics* (Seattle: University of Washington Press, 1958).

NOTES TO CHAPTER 16

1. *The Moral Decision* (Bloomington: Indiana University Press, 1955), p. 253.
2. Note Eli Ginzberg, "What Every Economist Should Know about Health and Medicine," *American Economic Review,* 44 (March 1954), 104–19.
3. See his "Metaphysical Pathos and the Theory of Bureaucracy," *American Political Science Review,* 49 (June 1955), 496–507.

Index

Aaron, Benjamin, 93–94
Abrams, Frank W., 35
Acton, Lord, 232
Adams, Charles Francis, 152–53
Adams, Brooks, 196–97
Adams, Henry, 133, 196
Adams, Henry Carter, 196
Adams, John, 146, 193
Administrative reorganization, 278–83
Advisory committees, 96–99
AFL-CIO, 50–51
Agar, Herbert, 285
Agrarianism, defense of, 148–49, 153, 156
Agricultural Adjustment Act, 80–81
Agricultural organizations, growth of, 77–78
Agriculture, Department of, 79, 82–83
American Farm Bureau Federation, 82–85
American Medical Association: nature and activities of, 106, 108–11, 314-(n17); regulation of, 260, 262
Anthropology, American, 129n
Antitrust policy, 260–61
Anti-urbanism, 153
Apathy. See Participation, political

Arendt, Hannah, 17, 28
Aristotle, 140, 240
Association of American Railroads, 91
Association of Land-Grant Colleges, 79
Austin, John, 141, 143
Automation, 23–25
Automobile dealers, 41

Babbitt, Irving, 197
Bailey, Stephen K., 287
Bagehot, Walter, 142
Baratz, Morton S., 100–101
Barker, Ernest, 142
Beard, Charles A., 131
Beck, David, 59, 307(n15)
Beer, Samuel H., 289
Bell, Daniel, 18–19, 28
Bellamy, Edward, 196
Belloc, Hilaire, 153
Bendix, Reinhard, 32, 37
Bentham, Jeremy, 141, 142
Bentley, Arthur F., 131
Berle, Jr., Adolf A., 207: on economic concentration, 28; on corporate self-financing, 40; defense of corporation by, 165–66

Bernstein, Marver H., 91
Bidney, David, 129n
Bituminous Coal Operators' Association, 63
Bowles, Chester, 281
Bowman, Jr., Ward S., 268
Borsodi, Ralph, 156
Brandeis, Louis D., 202
Brannan, Charles F., 84
Bridges, Harry, 53
Brownell, Baker, 156
Brownson, Orestes, 246–47
Bureau of Agricultural Economics, 82
Bureaucracy, in business corporations, 31–33. *See also* Oligarchical rule; Technology
Business Advisory Council, 96, 98
Business corporations: operations of, 39–48; state regulation of, 205–6, 210–11, 257–58
Business leaders as coordinators, 37–38

Cabinet, U.S., 278–79
Cahn, Edmond N., 293
Calhoun, John C., 151–52
California Teachers Association, 106
Campaign expenses, 291
Candidates, political, 290–91
Centralization, 274. *See also* Technology
Chase, Stuart, 169
Civil service, 282–83
Civil War, 13
Clothing Workers, 65
Cole, G. D. H., 142, 143, 145
Commerce, Department of, 96, 98
Commons, John R., 196
Community as basis for individualism, 220–22
Concentration, industrial, 28–31. *See also* Technology
Congress, U.S., 279, 281, 284, 287–88
Consensus and constitutionalism, 243–44, 248
Conservatism in social science, 128–29
Constitutionalism, 292–93; as proceduralism, 201; institutions of, 232–33, 238–51; theory of, 217, 229–31, 234–51

Consumers, 207; and technology, 24; and NRA, 73–74; consumer representation, 264–65. *See also* Business corporations
Cook, Thomas I., 193
Coolidge, Calvin, 193
Cordiner, Ralph J., 34
Corporations. *See* Business corporations
Corporatism, American, 158–75; and leadership, 122, 159–60, 166–67, 170
Croly, Herbert, 197–200
County-agents. *See* Extension Service

Dankert, Clyde E., 307(n27)
David, Donald K., 35
Decentralization, 74–75, 86–87, 269; and agricultural policy, 83–85; and river valley administration, 85–86; and federal range administration, 97–98; Jefferson on, 149; Fromm on, 155; Lilienthal on, 164; and irresponsible power, 184
Democratic Advisory Council, 286, 291
Dewey, John, 156, 220
Discrimination in licensing, 106
Dissent, 218, 237–38, 248, 284
Division of labor, 17
Drucker, Peter F., 25, 284
Dubinsky, David, 65
Due process. *See* Procedural due process
Duguit, Léon, 144
Durr, Clifford J., 279n

Eaton, Cyrus, 90, 95
Economic concentration, 28–31
Economic performance test, 167, 269–70
Economic structure test, 260, 269
Economics and pluralism, 167–68
Economy, governmental regulation of, 205–7, 260–72
Education, 236, 245–46, 290; administration of, 106, 274
Edwards, Corwin D., 30
Eggers, Rowland, 276
Elliott, William Y., 287
Ely, Richard T., 196

Empiricism: in social science, 293; limits of, 299
Engels, Friedrich, 17
Equality, 244, 272–74
Executive Branch, reorganization of, 278–83
Extension Service, 79–83

Factory. *See* Technology
Fair Employment Practices Commission, 265
Farm Bureau. *See* American Farm Bureau Federation
Farm Security Administration, 82
Federal Communications Commission, 89, 92n, 96
Federal Reserve Board, 100
Federalism, 9–10, 201; defense of, 147, 148–50, 157; Hamilton's view of, 194; obstacles to, 226. *See also* Decentralization; Sectionalism
Federalist papers: *No. 10, No. 51*, 150; *No. 23*, 194; *No. 70*, 195
Fellner, William, 87
Fenno, Jr., Richard F., 278
Feudal ideals in social science, 128
Feudalism; American preservation of, 11–12, 13, 14
Figgis, John N., 142
Fischer, John, 284
Fisher, Lloyd H., 74–75, 183–84
Florence, P. Sargant, 268
Follett, Mary Parker, 118; as neo-feudalist, 129; political theory of, 157–63; and industrial administration, 158, 161; idealism of, 160; and positive government, 196; professed antifeudalism of, 320(n34)
Food and Drug Administration, 309-(n4)
Ford, Henry, 319(n18)
Ford, Henry Jones, 284
Fortune, 34
Foss, Phillip O., 97–98
Foundations, 46–47, 304(n33)
Franklin, Benjamin, 149
Freedom of association, 12, 226
Friedman, Wolfgang F., 46–47
Frischknecht, Reed L., 82–83

Fromm, Erich, 129, 154–56
Functional representation, 277–78
Functionalism in social science, 114, 116, 125
Fuller, Lon L., 237

Galbraith, John Kenneth, 164–65, 167
Garrison, William Lloyd, 191
Gaus, John M., 79–80
Gellhorn, Walter, 107n
George, Henry, 196n
Gierke, Otto, 143
Gladden, Washington, 196
Goldberg, Arthur J., 64
Gompers, Samuel, 60
Gordon, Robert Aaron, 40
Gouldner, Alvin W., 300
Government contracts and large firms, 101–102
Grants-in-aid, 275–76
Grazing Division, Bureau of Land Management, 96–98
Green, T. H., 144
Groups: voluntary groups, 7–9; occupational groups, 105–7; study of, 116–17, 130–33; group dynamics, 120–21; extent of, 185; rights of, 12, 201, 226; public regulation of, 204–11; governmental protection of, 225; definition of public and private, 255–57; in government, 284–87

Hall, Bolton, 153
Hamilton, Alexander, 193n; 76–77, 194–95, 239, 318 (n2)
Hamilton, Walton, 73
Hardin, Charles M., 83
Hartz, Louis, 151, 301 (n3)
Hatch Act, 79
Health, state regulation of, 104–5
Hegel, G. W. F., 141, 143, 163
Henderson, Leon, 281
Hoffa, James R., 60–62
Hoover Commission, 281
Hoover, Herbert, 195n
Human nature and constitutionalism, 238–39, 243, 246–47
Human relations studies, 118. *See also* Social therapy

Hume, David, 185, 259
Huntington, Samuel P., 90–91, 319-(n8)
Hyde, David R., 105n, 108–11

Idealism: in social science, 126; in Follett, 160, 163
Ideology. *See* Technology
Immigration, 226
Independent regulatory commissions, 88–96, 279–80
Indian tribes, 323(n2)
Individual rights, 150–51, 216, 259. *See also* Procedural rights
Individualism, 231; and English pluralism, 140–41; and forms of government, 150; and pluralism, 179–80, 186–87; Croly's view of, 198–99; and public action, 208; in American political thought, 215–17; inadequacy of, 218–22
Industrialism. *See* Technology
Industrialization, process of, 16
Inherent powers, doctrine of, 195
Instrumentalism in social science, 115–23
Internal Security Act, 202n
Interstate Commerce Commission, 90–92, 94
ITU, 261

Jackson, Robert H., 203
Jacobs, Paul, 54, 62–63
Jefferson, Thomas, 148–49, 151, 239, 245–46, 319(n8)
Jessup, John Knox, 168–69
Jünger, Ernst, 17

Kaplan, Abraham, 135
Keiser, Norman F., 99
Kessel, Reuben A., 314(n17)
Key, Jr., V. O., 110n
Komaroff, Michael J., 93–94

Labor racketeering, 59
Labor unions: growth of, 51; economic orientation of, 50, 60–61; leadership of, 51, 56, 61, 65; internal government of, 52–55, 306(n8);

power of, 55–57; business investments of, 62–63; social orientation of, 61, 63–66, 307(n27); and corporatism, 169–70; public regulation of, 209–10, 263–64
Ladies' Garment Workers' Union, 65
Laissez-faire policy, 260
Land-grant colleges, 79, 80, 85
Laski, Harold J., 38, 142–45 passim, 259
Lasswell, Harold D., 115–17, 124, 131, 135
Latham, Earl, 78, 132, 261
Leadership, 245. *See also* Oligarchical rule
Le Bon, Gustave, 17
Lederer, Emil, 17
Leisure, 227, 275
Lerner, Max, 9, 71, 284
Lewin, Kurt, 117–18, 120–21, 315(n7)
Liberalism: 18th century, 14, 219; English, 141; economic, 183; as individualism, 215. *See also* Individualism
Licensing, 106
Lilienthal, David E., 164, 166–67
Lincoln, Abraham, 195
Lindsay, A. D., 142
Lippmann, Walter, 197
Lloyd, Henry Demarest, 196
Local government, 152, 275–77
Locke, John, 259
Long, Norton E., 281n

Madison, James, 150, 185, 226
Maitland, Frederic, 142, 143
Mannheim, Karl, 15, 17, 316(n29)
Marx, Karl, 15, 17
Mason, Edward S., 29
Mass media, 290
Mavrinak, Albert A., 204
Mayo, Elton, 118, 129, 170–75
McCloskey, Robert G., 203
McConnell, L. Grant, 82, 83–85
McDonald, David J., 53–54, 65–66
McKenzie, R. T., 289
McKinley, Charles, 97
Meat Cutters and Butcher Workmen, 55

Medical associations, 104–5, 106, 110. *See also* American Medical Association

Merriam, Charles E., 131

Michels, Robert, 32–33, 241

Mill, John Stuart, 20, 250–51

Mills, C. Wright, 28, 36–37, 38, 60, 102

Mitchell, Billy, 283

Monopoly. *See* Economic concentration

Montesquieu, baron de, 140

Morrill Act, 79

Mosca, Gaetano, 15, 241

Mt. Weather Agreement, 81

Mumford, Lewis, 156

Murphy, Gardner, 121–23

Murray, Philip, 53

National Advisory Board Council, 96–97

National Association of Securities Underwriters, 95

National Industrial Recovery Administration, 72–74

National Labor Relations Board, 93–94

National Mediation Board, 92–94

National Medical Association, 110n

Nationalization, 260

Natural law, 234–35, 236, 246

Niebuhr, Reinhold, 231

Nisbet, Robert A., 116–17

Northrup, Herbert R., 93

Occupational groups. *See* Groups

Office of Price Administration, 206, 280–81

Oligarchical rule, 69–70; in business corporations, 31–32; in labor unions, 51–52, 55; in agriculture, 83–85; in medicine, 111; and political parties, 241–42

Opposition. *See* Dissent

Pareto, Vilfredo, 15, 241

Participation, political, 182, 224, 240–43 passim

Party system: 240–41, 245; American, 201, 284–91; British, 289–90

Pension funds, 40, 272

Perry, Ralph Barton, 247

Petrillo, James C., 52

Physiocrats, 148

Pinchot, Gifford, 283

Plato, 224, 240

Pluralism: defense of, 2; image of, 71–72; and national emergencies, 72–75; in American agriculture, 76–87; as shield for private groups, 111–12; in social science, 130, 136–37; theory of, 144–45, 181; European theory of, 139–45; in economics, 167–68; and corporatism, 175–76; and individualism, 179–80, 186–87; need for and obstacles to, 226; and public action, 272. *See also* Decentralization

Political science. *See* Social science

Political thought, American, 11–12, 14, 138–39, 146–47, 192, 197, 213–17

Politics in administration, 281–83

Positive government. *See* State action

Presidential leadership, 278–81, 284, 286

Press, 290

Private groups. *See* Groups

Procedural due process, 201–4, 212; and discourse, 293; violation of, 327-(n40)

Procedural rights, 201–4, 212, 235–38

Professional associations. *See* Medical associations

Progress, 229–30

Property, 221. *See also* Equality

Public action. *See* State action

Public groups. *See* Groups

Public interest, 280, 283, 246. *See also* Constitutionalism

Public lands, 96–98

Public welfare, 226

Racial discrimination, 92–94

Radio Corporation of America, 89

Railroads, 90

Railroad unions, 92–93

Rand, Christopher, 272

Randall, Clarence B., 46

Range administration, federal, 97–98

Rarick, Donald, 53–54
Rationing, 206n
Representation: functional 277–78; in administration, 281
Reuther, Walter, 63, 64
Riesman, David, 28
Riggs, Fred W., 249
Rights. *See* Individual rights; Procedural rights
Roethlisberger, F. J., 315(n8)
Roosevelt, Franklin D., 80–81, 168, 282, 321(n52)
Rossiter, Clinton, 296
Rousseau, Jean-Jacques, 141, 143, 232
Royce, Josiah, 196, 250

Santayana, George, 250
School districts, 313(n5). *See also* Education
Schumpeter, Joseph A., 19–20
Seabury, Samuel, 156–57
Sectionalism, 151–52
Securities and Exchange Commission, 90, 95
Seidenberg, Roderick, 28
Selznick, Philip, 85–86
Separation of powers, 201
Shareholders. *See* Business corporations
Sharfman, J. L., 95
Shefferman, Nathan W., 58–59
Sherman Act, 261
Simmel, Georg, 15, 17
Simon, Herbert A., 315(n17)
Simon, Yves R., 6, 231
Skepticism, 224
Sloan, Alfred P., 34
Smith, Adam, 228
Social science, American: nature and characteristics of, 114–30, 135–37; quest for general theory in, 126–27, 133–34; as instrument of policy, 293–96; and politics, 295–96; need for humanism in, 296–98, 300
Social therapy in social science, 115–23
Southern Agrarians, 153
Southern Tenant Farmers' Union, 84
State action, American: theory of,

192–200; practice of, 200–212; proper scope of, 255–59, 266, 271–72
State governments, 103, 105n
State regulatory commissions, 103–5
States: as victims of pressure, 103–7, 111–12, 185; as social laboratories, 186
Stockholders. *See* Business corporations
Stockmen's associations, 197
Strasser, Adolph, 60
Strong, Josiah, 196
Supreme Court, U.S., 203–4
Sutherland, Edwin H., 115n

Taft-Hartley Act, 210, 263
Tannenbaum, Frank, 169–70
Tarde, Gabriel, 17
Tawney, R. H., 142, 144
Taylor Grazing Act, 97
Taylor, John, 149–50, 318(n5)
Taylor, Maxwell D., 283
Taylor, Overton H., 28
Teamsters Union, 54, 57–61
Technology: and pluralism, 15; social implications of, 15–25; and rationality, 16–17, 20, 22; and individuals, 17–18, 20; and planning, 19–20, 24; and ideology, 20; and centralization, 20–22; public control of, 253, 268; social technology, 293–96
Tennessee Valley Authority, 85–86, 184
Texas Railroad Commission, 103
Thompson, Victor A., 206n, 280–81
Thoreau, Henry David, 193n
Tocqueville, Alexis de, 70, 128, 239
Toleration, 218, 224. *See also* Dissent
Tolman, Edward C., 315(n7)
Trade associations, 31
Trade unions. *See* Labor unions
Transportation policy, 279. *See also* Interstate Commerce Commission
Truman, David B., 132
Truman, Harry S., 75
Tugwell, Rexford Guy, 153
Tyler, Gus, 66
Typographical Union, 261